ON
TRACK

JOHN BLAY is a writer, naturalist and walker. He has written extensively about the bush and its people in poetry, drama and prose. Since 2001, the south-east forests of New South Wales have been the focus of his work, often in association with local Aboriginal communities.

ON TRACK

John Blay

Searching out the
Bundian Way

NEWSOUTH

A NewSouth book

Published by
NewSouth Publishing
University of New South Wales Press Ltd
University of New South Wales
Sydney NSW 2052
AUSTRALIA
newsouthpublishing.com

© John Blay 2015
First published 2015

10 9 8 7 6 5 4 3 2 1

This book is copyright. Apart from any fair dealing for the purpose of private study, research, criticism or review, as permitted under the Copyright Act, no part of this book may be reproduced by any process without written permission. Inquiries should be addressed to the publisher.

National Library of Australia
Cataloguing-in-Publication entry

   Creator: Blay, John, 1944– author.
   Title: On Track: Searching out the Bundian Way / John Blay.
   ISBN: 9781742234441 (paperback)
         9781742242095 (ePub/Kindle)
         9781742247403 (ePDF)
   Subjects: Trails – New South Wales.
   Aboriginal Australians – New South Wales – History.
   Natural areas – New South Wales.
   Cultural property – New South Wales.
   Dewey Number: 333.7809944

Design Josephine Pajor-Markus
Maps Josephine Pajor-Markus and Di Quick, after John Blay
Plant drawings John Blay
Photographs John Blay except 'Walking the track around the bay' by Blay/Freudenstein
Cover design Sandy Cull, gogoGingko
Front cover image Leaving Geehi. Photo: Blay/Medvecka
Back cover image BJ Cruse explores the Bundian Pass. Photo: John Blay

The following text may contain the names or images of people who are now deceased. Some Aboriginal and Torres Strait Islander communities may be distressed by seeing the name, or image of a community member who has passed away.

The maps in this book are approximate representations of the areas they cover and should not be relied upon by those undertaking walks or visits into these areas.

All reasonable efforts were taken to obtain permission to use copyright material reproduced in this book, but in some cases copyright could not be traced. The author welcomes information in this regard.

*In memory of Beryl Cruse
whose intelligence and quiet determination inspired many of us.*

They are close observers of Nature and they have an intimate knowledge of the world about them. Surveyors mapping the country, travellers and botanists will receive from them much useful information, given with due modesty and which can be relied upon. This is not surprising, for every geographical point, every brook, every plant, even the different species of these same, have each their own name.

> Baron Charles von Hügel, 1833[1]

Contents

Acknowledgements *xi*
Map of south-east New South Wales *xv*

Introduction *1*

PART 1: THE HIGHER COUNTRY
A long walk *9*
High points *13*
Moth places *22*
The Pilot Wilderness *32*
Naming things *42*
Cultural matters *48*
The Man *58*
Byadbo trails *69*
Tingaringy and the Howitt country *77*
Through the Stockyard *89*

PART 2: THE MONARO
Merambego *98*
The way to Delegate *104*
The Maneroo *114*
Economy of the Maneroo *120*
NSW Aborigines Protection Board 1884–1942 *134*
The blankets of Delegate *140*

Across the Little Plains   146
Yamfields   154
The Very Reverend WB Clarke   163
Shifting 'tribes'   171

PART 3: THE COAST
Coming to Twofold Bay   186
Brierly at Turamullerer   192
Balawan and first appearances   207
Another side   216
Ways through Towamba   226
Master of all he surveys?   237
Scotsmen, rats and lice   242
In the shadow of waratahs   271
Turamullerer: Coming to Bilgalera   277

Afterword   286
Postscript: Keeping on track   293

    Notes   295
    Notes on terminology   306
    Bibliography   313
    Index   321

Acknowledgements

First, I am happy to acknowledge the traditional Aboriginal custodians of the land and Elders past and present. Many have spoken with me during the course of my research and I thank them for their support and assistance. Although I aimed to find a better understanding of the place and its people, there is another and greater book, perhaps many, waiting to be told from their point of view. Connection to the land and all that flows from it is at once as deep and mysterious as it is complex. The oldest continent on earth has many tales to tell. Those with connections to country have particular stories of their own, and a great store of knowledge.

Here, in working towards a shared history, I have many to thank for their assistance in helping bring this part to fruition. The New South Wales government generously provided two history research grants that enabled the first and most difficult walking stages. Both Bob Carr and Bob Debus took an interest in the project, and Bob Debus's practical suggestions put me in contact with key players. That financial assistance in the beginning bought extra time in the bush but, before that, ironically, sundry poets set me going in such a strange direction, people like Bob Brissenden, David Campbell and Manning and Dymphna Clark. A conversation with the American Gary Snyder showed me that Australians aren't as unique as we thought, while greater depth conversations with Roland Robinson sparked ways to seek out the Aboriginal connection, moving towards the interconnectedness of things, looking more closely at the old ways, and stories. Frank Moorhouse must take the blame for getting me into the bush over an extended time. Others like the ecologists Alec Costin, Alan Fox and my dear old friend and counsel, Dane Wimbush, helped me understand what I found there. Travels with Bill Gammage brought fruitful discourse. And very many of the old-style bushmen I met along the way have a special poetry in their souls, perhaps in spite of, or because of, their solitary consideration of the way of things. Their number includes: Keith Brownlie, Neil Platts, Allan Walker, Barrie Reed, Gordon Platts and Clive Cottrell, to name only a few.

The wit and wisdom of many women have been altogether vital, especially Jacqueline Medvecka for her too-little-acknowledged passion, commitment and transport, Jane Ulman, who 'got it' right from the beginning and has, like a recording angel, hovered over the project with spirit and a true ear, and Leonie Gale for her guidance, bush sense and down-to-earth understanding of conservation and its politics.

Of the many Aboriginal people who have made major contributions I must especially mention Guboo Ted Thomas, Percy Mumbler, Merv Penrith, John Mumbulla, Warren Foster, Darren Mongta, Aileen Blackburn and Beryl Cruse for their sagacity, understanding, wisdom and spirit. Other guides and survey companions en route bringing to light important aspects included Warren Foster, Darren Mongta, Quentin Aldridge, Derek Davison, David Dixon, Dennis Cruse, Colin Davison, Garry Mongta, BJ Cruse, Brian Mongta, Matthew Mongta, Dennis Arvidson, Lee Cruse, Jolene Brindle, Teneille Stewart,

Acknowledgements

Markita Manton, Brooke Mongta and Muriel May, Shirley Foster, Linno Thomas, Budda Mongta, Rae Solomon-Stewart, Michael Darcy, Sharon Anderson, Ellen Mundy, Margaret Dixon, Chris Griffiths, Bobby Maher, Joe Stewart, Shirley Aldridge, Lyddie and Ossie Stewart, Cathy Jones, Randall Mumbler, Rod Mason, Deanna Davison, Iris White, Cheryl Davison, Alice Williams and Graham Moore.

The survey process was extremely demanding, physically, culturally and intellectually and might never have got on the road without Franz Peters, Rob McKinnon and Pam O'Brien of the National Parks and Wildlife Service (NPWS) who have assisted at every juncture. The continuing assistance of Penny Stewart, Karen Cash, Paul Carriage, Marty Linehan and Brett Miners was vital. Education has always been a major factor. Acknowledgement and thanks for their practical, botanical and ecological contributions are due also to Paul McPherson, Jackie Miles, Rainer Rehwinkle, David Eddy and all those others with local knowledge who have offered assistance.

Many others have made invaluable contributions in so many ways, including Annabel and Imogen Blay, Rodney Hall, Geoff Page, Wes Stacey, David Malouf, Brian Egloff, Sue Feary, Jean and Janine Cleret, Angel John Gallard, Fred Kozak Eleanor Williams, Bet Hall, Noel Whittem, Heather Kozak, Mark O'Connor, Det and Hemmi Voges, Kate Sullivan, John Clegg, Bob Makinson, Ian Telford, Les Kosez, Keith Muir, Fiona McKenna, John and Bini Malcolm, photographer extraordinaire John Ford for his sense of the bush, Heather Ford, Pete Sands, Josh and Annabel Dorrough, Steve Gale, John Reed, Pat Ryan, Fred Maher, Graeme Worboys, Dave Darlington, Tim Shepherd, Dan Lunney, Ken Green, Marcus Sandford, Barbara Brownlie, Danny Corcoran, Lee Chittick, Sue Wesson, Bombala and District Historical Society, Delegate Progress Association, George Schneider, Tanya Koeneman, Isabel McBryde and the librarians and staff at the Mitchell Library, State Library of

New South Wales, Sydney and at the Petherick Reading Room, National Library of Australia, Canberra.

Some parts have already been published, often in different form in *The Canberra Times*, the *Australian Literary Review*, *Historic Environment* and the Watermark Literary Muster, as well as the proceedings of WILD10, the Tenth World Wilderness Congress, Symposium on science and stewardship to protect and sustain wilderness values. Thanks also to the Clark family for permission to quote from Dymphna Clark's *Baron Charles von Hügel: New Holland journal November 1833–October 1834*. Elspeth Menzies at NewSouth Publishing has accommodated the eccentricities of my vision and editor Jessica Perini has not stinted in support.

To the end I also express a great debt to NPWS and Mike Young for his *The Aboriginal People of the Monaro* which documents so many of my sources that are generally otherwise inaccessible and to Mark McKenna for his book *Looking for Blackfellas Point*, both are key texts in my explorations. I recommend them whole-heartedly. My friendship with Mark McKenna has sustained many journeys and given the writing muscle. At his home near Towamba, overlooking two of the ancient routes, the hospitality and support have been boundless. This walk would have gone nowhere without the persistent courage and determination of BJ Cruse and might never have developed without the richly layered guidance of his father, much respected Elder, Uncle Ossie Cruse. But especially I have to acknowledge the many beauties of Christine Freudenstein whose overview and love have been quintessential in advancing the quest through to a conclusion.

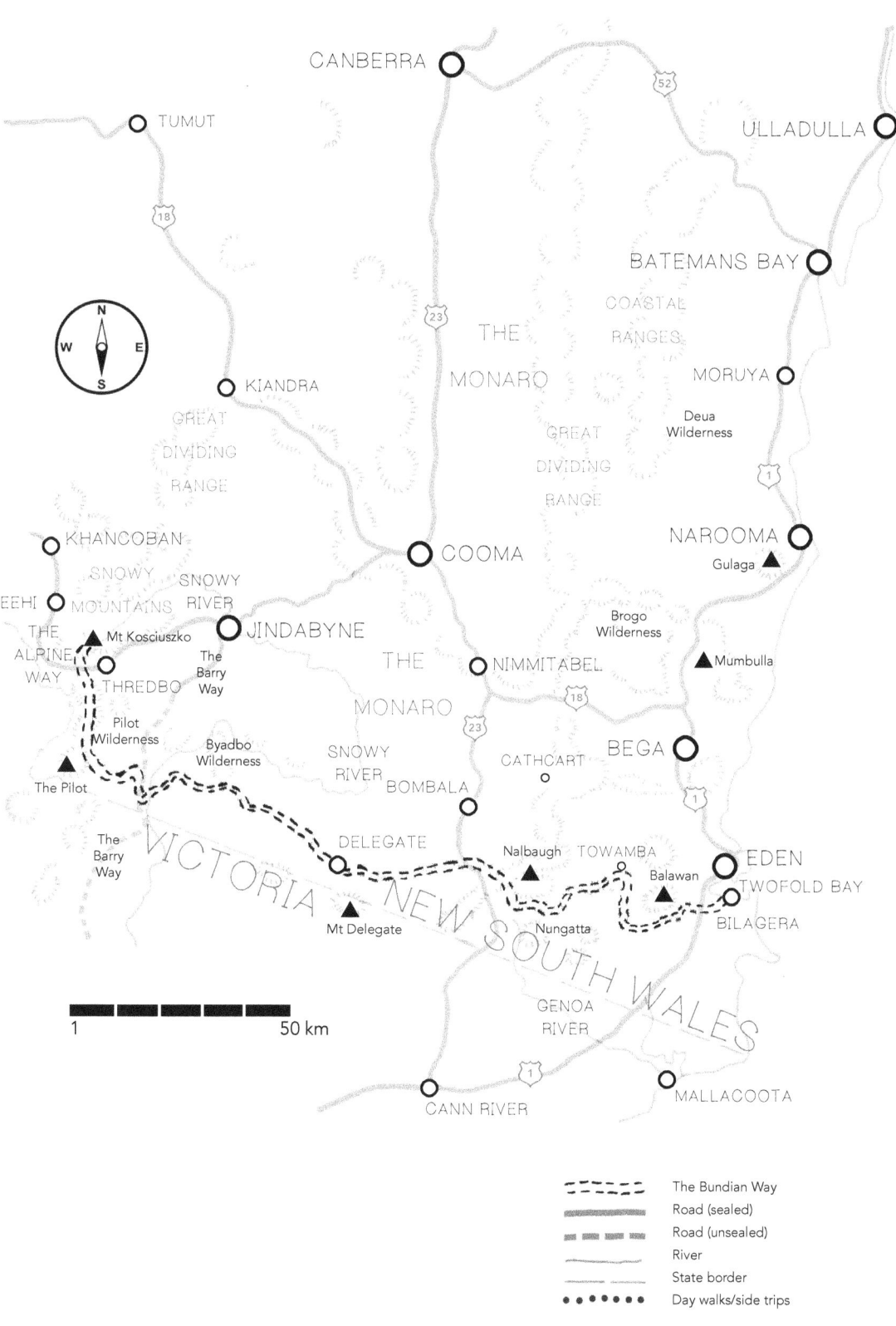

Introduction

Into the night I can't take my eyes off that sawtooth line of mountaintops that over-reach, perhaps overwhelm, my campsite. The Murray River, marking the border between Victoria and south-eastern New South Wales lies a few kilometres to the south. The Snowy Mountains surround me. But none are higher than those towering directly ahead. Moonlight picks out the savagery of slopes. Stars – more brilliant than city lights – set the heights aglow, add complexity I don't need tonight. How can I find the ancient ways? It suddenly seems impossible. A pipedream. And is it possible to scale that dark mass, the highest part of Australia, and then walk all the way from the summit to the sea as the old people are said to have done? The challenge has always been there. Many years walking the region pointed me in this direction. But such a distance, such a tangled history, such complicated, strange country, the hardships along the way will be demanding, perhaps too demanding. I have no idea how long it's going to take. Unknowns threaten. And yet something about the prospect has me breathless with excitement.

From the time the first Europeans walked along the coast

after surviving a shipwreck in 1797, to the period of early settlement of the region 20 to 30 years later, I find accounts of the difficulties of travelling between the tablelands and the coast. Scrubs combined with the irregular, steeply dissected landscape to present near-impassable obstacles. The earliest settlers of the coastal districts used the waterways while those from the Monaro found the ruggedness of the coastal ranges an absolute barrier. At Badga, Dulundundu, Greenlands, Nunnock, Badgerys, Maharatta and Bendoc they could go no further: the limits to their settlement appeared physical.

Many accounts tell how the old Aboriginal clans stepped in to show the explorers and squatters the ways to go, most notably by following pathways that had been used for thousands of years. 'Why it was the blacks, and nobody else who opened up the country...' said Bernard O'Rourke, one of the first to settle the region, in 1843. 'They led him, and you, and everyone else here and there.' He also told how, in the days of first settlement,

> The blacks ... would yabber about a big fellow station out there (pointing in a particular direction), and the settlers, desirous of increasing their territorial possessions, would implicitly go after them. In the course of a few days or weeks the 'promised land' hove in sight, and there the land grabbers pitched their tents and regarded this the ownership of the many acres which appeared to serve as a panacea for their adventures.[1]

I had been undertaking numerous long-distance bushwalks, mostly from north to south through the south-east forests and the time had come for me to try west to east. In between walks I was researching, undoubtedly spending far too many hours poring over journals, parish maps, survey field books, talking with the old families and tracing the many links between the settlers and the Aboriginal people. About 40 of the region's

Introduction

early edition parish maps showed exciting prospects. It became clear that in south-eastern Australia – typical of elsewhere in the country – a network of ancient pathways crisscrossed the region. Four names stood out among those who chronicled the early days of settlement in the region: Oswald Brierly, GA Robinson, AW Howitt, and the Very Reverend WB Clarke. Their works fascinated me. And of all the places they mentioned, one stood out – the Bundian Pass – legend claimed it as the easiest route from the Monaro tablelands to the coast. Only problem was, its location had been forgotten. Our fascination with motor vehicles made us blind to the nature of the old routes. Where was it exactly? What was its function? Whose pass was it? Mystery gathered round it as though it were a doorway to a lost, golden age, some kind of Camelot. My dreams saw the magic in antipodean terms, down-to-earth yet wonderful; the deeper I searched the more they revealed. Suddenly the purpose of the pass became evident; it binds the strands of countryside together. Deep inside, I knew I could find what I needed.

The walk I was proposing to follow ran from the highest part of the continent all the way to the coast at Twofold Bay over a distance of less than 300 kilometres, starting from the alpine meadows, on through tall montane forests, across Treeless Plains to the wild coastal ranges, and finally to the coastline near Eden. I had only a general route in mind. *The details will fill themselves in*, I thought.

When I am about to set out walking, I describe my plans to a friend, who responds, 'You have to meet BJ Cruse. He's the chair of the Eden Local Aboriginal Land Council.'

Our meeting comes when I am almost prepared to start walking. We talk about forbidding country, because not far inland from Eden and Twofold Bay the geology complicates life. Patches of basalt and rhyolite characterise the volcanic rift and mighty upliftings of mountains that happened round

350 million years ago and still make passage difficult. In only a few places can you find the rolling flatlands people nowadays generally regard as *hospitable,* and they lie most notably along the Towamba River which follows a geological fault running directly north-west to the abrupt cliffs that mark the edge of the tablelands. On top is the Monaro, the tablelands, a series of downs that includes the Treeless Plains. For the early white settlers who arrived in the 1820s this was very productive farming country with one major drawback: they couldn't get their produce to market. The port of Eden in Twofold Bay offered safe anchorage not much more than 50 kilometres from the eastern limits of the Monaro tablelands, but it was an exceedingly mean and difficult 50 kilometres given the elevation exceeds 1000 metres. Furthermore, despite impressions that Australian forests were open and park-like due to the influence of regular Aboriginal firestick farming, in the south-east forests only some parts were. My familiarity with the regional countryside kept showing me all manner of Aboriginal influences beyond fire and so, as I go, I determine to express as best I can the people's connection with those landscapes.

Hidden away in the countryside many things remain to be found. Some half-remembered or forgotten. Some as natural as plants or animals, while others are more abstract or mysterious, I could even say, *enchanted.* They're like secrets but they have names, expressed with all the beauty of language and an ancient respect for the complexity of life. This land is inhabited by spirits from time immemorial, and each has its own story. After many years of experience in the bush I well understand that you only begin to find the interesting things after you've been by yourself for some time, the longer the better. The more intimately I come to grips with places on foot, the more their special qualities appear. No mere curiosity pushes me; more a compulsion. Retracing my steps and going back to places many times is often necessary to find a clear picture, the essence of

Introduction

the place, and yet the freshest account usually comes from my first visit. Even so, it often seems that everything arrives piecemeal, some details more hard-won than others, and as I consider the many voices and tenses of my notebooks key to recapturing the sense of my walking from moment to moment, the accounts gel best into an all-at-once present tense.

Those various old heroes of mine who inspire and sustain my perambulations from moment to moment will have to live with me in this strange timescale. We journey together in the here and now and move into the timelessness of place as it is lived. How better to find the honesty that illuminates such moments? Why not attempt to find the freshness of first sight, layered with further discoveries and history?

My conversation with BJ only heightens my excitement to begin walking. Although I only vaguely know which way to go, he can't help me with more precise routes and so I will have to study the oldest maps and journals intensely. In the times that follow I meet his father, Uncle Ossie Cruse, a respected Elder with whom I find a close connection, and others. They tell me stories that have been passed down to them, most of which I will not repeat as they belong more to the Aboriginal traditions.

Although I can see BJ holds a special regard for the old routes, he has a big job to do and it goes without saying he feels the weight of his responsibilities. On top of its social, heritage and cultural responsibilities, the Eden Local Aboriginal Land Council superintends a vast tract of land. The southern boundary runs from Cape Howe for over 190 kilometres along the New South Wales–Victoria border. With an area of some 8260 square kilometres, it takes in not only Twofold Bay and Cape Howe, but also Mount Kosciuszko and Thredbo in the high country as well as the Murray River gorges and whole sections of the Snowy River at its wildest. Almost one-third of that area is declared wilderness and one-half is national park; some of the most rugged country in Australia. I am proposing to walk through the centre of it, towards the Bundian Pass, a place that might nowadays only exist in legend. Or in my mind. How crazy must that have seemed? BJ's farewell to me is: 'Yeah, go on, do it. Who knows what you'll find,' then he pauses. Comes that cheeky smile and he adds, 'just you stay on track.'

PART 1
THE HIGHER COUNTRY

The high mountains ... isolated the tribes of the coast from those inland, though there were tracks here and there by which friendly meetings or hostile raids took place between some of the tribes. The character of the coastal country itself also frequently isolated the tribes to some extent from their immediate neighbours.

AW Howitt, 1904[1]

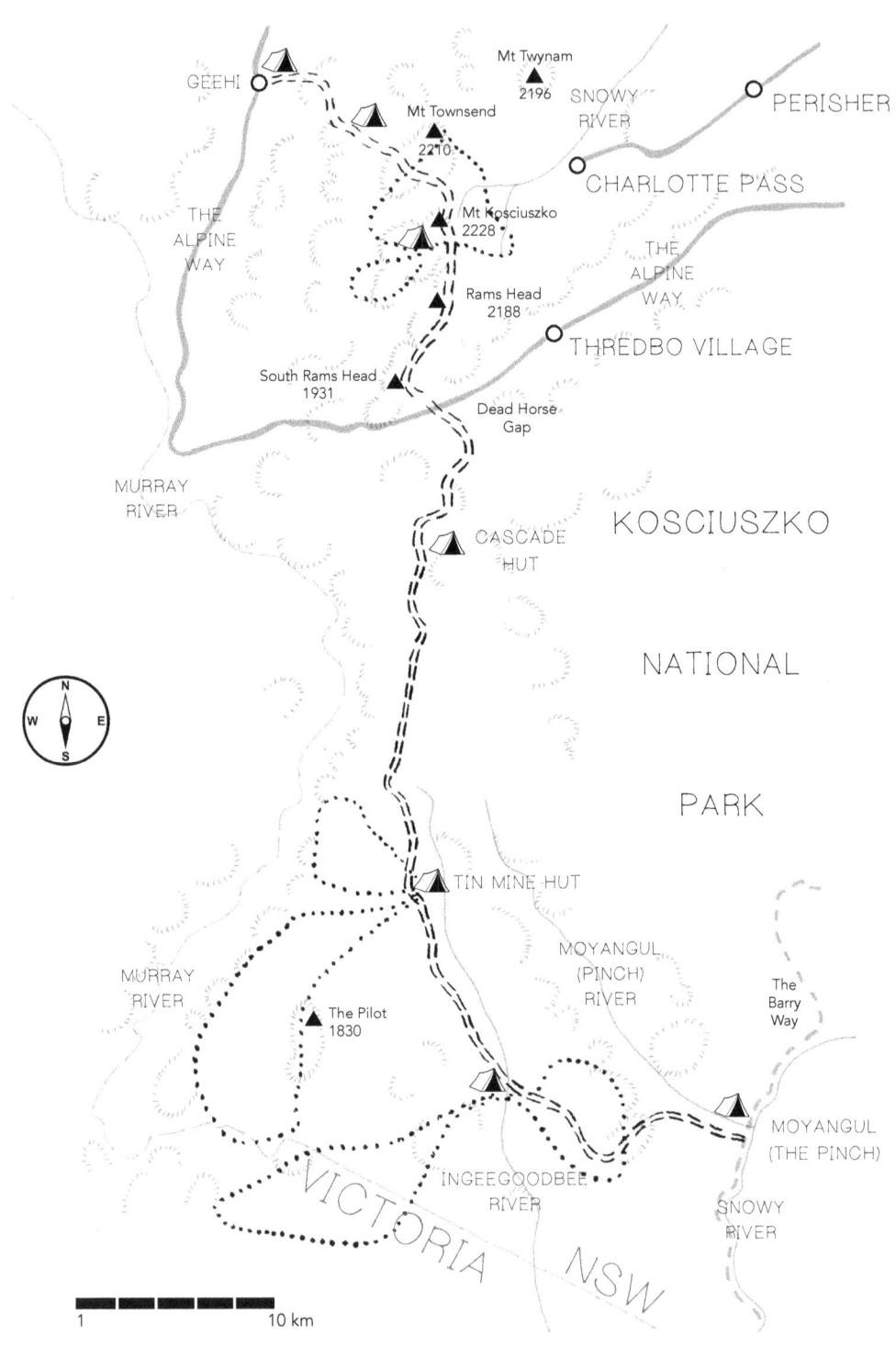

A long walk

When I was young my friends and I used to go bushwalking. It was fun, a few days here, a few days there, just one of those things you do for recreation, until 1982 when I began an extreme walk through the south-eastern coastal ranges. Sometimes I passed many weeks without seeing anyone. The aim was to find how an extended period in wilderness would influence me, and I tried to show this in my book *Back Country*.[2] But the experience went deep. My eyes began to open. And some of what happened back then is only now beginning to make sense to me.

I couldn't stop there. One year stretched to two. Then another. My journey has continued through the wild countryside of the region and I still can't see it coming to an end. Step by step the walk becomes a meditation, at times more like a pilgrimage. It develops its own rhythms, it sings to me, takes me where I have to go and, for reasons that might become clearer as this walk continues, I feel obliged to follow. But, I must confess, most times I prefer not to take an unnecessary step, even in the course of walking hundreds of kilometres. Maybe I need to feel that each step is special, it's another part of the exploration.

Even when I'm exhausted the excitement of each new pace carries me forward; that keeps me going from day-to-day. I'm never afraid of being lost. I can happily let my feet find their own way through difficult terrain rather than following the line you might draw on a map. This is often what leads me into the Aboriginal connections that have been an essential part of the walking and my journey of discovery. They are everywhere.

Once I had begun searching out the walking route that goes by way of the old Bundian lands, it took some time to realise what was happening to me. Something strange must have been there during my earliest walks. I could call it something of a thrill. A tingle. A special buzz of excitement. Maybe a touch of magic. With time it is more and more recognisable. Then comes an occasion when, in the wild dingo country of Kosciuszko National Park, I realise what it is. My Koori friends figure it is the Bundian Way singing to us. Each of us feel the sensation, whatever it is. It continues, especially in the wilder, most remote country, and, even later, it stays with us through some very difficult times as we work towards official recognition of the route.

I go back to see BJ Cruse in Eden a few days before I start walking, as I have more questions. We sit overlooking the surf of Twofold Bay while I tell him I've read about a place called the Bundian Pass and wonder whether he knows anything about it. Its location? But he just shakes a mop of curly hair that is beginning to whiten round the sides. He listens patiently as I describe my intentions in walking through the national parks of the region while looking for signs of old pathways.

He knows exactly where I am talking about. 'Hmm!' he mutters, squinting at me to check whether I am some kind of crazy man. 'Tough country up there alright.' Emotions play across his face, as I mention the newly declared national park, then comes his wild smile. 'Those national parks don't have anything special to do with us. They run north and south along where nobody else wanted the land. Our people used to go east and west. The way those parks run has got no connection with the old people.' He laughs at the thought of those steep mountainsides, shaking his head. 'Most places there you can't walk. No way.'

'But I reckon there's stuff from the old days still there in the wild country,' I say. 'I've been checking the history, there are places all through, signs, complete pathways even. It's not wasteland. There's a lot more to all that back country than meets the eye, I can tell you that for sure.'

'Yeh, that's right,' he says, a glint in his eyes. 'Old Kooris from Twofold Bay used to walk all the way from here up to the high country. After moths. Them bogongs ...' he pauses. 'They used to feast on 'em. The people came from everywhere, gathered together for the ceremonies and trade. They even played football ... Before the whitefellas caught up with it.' He gestures, showing some AFL moves, before he narrows in on me again. 'No one else'd believe you can still find those routes the old Kooris went, but we know about them. I'll tell you what, you find somewhere like that, I'll come up and walk it with you.'

When I speak with Elders about searching out and mapping one of the old routes and what should be done if its location can be found, we consider the possibility of establishing a public walking route, perhaps even seeking heritage recognition. Ossie Cruse says, 'It's there. It's always been there. We know that, so we don't need recognition.' He pauses, searching the far distance before turning to directly engage me. 'But it could help others understand. What means the most to us is the kinship. It's what connects us Kooris. The way's a symbol. And for the whitefellas, we should do our best to get it recognised.'

When I ask Ossie who owns the pathways, he responds, 'We all do. Or nobody does, unlike the way Europeans own their land, we're custodians of it. We have a responsibility to look after our part for future generations ... You see, we're all one family round here, we're all related. We're proud of what we've got. Sometimes we fight, but we all get on together again afterwards. That's the way things are.'

Then there is the difficult point, how the media focus on the most heart-wrenchingly difficult issues of the Aboriginal Australia – especially from northern parts of the country – and it is as if the Aboriginal people living in south-eastern Australia don't count. In fact, they outnumber those of the north many times over. And while the situation of the local Aboriginal people is downplayed, they are time and again dealt out of the equation, as if invisibility is to be their fate. National Parks have been declared without taking account of Aboriginal interests. Customary work – most recently in the bean-picking, fishing and timber industries – has gone and they seem to have no place in the coming, more high-tech workplaces where, for example, machines clear-fell the forests. It's only too easy to sit back and paint the nation's first people out of the picture. 'They don't fit in anymore,' I'm told by an official who should know better. 'We're in a computer age. The world's moving on.'

Both Ossie and BJ would disagree. Vehemently, I believe. But I don't burden them with it.

We agree that we still have a lot to learn about the countryside and its people. One of my aims in the walk, I say, is to look at our shared history, see how it applies in the countryside. Before I leave, as if in approval of my trek, BJ says how his people were never in the habit of sitting in one spot, they didn't wait for the world to come to them. They used to be able to move on. Find whatever they needed.

In a different world, on top of my historical research, I have to establish an elaborate network of food-drops, water caches and lifts before I can start walking. But one issue that unsettles me is that I still don't exactly know what route I'm going to follow. As the day of departure beckons and I'm feeling stronger pangs of anxiety because I still don't know how far or where I'll be walking from day-to-day, I suddenly think: *to hell with it. I'll go in the spirit of the old people.*

High points

The Geehi Flats appeal to me. They teem with life at this time of year. Trout fishers wade the fast-flowing streams. Campers make themselves at home on the sprawling, flower-studded woodlands, as do many hundreds of kangaroos. The eurabbie and red box eucalypts of the flatlands by the river are loud with birdcalls. At 460-metre elevation, it is a Shangri-La walled in by a line of rocky peaks that rise to a height of 2229 metres and comprise the highest part of the Australian continent. The mountainsides also make an inspiring sight, where a patchwork of forests stand out – the tallest as alpine ash – reducing in height as they approach the subalpine communities of the snowline where ground-hugging alpine species predominate. My eyes scan the daunting walls looking for a way up; there it is! A single long ridge continues all the way to the top. Various huts around the flats were used after World War II to accommodate workers – many of them migrants – for the Snowy Mountains Scheme, whereby the major streams were turned westerly, generating electricity along the way. The signs of earlier occupation by cattlemen are evident, along with the legacy of explorers such as Baron Sir Ferdinand von Mueller who spread blackberry seeds in places like this so they would grow in abundance for those who followed. The old Aboriginal people left more subtle indicators of their occupation.

Today is 16 February. Upstream, away from the campsites, is a hut I want to inspect; a curiosity to mark the start of my walk to the coast. But the signs are not good, maybe. Snow melt and storms have flooded the creek to a chest-high torrent. Keen as I am not to get my clothes and boots wet at the beginning, I detour further upstream looking for a shallower crossing. Of course, midstream, I slip and get soaked anyway. The passage from the creek is blocked by blackberry thickets dense with fruit. Why hurry? I decide my best remedy against the wet and cold is to eat as many blackberries as possible, to pick my way out. An hour later I arrive back at the point across the stream from where I started. The hut, named after a Dr Forbes who used it as a fishing refuge, is as charming and as generally dilapidated as the many other huts of this country that can provide shelter when the weather turns bad. Part cemented riverstones and part weatherboard, it would be a haven with its huge fireplace and improvised furniture. It signals: be alert to the dangers. A strange feeling takes hold of me. The walk, which I thought I had started, has become a dream that moves through time and space randomly, more a meditation on country than its history. I have become an audience for a natural repertory that comes in ancient rhythms, cycles that defy imagining. Time has become irrelevant. Thoughts mingle with place, the landscape is alive calling me forward. But I cannot tell where it will lead.

My clothes begin to dry as I pass beyond any influence of the bustle of the camping areas and thread my way to the track, ominously marked by a line of tall, orange-coloured snow-poles, that leads to Hannels Spur. A sign announces bluntly:

High points

Moira's Flat 6.5 km
Mt Kosciuszko 15.5 km
1800 m ascent

Where it starts to climb steeply, the recent rains have bent trees and shrubs over the track. They hold such a quantity of water in their foliage I'm soon soaking wet again and stay that way the rest of the day. Even though the route goes up and down all the time, it's a reasonably direct way to the top of Australia. By this time after years of explorations in the south-east forests I have found a lightness in my walking. It has become easy, a means to see better, to find out, to know the way of things in my country. This is not to say I desperately need to keep walking, for indeed I am as happy as anyone else to find a shortcut or lift. Walking has become thought. I feel I am in dialogue with nature, I understand it is telling me what I need to know. Unfortunately, my path is not as simple as it appeared from the Geehi Flats. Frequent variations in forest vegetation such as I expected are interesting enough, the scrubs are not. Only too often when the path confronts a wall of the scrub, it splits into byways going in different directions, each of which peters out in the water-laden tangles of leafy bossiaea. This might not sound so bad but the experience is daunting for it grows thick and high. All I can do is choose whichever route seems the easiest and push through as best I can, as often as not resorting to a crawl through its prison-like bars. But so doing in backpacking regalia that includes walking stick, camera and hat, is not an experience I'll look back upon with relish. A few hundred metres later I rediscover the track, so broad and comfortable to walk that it surprises me yet again at how quickly the brain will let go of pain.

There's a very personal side to this part of the walk. I'm looking forward to an extended time to absorb the spirit of the high country, to spend time and get the unique feel of the place. It's something I have experienced before but it all happened so quickly I've been left wondering whether I had really seen those alpine gardens light up, glow, luminesce, shine ... And so in my pack I carry the extra weight of a few weeks' food. It should be enough to buy me all the time I need to find whether that fleeting blissfulness was real, just as it will be a time for refreshment while I gather my strength in preparation to walk that next 285 kilometres through the wild country on my way to the coast. But the eagerness in my steps begins to wane during the long, very testing way up.

Exhaustion hits me just before I stumble upon Moira's Flat, a reasonable camping spot with water only 100 metres away. A sign announces Geehi Flats 6.5 kilometres, Kosciuszko 9 kilometres. The little flat is hemmed in closely by walls of the dreaded scrub. Only a few escape doors are provided. The mistiness thickens. Everything's wet.

This way has links to the old Aboriginal people as an obvious route to the top from the river flats. The cattlemen also started to use it for summer grazing in the late 1800s. In 1930 a newcomer named Hannel was persuaded by an old hand to finance the clearing of a track from the flats to the good summer pasture on top. But his cattle couldn't be persuaded to climb the steepness in the first sections and the route was seldom used. His folly was rewarded by the spur being named in his honour.[3]

In the morning when I lift the tent-fly I'm sitting on, the biggest, most aggressive funnelweb spider dances towards me. It's black and half the size of my fist, fangs dripping poison. Its savage display fascinates me; I back off. Having made a point about being so rudely disturbed, after a while it relaxes, then takes its leave. Further up the track, after I pass the 1600 metre elevation point, the scrub thins somewhat but many trees have fallen over the track. Low-growing snowgums and scrub are a consequence of the terrible 1939 bushfires, which ravaged places on the southerly aspects that are dry enough to burn perhaps once in a lifetime. The snowgum woodlands however would sustain fire every few years, and the old summertime graziers used to burn here whenever possible, firing from the gullies up the hills to get the greatest intensity and heat, with an aim to produce sweeter grass for their cattle, which further trampled and removed the herbaceous groundcovers to bare the soils. After heavy rains the cumulative result was sheet erosion and gully erosion and, later, a 'scrubbing up'. It can take some 40 to 80 years after the earth is scorched for these forms of scrub to die back. Ironically, the withdrawal of cattle grazing after 100 years was another disturbance that resulted in further scrubs.[4]

The only way I can make my way through is to climb and crawl again, which I hate even more than funnelwebs. Traces of the old track, put in by the cattlemen's axes and mattocks, remain. It went straight up whereas this more foot-oriented version winds all over the place. By 1800 metres I can see that far below mist still blankets the Geehi Flats. The flora is now more clearly alpine, lush with billy buttons, dianellas and geraniums. Round midday I arrive at the head of the track and a place known as Byatts Camp, with brilliant views along the Abbott Range. Already the light is infecting me. Everything looks so very beautiful. Sphagnum bogs and the gorgeous new foliage of pineapple-grass lies beside dense low scrubs of mostly alpine shaggy pea. A few cairns stand to mark the way but I distrust them. I have talked with men who claim to have made false cairns and destroyed the proper ones. In the wilderness, they claim, you have to be self-sufficient; we shouldn't 'mark' the landscape. My attitude is it's best to trust my resources and make my own way. I certainly wouldn't like to be following false cairns in a blizzard.

It's my great pleasure to walk on the snowgrass mat through the bowl of Wilkinsons Creek, a cirque valley ground out by the movement of long-ago glaciers, right beside the continent's highest peak. So many contrasts, colours, and sculptural shapes assail my senses. It's so green. So rocky. With so many wildflowers.

Such variety. The sky is a savage blue. Ice patches, some the size of football fields, bring another contrast. The steepness never lets up and yet I walk on as in a dream, far preferring the magic to what might be the shortest route. My destination changes as I go. Grades no longer matter. I want to go everywhere at once. At this stage it seems I am climbing the generous slopes of a living creature, onto the waist and then the hips of some great woman; a feeling all the more exaggerated when I come to the crest of Targangal – a mother, I decide – on top of Australia. But it doesn't feel like the summit, which more belongs to Mount Townsend, only 18 metres lower and the next peak northwards. So many parts of the high country have their enticing human form-like roundnesses mixed with stony prohibitions. It's so late that all the day-walkers have long returned to their villages. With no distractions, I continue in my mood – I was going to say elevated – from the top, so as to avoid the man-made tracks and find my own route down over a few kilometres to pass beside the glacial lake and on to the odd, red-painted Cootapatamba Hut. The colour makes it stand out in the blizzards that can come at any time of year, when access is through the chimney-like tower, maybe 5 metres tall. It is no place to camp, but only to take shelter. A cave, not much more than 2 metres square, its visitors' book says it has saved many from freezing, even sheltering a group of some 16 schoolgirls caught out during an adventure trek. One large group were dismayed to find the expected six by six dimensions were expressed in feet, not metres. It saves perhaps one person a year, usually cross-country skiers or snow boarders caught out in extreme conditions. My camp is within 50 metres but looking away from it, so it doesn't spoil the wild vistas.

At first imagining it all seemed simple. Walk through wild parts of south-eastern Australia keeping an eye out for its Aboriginal qualities, especially its old pathways also known by other names such as Dreaming routes and songlines. Soon I'm noting

High points

Aboriginal landscapes. Then I'm also looking at how the country used to be before European settlement, and how it came to be the way it is today.

The cold bites once the sun goes down. Mist flows over the crests yet the air is quite humid. From my tent entrance looking southwards the Swampy Plains appear wild and primitive in the fading light, like a considerable area of planet earth with its own entire river system seen from space and from which all human interventions have been removed. Masses of snow daisies shine a silvery light, playing with the rockiness, the crevices and cracks. Sleep comes soundly but dreams of practical, social matters invade: I can't remember where I parked the car and search for the right person to ask for help. It's a strange town. Lost. I panic.

Kilometres away from popular tourist trails, the wild ecstatic beauties of the plateau next morning are more dramatic than I could ever have anticipated so I decide to stay here for a few days or as long as it takes to familiarise myself. It's as if I've come under a spell, just as it is very heaven to walk with a light daypack. The Leatherbarrel is a shocking reminder of how high this country is: a water-engineered gash between the plains and the massive granite formations of the southern Ramsheads which rise to heights that rival Kosciuszko. Leatherbarrel Creek divides the ways, for upon the ridge on the far side of the creek is another route followed by the old people to gain the high country.

Opalescent woodlice, deftly organised brumby trails, fields of mountain celery, fat wingless grasshoppers black and green and shimmering, then fields of gold. One marvel follows another. As I wander southwards to the extremity of the high country I think of the changes that take place here from day-to-day, how the flowers might this day be golden, the next day brown, and soon enough overtaken by the white or purple of another species. But the light is like nowhere else in Australia, bringing such changes, such diamond clarity, such brilliance, all in time-frames that are so small. Blizzards and cloud can overtake you so completely that you have to hold the compass close to your eyes to read the direction. And so the generosity of such a place is counter-balanced by the threats it poses. The resulting mix of bounties and dangers somehow add to its strange beauty. Some weeks ago near Charlotte Pass a friend burst into tears, overwhelmed at the beauty of the fields of snow daisy that patchworked the bowl of the upper Snowy in the direction of Kosciuszko. I came with a group including my old friend Dane Wimbush to assess the alpine flora in a plot on the lower slopes of the mountain. Since 1958, as a botanist attached to the CSIRO, Dane has annually surveyed the same transect, marked by string and tape strung between a line of permanent pegs that runs for some 200 metres down the hill and across a small creek. He logs the fine details of its plantlife. The constancy of his study makes it a long-term tool to measure changes in the vegetation and climate. Strange to say, I now have visions of the high country in very slow motion – species come and go, grow taller and shorter, move uphill and down – a constantly changing cavalcade.

Arcade-like runways that twist through the taller heath shrubbery are made by the broad-toothed rats that survive here under the deep snow through winter. The lower subalpine tracts are the country of the corroboree frog, unarguably one of the most beautiful creatures on earth. Warming of the climate coupled with the *Chytrid* fungus, even in a place as cold as this, is the reason that I will most likely never see one in the wild.

The second highest mountain of Australia, the one that looks taller than Kosciuszko, was named after the surveyor TS Townsend who mapped the range in February 1847. The peak is a total contrast to the enticing Kosciuszko, being wild, mad and rocky with jutting slabs of granite in all directions. In this place you feel on edge; the fragility of life is emphasised,

High points

risks threaten in all directions. Time is suspended. There is no rush or desperation. Perhaps I have been taken into the high country's own rhythms.

Beyond the line of rocky hills below Cootapatamba I find discrete pastures, and then even more fields of pasture occupied by herds of brumbies that thunder away upon my approach leaving behind stinking piles of their manure. I find dog scat full of moth parts and, then look up to see stunning views across the grassy flats of Tom Groggin station and the Murray to the Victorian Alps; east and south, only wild limitless mountain ranges, but west, a hint of the flatlands beyond. This is a time of intense reflection for me. The state of mind most suited for this place gradually comes to me. The desperations and deadlines of civilisation, its news and relentless conflict and violences, fade into the patterns of my place in nature. Somehow I have become watchful and unhurried but deliberate. Wonderment has time to happen. I can pause whenever the moment demands. I carry something like that deep sense of awe reported of the old Aborigines when visiting this country, how they walked with their heads bowed during their excursions. Back above the plateau on rocky hills, I find bogong moths in the crevices, and ancient mountain plum-pine clinging to the warmest side of rocks along with a few snowgums in the sheltered places. Towards the end of the day I can make out dozens of people on the track to Thredbo, bustling back to civilisation, as small as ants scurrying along their ant-path. My heart sings, I am free.

Moth places

Over the next days, following the new time scales, I ramble widely across the high country, cutting round Kosciuszko to the turrets of Mount Townsend, finding the strange peacefulness of Lake Albina and the force of the rockpile that is North Ramshead. In many moth crevices countless bogongs still linger after their summer hibernation or aestivation, plastered thickly on the granite walls, overlapping each other with a mutual grip on suitable rockfaces that is oddly co-operative. One of Kosciuszko's Aboriginal names was Targangal, which would associate it with other parts such as Dargal, Jagungal, Moyangul and Youngal by the suffix that refers to 'place'. I imagine here how in the early summer the Twofold Bay people would arrive for their bogong celebrations and I can almost hear the excitement of the old tribes as they gather together on warmer flats below the snowline.

In her 1980 book, *The Moth Hunters: Aboriginal prehistory of the Australian Alps*, archaeologist Josephine Flood drew attention to the moths and cultural issues of the region. Since its publication Aboriginal people, including descendants of those from whom the early settlers gained their sketchy information, have been able to further contribute to what is undeniably a remarkable story.

As I have come to understand it, the people used to come from very long distances away. They stopped at certain places to observe formalities. Then all the clans moved elsewhere, gathering to participate in the social activities and ceremonies. It might be nearer Jindabyne or up on the Snowy Plain, probably a different place each year on a rotational basis, so long as there was wood and water available and bogong peaks were nearby for the men to fetch sufficient quantities of the moths to feed the crowd. The important thing was the inter-tribal contact and shared ceremonial life. People came to participate from across the region, from Braidwood and the coast, from Twofold Bay, from along the Snowy, even from Omeo on the other side of the mountains and the western districts. They were kith and kin, they shared ceremonies and their gatherings served many functions by allowing, for example, different languages to be spoken, marriages to be arranged and knowledge to be passed on, as well as various forms of dispute resolution, trade and sport. Spiritual and kinship connections were also explored, but the much-renowned displays of storytelling in music and dance were most prized.

Later accounts of the gatherings in the mountains talk of friction between various groups, even suggesting animosity between the coastal and mountain people. No doubt it existed at certain times, but much had changed by the time ethnologists like AW Howitt and Richard Helms started collecting their information 50 years after the fact. Competition for localities not taken up by settlers had increased. The earlier records are probably the most candid.

One came from George Henry Dawson who, after arriving in Australia in 1834 with his parents, brothers and sisters, soon settled on the Monaro. He describes how the people came to feast on the moths for weeks at a time, drawing attention to the vivacity of these gatherings, the 'great merrymaking and corroborees', and how the women played 'drums made out of a piece of skin or hide stitched tight across a piece of bark curled before the fire'. These were beaten with their yam sticks while they chanted 'a native tune running like this – belly belly hander yar yar sone'. He added that they also 'played the reeds with their fingers and played them very well, their tunes being mostly of a plaintive kind and weird in the extreme'.[5]

Another came from William Jardine who was born in Scotland and came to the Monaro, starting a flour mill in Jindabyne with Stewart Ryrie in 1846. He recalled how in 1844, when he first knew the tribe, it was numerous and could, if it wished, have kept the white invaders back. Then after 1845, when the snow began to thaw, he would see 'the different sections of the tribe collect together and resort to the mountains at the foot of Mount Kosciusko to regale themselves on a kind of moth'. He saw how a couple of men would take a net made for the purpose, and catch moths 'so numerous that when they rose in the air they looked like a dark cloud. During their two or three months stay the aborigines must have eaten several tons of them each year.'[6]

The many accounts are similar, although George Bennett, who would go on to become director of the Australian Museum in 1836 gave a more technical view. He undertook an expedition into the moth places of the north-western high country in December 1832 accompanied by local Aboriginal men. He noted that because the bogongs (bugongs, as they were also known) congregate at various places along the range during November, December, and January, this time became 'a season of festivity among the native blacks, who assemble from far and near to collect the Bugong; the bodies of these insects contain a quantity of oil, and they are sought after as a luscious and fattening food.' He described how after cooking, the bogongs were winnowed to remove the dust and wings, then pounded into cakes resembling lumps of fat which would not keep more than a few days, 'but by smoking they are able to preserve them for a much longer period'.[7]

A westerly springs up early. The tent billows its gale warning as I battle to get it stowed and break camp as quickly as possible. It's time to move on, I understand, and make for the sheltered country on the other side of the range. Part of the way up the steep slope to the crest of the Great Divide, a satiny snake lies curled between clumps of the grass soaking in the early sunlight. It's one of the white-lipped snakes that feed upon the smaller lizards not uncommon in these parts. It appears asleep. As I bend to touch it, in a flash it disappears under a poa tussock. The wind howls across the snowgrass, and helps push me up the slope. Near the crest, at close to 2000 metres, I come across an ancient Aboriginal stone arrangement, a simple enough gathering of stones, with a westerly view towards the plains country. Even the little buttercups, changing from one species to another as I go upslope, are keeping their heads low. To retain my last views of all the majesty to the west, I pass round the steeper slopes of the Ramshead, trusting all the while that the boulders are firmly anchored against an immediate 700-metre fall into the Leatherbarrel. But there's little risk as the gale pushes me hard against the slope, keeping at bay the bush flies and march-flies that so plague a stationary figure. Alpine sunrays, as delightful as any plant on earth, scarcely move their papery white daisy flowerheads, but across the feldmark on the way to South Ramshead, all the other fields of flowers – so bright before – begin to glimmer.

Then as I swing into the saddle that leads towards South Ramshead I am back following the footsteps of the pioneering anthropologist and bushman, AW Howitt. He followed this route in early January 1866 and, importantly for me, described his climb along an old track that led upwards from the river flats of the Murray River near Tom Groggin homestead. The beginning of this track was signalled by 'a very old mark made by the blacks who used this very track in going to Maneroo – it was a piece of bark taken off a tree'. And soon 'we then found ourselves on the old blacks' trail – a dim half obliterated track through the grass and bushes such as would be made by bare feet'. His party crossed the Leatherbarrel and slowly climbed the steep ascent until 'again on the summit of the ridge found the old track and the tree marks. From here we followed the line – indeed there was no other as the crest of the ridge wound along – ... till after about eight miles from the station we found ourselves in the first of the open patches that connect the forest with the open summit.' And it is immensely satisfying for me to follow just such a line of track in the knowledge people have come this way since time immemorial.[8]

In the afternoon sunlight a few days ago, upon glancing up, I saw the actual ram's head revealed in the formations of stone and grass; a merino with curled horns. All features – eyes, mouth and woolly texture – were clear to see, but it lasted only a short while before the sun dipped lower. There is something warm and soft about the Ramshead, but not the South Ramshead. At close enough to 2000 metres, it is savage and stony, where the tumble-down granite boulders form the niches, crevices and caves in which the clustering bogongs shelter. In one cave about the size of a motel bedroom, the walls are lined thickly with the moth. The effect is not unlike some blotched pub carpet covering walls and roof. In touching them to make sure they are actually alive, I dislodge a few, and the next ones lose their grip on each other. Then more and more: thousands peel off and tumble in turn to the ground where they form a slow, writhing mass. It's a demonstration of how readily they might be harvested.

The old route to the top taken so many years ago by Howitt passes the southern ramparts of the Ramshead. From here the Divide leaves the main range, turning easterly towards Dead Horse Gap and The Pilot. Traces of stormcloud appear on the horizon to the west. I could take shelter in some caves, but it's time to be going. Snow-gentians and the waxy brilliance of anemone buttercup light my steps along the steep grass-covered slopes that lead to the tree line and its snowgums. If for no other reason, the flowerings here make me want to stay as long as possible. Looking south-eastwards along the crest of the Divide the winds have cleared most of the blue haze that usually blots the distance and I can make out the mountain landmarks of my journey to the coast. The Pilot, closest, is the first, then Tingaringy and Bendoc or Delegate Hill mark the southern limits of the Monaro, and on the far side Nalbaugh stands out with, perhaps, the faint outline of Imlay in the farthest distance. This is the way to the coast, it's my walking route, a little less than 170 kilometres as the crow flies, and it's so obvious. From up here, on top of Australia, the way seems benign. Well, rather.

Heading easterly, it's steeply downhill as I come out of the alpine pastures into snowgum woodland and find a reasonably obvious track that leads along the crest of the ridge to Dead Horse Gap. Splashes of wildflower adorn the route – golds, reds, purples – more boldly than in the higher country. I see signs of brumbies, wombats and kangaroos. Of course, it's not strange that so many creatures use this trail; man is undoubtedly one of its least frequent users, nonetheless it stands out because it follows the easiest and best way to go.

In the glare of afternoon sunlight Dead Horse Gap – at an elevation just under 1600 metres – is still a beautiful place in spite of the road. Colourful alpine flower carpets open upstream along the Thredbo River into the intensely beautiful, treeless Boggy Plain. It was a crossroads for the old Kooris, as well as the white explorers and cattlemen who followed their paths.

The higher country

One route goes east–west along the Divide, while the road from Thredbo roughly follows the path Howitt used to come up from to the Murray. Despite all the works necessary to build the road, rich evidence of Aboriginal use may still be found. As I hunt round, looking at the flat places for signs of artefacts, a group of young men shamble past along the path that leads beside the river from Thredbo. They're a real mess, red faced, out of breath, limping, dirty. I nod my greetings as they bustle past, totally mystified by their condition and their haste. A couple of older men are waiting near the road, so I chat to them and mention the youths.

'They're our students,' one teacher explains. 'It's an extreme adventure experience. We've been following the Alps Walking Track for a week now and this is the closest we've come to civilisation. Our next stage is to go along the Divide past Kozzie [Kosciuszko] to the Jagungal Wilderness. The boys pleaded and pleaded, so we let them detour to Thredbo provided they don't delay our progress. They've just run a very steep and rugged 8 kilometres to buy Coke and Mars Bars.'

'I hope it was worthwhile for them,' I venture.

'Oh yes,' says the other. 'Wouldn't you have done it at their age?'

The young men, strengthened, I suppose, take up their backpacks once more and continue up the steep slopes the way I have just come. The meeting makes me wonder about the human condition. Maybe this is how it has always been. Maybe the young Koori kids would hurtle down the hill from their camps here to a patch of the very sweetest yams. Certainly this is one of the important junctions.

On 1 March 1834, Dr John Lhotsky was the first European to come this way and write about his experience. At Mutong he threw a packsaddle on his cart horse and set off for the high country, following the old way across Grosses Plain, then cutting across to the Mowamba River, which runs northwards to the

Snowy from the Boggy Plain, skirting east of the high country. He refers to a 'Black Path', which suggests he followed an Aboriginal pathway leading to Wombat Gully and then along the Boggy Plain to the Gap and was told about it by local Aboriginal people. It appears the highest peak he reached was the Drift, of 1931 metres, from which he would have seen the full panorama of the high country, Kosciuszko and the Ramsheads, occupying the skyline across the Thredbo River.[9]

In the course of surveying the Great Divide TS Townsend followed the same route 14 years later, but continued across the Boggy Plain to Dead Horse Gap and then onto the Ramsheads. He then followed the Divide south towards the head of the Murray, not an easy journey with pack bullocks and considering it snowed for 3 days in the middle of February. He reported that

> The Blacks had visited the Snowy Mountains, a short time previously to us, for the purpose of getting 'Bogongs' ... and the consequence was, the country throughout the whole survey was burnt, leaving my bullocks destitute of food. During the time I was on the range the lower parts of the country were burning, and I was prevented, in almost every instance, from getting angles on any distant points, by the dense masses of smoke obscuring the horizon in all directions.[10]

His observations were echoed some years later during Howitt's visit, when 'tremendous bushfires which have been raging in these mountains all summer ... produced smoke like a London fog'. Regular burning as people passed by, favouring patches here and there, would have kept the lower slopes clear of scrub.[11]

The Reverend WB Clarke was a man of scientific bent whose travels are inspirational. And the more I read of his writings, the more I like him as a person. He was foremost a geologist, the man who first found gold in the colony but was asked to keep it secret by the governor. He travelled the region as the government's scientific adviser and geological surveyor from September 1851 to July 1853. He went by foot and horseback, with two servants, during his reconnaissance across the Alps to Omeo and east to Twofold Bay, attempting to contact the local Aboriginal people wherever he went. In his progress reports, first published in newspapers and as parliamentary papers, he outlined the structure of the country he had seen and its metalliferous resources. In 1851 he published *Plain Statements and Practical Hints Respecting the Discovery and Working of Gold in Australia* and in 1860 *Researches in the Southern Gold Fields of New South Wales*. When his party camped at Dead Horse Gap he wrote:

> In the month of March preceding, a party of Aborigines coming from the Murray River to Maneero, were overtaken in a snow storm and that, whilst one man was severely frost-burnt and crippled, two others were completely smothered in the drift, within a short distance of the very spot upon which I and my party encamped on the 22nd and 23rd December, 1851.[12]

He goes on to note meteorological details and how Surveyor Townsend suffered considerable snowfalls in mid-February at the same time as there was smoke from Aboriginal burning. He builds his portrait of the region detail by detail. Many of the journalists didn't note occurrences that were frequent or common. And so this detail of the late summer–early autumn burning is very interesting, but it's common in the less-windy seasons for the smoke from one burning gully to blanket the region. What I find most surprising is that in my experience over the seasons the higher country is very seldom susceptible to fire. Most often, it has been difficult for me to start a campfire burning. The clouds come down frequently enough to keep the fuel damp. Only towards the end of summer in the driest times will the high country burn, especially the alpine ash forests. Similarly, the open plains of snowgrass above the tree line are hardly a fire risk, even though I know some patches have burned during the extreme bushfires such as happened during 2002–03. The snowgum woodlands will however burn more often, and the old clans certainly started fires as part of their attention to country, which involved discrimination and a knowledge of how fire would behave. I understand that the country beside the pathways was burned more frequently, in part for reasons of keeping the track clear, but also to rekindle the firesticks. Perhaps burning was the responsibility of one clan, the home clan, or perhaps it was the collective responsibility of all who passed through. In my desire to understand the places I'm traversing, I'm increasingly plagued with questions.

The Pilot Wilderness

From Dead Horse Gap a trail leads eastwards beside one of those high country paradoxes. No trees inhabit the highest parts, but then you find bands of trees lower, on the more sheltered hillsides. On the Boggy Plain, the floor of the valley, the area is also devoid of trees. This is due to the frost hollow effect whereby the extreme cold falls into the hollows and spoils their growth. On the grassy flats the walking is good but unfortunately they provide a great number of brumbies with pasture. Hereabouts, National Parks and Wildlife Service lure a few at a time to trap yards using salt as the bait. They are then transported out of the park and sold to willing purchasers. The numbers are reduced, but not to the extent of their natural increase. Dead horses in the Dead Horse Gap would be a bad look indeed. After crossing Boggy Plain the trail zigzags roughly east and south along the crest of the Divide. Maybe it's because the air's thinner here, maybe you are closer to God, but I'm filled with elation, my senses soar, my steps float. Many of the snowgrass patches are golden with daisies.

At Cascade Creek I stop to marvel once more. Maybe it is

because life here is concentrated into a warm season so short everything has to take advantage while it lasts. Thousands of large rusty wasps fly close to the ground. White-throated needletails (swifts) in their hundreds fill the skies as high as I can see but some are so close overhead I can hear the metallic rattling of their feathers. Then, most curiously four women come walking towards me along the track. They stop and we marvel a while together like old friends before they walk on. Then another few cross my path, and another, until in all some 18 very happy women of varied age and disposition have come by in assorted groups, all as excited as me, and we invariably swap our delight before they proceed. Once the last of them have gone, I miss the instant companionship. And it's as if the marvels have gone with them. Camp comes near Cascade Hut, a cattleman's split log construction, where I have a fire burning strongly, when three campers from Canberra arrive. I invite them to join me by my fire and we have intense discussions into the night as we finish their bottle of port. Just as well, for the air is freezing. Later, brumbies stomp round camp, sheltering under the trees I guess. Come morning the frost is thick and white all across the flats, remaining even as I depart.

After Cascade I expect to see fewer people. The country gets wilder. This is the only formal track through this part of the ranges and it serves as the Australian Alps Walking Track. Soon I am passing through a tall forest of alpine ash. Many trees could be over 60 metres. Where one has been chainsawed from the track recently, I pause to count its growth rings: 93, in a tree less than a metre in diameter. Later, on a bigger tree, I count over 100 before I'm two-thirds of the way in and the rings become indistinct. The woolly teatree is in flower making white splashes along the creeklines. Splats along the track the size of an ice cream cone and full of seeds, grass, currants and undigested geebung fruit have me expecting to meet up with emus soon.

The march-flies (Tabanidae) are attracted to anything blue, especially denim jeans. Even through fabric their bite is ferocious. They seem to adore the blue of my backpack. They're in their thousands, perhaps attempting to mate with it. So long as they keep off my skin; and yet I wonder about the extra weight, and the possibility of breeding a hybrid between my pack and the flies. They lay their eggs on plants and would therefore be a lesser villain than the bot-flies (Oestridae) which infect the horses with parasitic bots. These maggoty larvae are the reason why so many of the brumbies are in bad condition.

There are fewer patches of white sallee now and more of the tall candlebark and mountain gum scattered about countless little swampy flats with a great variety of wildflowers. I keep diverging from the direct route, on one occasion to visit the gauging station on Tin Mine Creek and its ramshackle hut; just big enough for two men to lie down. A few people have scratched messages into the Masonite wall. One is, surprisingly, for the irony I suppose, the complete Keats poem: 'On First Looking into Chapman's Homer'. Someone else has added, 'Mar '88 – cross creek, up ridge to view falls.' Another adds: 'Be sure you don't follow ridge, go WSW...'

The Snowy Mountains Hydro-electric Authority used many such huts during preparations for the Snowy Scheme and put in the rough tracks to allow access to streams and gauges for hydrographers to research stream flows. But before the Snowy Scheme cattlemen ran stock in these places during summer; their rude structures, such as the Cascade Hut, often remain. Those at the Tin Mine by the Ingeegoodbee River have been restored to their make-do, ramshackle beauty under the guidance of National Parks. For reasons I don't understand, I feel compelled to make the Tin Mine huts my base during wilderness explorations in the vicinity. Signs of rats don't daunt me, there are advantages: plenty of air gets in, the earthen floors have been oiled and can be swept and, best of all, chairs to sit on. The location is remote, even today, at a very good day's walk from the nearest road, but when the home-spun philosopher Charlie Carter lived here before his death in 1952 they were a 3-day ride from Jindabyne, a journey he undertook once or twice a year for supplies.[13]

This is one of the places where scientist and geologist Reverend WB Clarke visited in 1852 and that is reason enough for me to celebrate his passage. Every day, wherever he was, he methodically recorded the details of the weather, including rainfall, temperature and cloud cover over a period of very many years. Today he'd be called a geek, but his observations were invaluable because so few other reliably consistent records of this nature from the early days of settlement exist. That he took the wider view made him the prototypical ecologist. He communicated readily with the Aboriginal people, seeking them out and recording their local details, the way they went, what things meant. However, it was as a geologist that he most touched greatness. Having had his discovery of gold suppressed for political reasons, once the rushes were under way everyone turned to Clarke. He was commissioned by the government to investigate the south-eastern regions. In his own meticulous way he noted a lot more than the presence of minerals.[14]

On his journey from Omeo to pass The Pilot he recorded: 'One might expect tin in the vicinity. I obtained one small specimen from the granite – none was, however found amidst the detritus.' The book and its maps detailing his journeys and discoveries, *Researches in the Southern Goldfields of New South Wales*, came to be regarded as a bible by the prospectors, and resulted in their activities continuing down the years. Ironically, the lasting result of his travels was not the metals he found but that he methodically maintained his records. Although many of these survive, it seems the essence of his discoveries in the form of his unpublished writings, field books, original maps and such were lost to fire in 1882. Beyond his published work, it is the surviving bits and pieces that suggest the scope of his achievements.

Over several days I ramble to Cowombat Flat, a great camping place close to the head of the Murray River and then check the border post that marks the official head of the Murray River before inspecting the cairn on Forest Hill. This reveals the western end of the Black-Allan line that delineates the border in a direct line to Cape Howe. From here, roughly following the border, I plunge through the forests to a creek that holds a more interesting connection with history, for I am using a copy of the first edition of the Beurina parish map. I'm trying to find a route mysteriously shown as a dotted line 'from Gippsland via Omeo' and at its other extreme, 'to Cooma'. It continues onto the adjacent Moyangul map, and so on.

On the creek I find old stopping places and then tracks leading up the ridge indicated in the first maps of this region. I follow it up onto the Berrima Ridge. It is like a roadway, one untroubled with human traffic since the old days. I even see signs of the twin tracks from long-ago horse- and bullock-drawn carts; the route first marked by surveyor TS Townsend and recorded in the travel journals of both WB Clarke and GA Robinson. In fact, stories, backed up by the first maps, appear to confirm this is an ancient Aboriginal route, one showed to the explorers and settlers of the 1820s and '30s, and followed by many thereafter as it became known as the best way to Omeo from the Monaro. An inconvenient, out-of-the-way place, the middle of a formal Wilderness Area today, 150 years ago it bustled with people coming and going. Many Aboriginal people used it to go to the Snowy for refuge during the cold weather. For the graziers it was the way between the Monaro and Omeo and on to the rich grazing lands of East Gippsland. For the gold prospectors, it was the best route between the Monaro and Omeo and the Ovens fields and those further west.

But doubts linger and gather strength as I make my way back to the huts. I'll be on paydirt, I decide, if I can find the

The Pilot Wilderness

other end of the track at the top near the Ingeegoodbee. It can't be that hard as the first maps are specific enough. All those journals can't be wrong. The route I have just experienced in The Pilot Wilderness even today is as far from settlement as it was in the mid-1800s, and yet it is the most reasonable way to go from Omeo to the Monaro. It would be the route most likely taken, for example, when GA Robinson recorded at Twofold Bay on 14 August 1844 that he witnessed how some natives had come to visit their coast friends for a corroboree, 'composed and arranged by Al.mil.gong, an Omeo Black from Tongio-mungie ...'[15]

The next day I have to choose between making the big climb onto The Pilot, at 1829 metres, a much harder walk, or diverting to Tin Mine Falls for what I suppose to be their remarkable beauty. I head for The Pilot because it is important, it commands the countryside, and it will help me better understand where I am. It shocks me to think that I have chosen understanding over beauty for beauty's sake. Or that is my suspicion. And doesn't it pay off for me.

Maybe it's luck that gives me a really clear day and all I'd hope for plus beauty, for it is home to a mass of wonderful shrubs and wildflowers with the added bonus that, being above the snowline, it is clear of trees on top. This is one of very few stand-alone peaks of the region. Vistas lie in all directions. Even Kosciuszko looks impressive. The sense of the Ingeegoodbee running along a high, limitless plateau when you're by the river is put into its true perspective when it is shown to be a fool's paradise, for in actual fact the land soon enough falls away savagely from either side. The drop off to the Murray is also very, very dramatic. Southwards, only a few kilometres away across Cowombat Flat, the peaks of the Cobberas are rugged and stony and unforgettable. Tingaringy, is most prominent in the eastern vista. Its rocky walls facing this direction mark the southern end of the Monaro's Treeless Plains. Behind it stands alone Delegate or Bendoc Hill, from whence *Eucalyptus delegatensis* (alpine ash) gets its name. The line of mountains blocking the south-eastern Monaro (Coolangubra to Wog Wog and Nungatta) makes better sense of the lay of the distant land than I have found anywhere else, but it also puts into perspective the closer Berrima Ridge and its associated clearings and flats and the form of the forests. The countryside is laid out more clearly for me than if it were signposted on a map.

My next destination is the nearby tin mine. It is not much more than overgrown scrabble, a few aqueducts here and there. Some tin was recovered over the years, along with a little gold. Though the mine was located near the conjunction of the slate and granite, most of the ore recovered came from the alluvial leads. The Mount Pilot Tin Syndicate went into liquidation in 1938 after spending too much money on roads that soon became impassable. Snow plagued their efforts in winter. Like so many other prospects through these mountains, the miners' expenses were not covered by their returns. Following the Great Depression prospecting continued to represent work for self-reliant men like Charlie Carter who stayed on, eventually to die of starvation in his hut in the winter of 1952 after his horses bolted and he was not strong enough to recapture them.

Then I walk for a few hours towards the Tin Mine Falls through swampy flats splashed with all manner of wildflowers before cutting onto a forest ridge parallel to the creek when the swamp narrows, climbing all the way. A lyrebird scampers away in alpine ash. Then suddenly there is the edge, a gut-wrenching view down into the Murray River, like a hole at my feet. The clouds lift as I cut around the clifftops above the remarkable canyon of the Tin Mine Creek. Rock faces show where shale has been sheared to a depth of hundreds of metres. Some great distance below me the falls begin their drop of a clear 120 metres in veils of droplets and shifting rainbows to rainforest far below. This one vision says so much about where I am, what a perilous plateau I've attained and how far down it is to go back to the reality of the lowlands. Spiderflowers pepper the slopes with crimson dots.

Stepping lightly on the way back I find parsons band orchids and rose quartz. The stone underfoot is often coloured with the glint of minerals. The silvery blue leaf forms of spinning gum excite me. Back at the huts for lunch, I pack up and head eastwards.

The Ingeegoodbee is an intensely beautiful stream, set amongst grassy flatlands with only the odd black sallee placed as if beside the lawns of some vast estate, and it makes for easy walking whether I follow the trail or the stream. Further up the slopes woodland gives way to mountain gum forest. It's great to be free to go as I please on foot, not tied to finding a roof for the night and unconcerned with traffic and work. Five-star camping places present themselves but near the end of the day I have to select a 4-star spot amongst fallen trees beside a stream. I'm really thirsty, so I go to the stream and slake my thirst. Towards the bottom end of the pool I notice a few brownish feathers. A long dead emu, partly submerged, lies amongst the tall sedges. The water for my tea comes from a distance further upstream.

Using the map again next day, I diverge from the Ingeegoodbee to follow the old route to Omeo Flat, a long grassy sward on either side of a meandering creek occupied by brumbies, emus and grey kangaroos. Then past a small gorge there's another part of the flat, green and brilliant, on the top of the ridge. I trace the Berrima Ridge to where the route drops to pass eastwards of the Cobberas, then return to where I left my backpack in less than a few hours: a gorgeous diversion through open forest. It's the route followed by Surveyor Townsend and his Aboriginal guides. Trees he marked still survive on the Surveyors Flat and at other places along his route.

But this is the heart of The Pilot Wilderness, and I am disturbed to find even at the head of creeks that the banks have been wrecked by horses. The ponds and swampy vegetation are trampled to a mush. Erosion gathers pace. Then the vision of another dead horse, one that from its posture has met an agonised fate, plays on my mind. Too many beautiful places hereabouts are in a bad condition due to the brumbies, which are in greater numbers than the countryside can support. Their hoofprints cut across the country everywhere. They still manage to also follow the old Aboriginal route, probably because it remains the best way from one point to another. The hundreds I have chanced to see in past days are far too many.

Freebody's Hut is marked on the maps but it's a ruin, just a pile of iron and primitive building materials. It's hot. There are masses of flies. It's like the farmlands of the Monaro, with weeds and willows and cowpats and deer droppings. I'm ready for more than this kind of clapped out country when I sense a great commotion in the air. Thousands more of the swifts appear, swirling high up and generally heading northwards. Then they're gone. I won't see them again. This part of the track is not pretty, merely a management trail that shows the impact of human usage because it's convenient for the passage of machines. Soon after these flats the track splits, one section leading to Suggan Buggan and Wulgulmerang. I take the branch that heads towards the Nine Mile Pinch walking past a dead dingo lying beside the track in the tall mountain gum forest.

But there is another alternative; the old way that came from Omeo via the Berrima Ridge and runs from Surveyors Flat, across Omeo Flat, crosses the management trail and the river before taking a direct route towards the Pinch. This is the way Townsend and all those others came. And it remains a wonderful way to walk. It's usually a metre or two wide. Artefacts appear at regular intervals. Grassy flats punctuate the forest. It rejoins the management trail just as the track tilts downwards, with a vengeance. And the ancient way clings to the top of the ridge that now takes me into radically different, desert-dry rain-shadow country. All the way downhill over some 8 kilometres (9 miles from one watering place to the next, it was guessed long ago by the cattlemen, who called it the Nine Mile) and an 800 metre fall to the Snowy River. Once out of the tall forest of the crest, blue leaves of the Snowy River wattle surround me, then I enter box and the white and black cypress country.

Its steepness is oppressive, the views frightening. Each step needs care my feet don't slide out from under me. Only zigzagging keeps traction. But, at the end, near the junction of the Pinch River and the Snowy, I find great camping spots. The pains ease. I feel connections deeper than I can readily say.

Naming things

Under a white box at the Pinch River camping area, I take in this beautiful place just upstream from the junction of the Pinch (Moyangul) River and the Lower Snowy (which people tell me used to be called Nurudj Djurung). Sitting at the picnic table, I reflect, write notes and generally replenish my reserves. I have food, there's plenty of water and nobody to disturb me. These are the times I enjoy most. The whispering of the river is punctuated only by birdcalls that tell the richness of the Lower Snowy. Just across the stream is a place that would easily serve as an amphitheatre. Goggle-eyed and nervous emus visit regularly, ignoring me due to my stillness, which suits me. White box, yellow box, white cypress and bundy are the most common trees, presenting a much more sombre landscape than the high country. Across the Snowy lie the sparsely vegetated and forbiddingly dry mountains of Byadbo glowing reddish in the afternoon sun.

I think back to my conversations with BJ, and how – in spite of the evidence I'm stumbling across – many people consider the living presence of his people in these wild places has been erased. But they're wrong. You just have to develop an eye for the signs. The ground is still littered with artefacts. Scarred and marked trees stand nearby.

And among the other persistent signs of the Aboriginal presence, place names are the most significant for me. I'm coming to realise that nothing to do with my walk is quite as clear and simple as I would prefer. To find the right track I often have to put up with a great many discomforts, stressful byways, dead-ends, braidings and general discombobulations, as my way leads through time as well as space. The history is not conventional, and the more I research, the more I am plagued by the names and their much-varied spelling, that is until recent days when something strange starts to happen. The particular beauty of their local character strikes me. I begin to hear the music of the syllables, the song of place. I realise many of the variations in accent point to the old, unwritten Aboriginal pronunciations, and so therefore I make a decision to keep the spelling used in my sources wherever possible, even using the older names inter-changeably. The different spellings can point to different shades of meaning, as with a temporal understanding, tribal characteristics, topographic features or aspects of Aboriginal landscape. The realisation immediately helps my growing appreciation of Country even though it's painful for me, after a strict schooling in regular, correct forms, to give up the consistency of spelling.

It's one aspect of the symbolic leap I have to make to continue my journey and find Aboriginal qualities – maybe I should call it spirit – in the countryside. Although it's central to my explorations, does that spirit live on in wider Australian culture, the way for example 'The Man from Snowy River' persists?

It is especially interesting to look at what society has chosen to forget. National myths become part of the nation's forgetting when they over-write the Aboriginal stories. Take the Snowy, a word vaguely descriptive of its source. Before the Snowy Hydro

Scheme, which diverted most of its waters inland, the river had seasons when it raged down the gorge, when it was a roaring, tumultuous 100-metre-wide torrent. An Aboriginal man told me that his people called the stretch of river between here and Jindabyne 'Nurudj Djurung', which has a quality of sound that feels just about right. Parts of the river had different names in a variety of languages. Some might refer to its source, some its destination and others to its current locality or particular qualities.[16]

Then again, the Moyangul also received a European name because those first exploring cattlemen called it the Pinch, beating the surveyors to the punch. At about the time the first whitefellas were venturing into these parts, Thomas Mitchell became surveyor-general in 1828 and, while overseeing the first general survey of the colony, he expressed a preference for Australian place names. Although it would be too late for those already named, such as Kosciuszko, places would no longer be named for heroes and patrons. He wrote instructions to his assistants to put this into effect. The field surveyors' standard monthly report form indicated that native names of places were to be inserted in all cases when they could be ascertained.[17]

Mitchell's requirements concerning place names were spelled out frequently enough:

> I have now to add that you will be particular in noting the native names of as many places as you can in your map of that part. The natives can furnish you with names for every flat and almost every hill and Settlers select their grants by these names; the names of new parishes will also be taken in most cases from the local names of the natives ...[18]

It was a theme to which Mitchell returned many a time; on 5 September 1829 he issued a circular to all surveyors and draftsmen with rules to standardise and simplify spelling, adding:

Naming things

'And many other words in which there are letters as superfluous as gum trees on the hills.'[19]

But of course over the years many recorded the names of the same place in different ways. Phonetic spellings varied. They were often then simplified. Sometimes the original pronunciation remained. Likewise, the naturalist von Hügel like WB Clarke and surveyors knew from first-hand experience that the Aboriginal people had names 'for every geographical point, every brook, every plant, even the different species of these same'. Unfortunately, too few of the original names were considered significant enough to be recorded, and where another name from elsewhere was known it became generic. Hence, for example, 'boomerang' became the name for an immense variety of throwing sticks in all shapes and sizes, each of which had a different name and use.[20]

On 6 August 1841 surveyor TS Townsend received instructions from Mitchell to map out the best line of route from Corner Inlet, Port Albert, near Wilsons Promontory, through Gippsland and Maneroo Plains, to the head of the Shoalhaven River. In his report of the journey from his camp at Coolringdon on the Monaro, he noted how he marked trees every mile. At 100 miles he crossed 'Bruthen Creek, of the Omeo natives', passing through Omeo at 167 miles, where the now-dry lake was a morass of pools, to the Playground and east of the Cobberas, crossing Freestone Creek, on his way along the traditional route through the Ingeegoodbee. At the foot of the cattlemen's Nine Mile Pinch, 218 miles into his journey, he recorded the name of the river as the Toonginbooka, 'a mountain torrent about eight yards wide'. It is one example of the trouble these surveyors took in establishing the names, that when he revisited in 1847 he revised his naming of the Toonginbooka to the next major stream southwards (noting 'vulgo, Suganbooka', then in his journal as Sugganbooka) which became the Suggan Buggan, of which Freestone Creek and the Ingeegoodbee are tributaries.

Thereafter, his first parish map records the name Moyangul River, and yet the alternative 'Pinch' appears to have been adopted because of its common usage among the cattlemen. He found the Snowy at their junction 70 yards wide, 'the waters rush and roar with fearful velocity and noise'.[21]

Not that Townsend was the first European to come through this route. The cattlemen and shepherds often had good relationships with the Aborigines, who showed them new, good places to go. They were not learned people and few records exist of their travels in search of new pastures. Richard Brooks, who was born in Surrey in 1812, became one of the earliest settlers of the Monaro when he arrived in 1827 with his father and cattle. His first intentions were frustrated when they were attacked by hostile blacks and 'he lost his cattle, which he found later on Gejizrick Flat, where the rich pastures that then existed caused him to determine to settle'. Today, the property is known as Gegedzerick near Berridale. The tribe continued their hostilities, but, rather than take the more usual extreme recourse, he presented an inscribed brass plate to a leader, naming Blueskin as *King of the Monaro* and thereafter gave the people a bullock every year, which was roasted whole at a feast near the homestead. Having paid his respects and made a good working relationship with the local Aboriginal people, he quickly turned this to his advantage by taking up the Jindabyne run. Soon afterwards, as settlement filled in the patchwork of the Monaro's best country, his friendship with the Aboriginals led to him being shown the part of the Snowy between Biddi and Willis, where he was first to run cattle, perhaps to the point of depleting its grass supplies, and then in 1834 he drove his cattle up the Nine Mile Pinch and along the Ingeegoodbee to occupy the first station on the richer high plains further south at Wulgulmerang. In 1851 he accompanied the Reverend WB Clarke who was researching the southern goldfields. They went over the range, sleeping one night on Kosciuszko, and returned from Omeo, via the Playgrounds and the Pinch.[22]

Although it had been used for many years at the time, 640 acres at the junction of the streams were set aside as a Travelling Stock and Camping Reserve to serve the Pinch in 1883. Townsend's route appears as a dashed line noting 'from Gippsland … to Cooma'.[23]

Still a camping place, my strip of white box–white cypress woodland near the Snowy occupies some of the flatter parts of this exceedingly steep country, and it is also visited by a north–south unformed road of breathtaking zigzag steepness called the Barry Way. The strip is part of the Kosciuszko National Park and forms a buffer between two Wilderness Areas, Pilot and Byadbo, both wildly different from each other. The location is far from the nearest town and most times of the year no more than a few cars pass by each day, the sort of place where you meditate on how you stand in the scheme of things. Somehow, I understand it is a critical locality in my travels. The reason why is not so easy to comprehend. It's a feeling I have in my guts; no word does it justice.

Cultural matters

The earliest accounts of the old Aboriginal people of the greater region generally referred to them as the Maneroo, and later they were usually described by where they came from, as in the Monaro (or Monaroo) tribe, the Omeo tribe, the Twofold Bay tribe. Later came a more subtle differentiation, with AW Howitt's description of the region's people as Ngarigo (of the Monaro), the Yaitmathang (of Omeo), Yuin (of the coast between Shoalhaven and Cape Howe) and Biduelli (south of the Monaro/Yuin) tribes. Each spoke their own language and could converse fluently in neighbouring languages. My aim is to use the name most commonly employed at that stage of the written history. One thing is certain: their numbers were very much reduced when the Europeans settled. This was most likely due to the introduction of new diseases such as smallpox, tuberculosis, measles and flu.[24]

Then, it's only too easy to lump all the settlers in one bag as heroes or villains. But they had more than one approach to the new lands. Similarly, the first Australians weren't a single people. They were many, each tribe and clan had their own understandings, differences, conflicts and comings together. Likewise, the British were many. How well did the English see eye-to-eye with the Irish and the Scots? Were they not riven by class and religion? The free settlers versus convicts and emancipists? Even the Scots were divided into Highlanders and Lowlanders, and so it goes. People are not always agreeable. Even though making distinctions between the various local identities is a complex task, it should pay dividends.

Over the years, many factors – from dispossession of the lands on which their identities were based to land rights legislation – have introduced hostility between some clans where there was none before; the possibility of financial compensation adds bitterness to their competition. Clans turn inwards against each other. There is a continuing dissociation. The background to all this plays a part in my explorations. The cultural richness of Nurudj Djurung lifts the stakes.

And so, considering the antagonisms in society then as now, my position here on the Snowy at Moyangul lies not only between wildernesses but also between a rock and a hard place. Such is life. I have to keep reminding myself that the reason I am here is to explore the values I find in this countryside, its peoples and wildlife, illuminate them perhaps, and I see the Aboriginal elements as a living part and parcel of the whole, not just some forgotten pre-historic circumstance.

In a conversation with an Aboriginal friend, we talked about routes between the east coast and Omeo, from where her mother had come. We mulled this subject over a number of years. But this day she related how they used to take her mother back to Omeo by car every year or two for a visit and how, usually when they were driving up the Drummer (a significant mountain of East Gippsland), her mother would break out, waving her arms about, saying, 'No stop, we're goin' the wrong way. Stop, stop ... We have to go across that way.' She was always pointing out a more direct way to go in preference to the roundabout highway route. She knew the right way to go. When later, I showed her a copy of the first parish map of the Byadbo section of the Snowy River, she went quiet. Ten minutes and not a word, so I looked over her shoulder to find whether there was something wrong: the page was spotted with tears that had dripped from her eyes.

'What's wrong?' I asked.

'See all these names on the map?' she said. 'Well I know all these places. I been given their stories. This was the way me old Mum was always talking about, the way she wanted us to go on the way home.'

She pointed out a route on the map. It was the same way those explorers had been shown, the way that went up the Pinch to the Ingeegoodbee and on past the Cobberas via the Omeo Flat. More confirmations would come that these ways remained alive in Aboriginal culture even though few nowadays actually walked them. Things may well change again, as they always have.[25]

The old Aboriginal people from places all about the greater region were compulsorily moved to mission-type stations at places like Wallaga Lake, Ramahyuck and Lake Tyers, and an Aboriginal Reserve was set aside near Delegate in 1892. Using the old languages was prohibited, as were ceremonial and cultural activities. The culture didn't go away; it simply changed. Even the old clan and regional groupings somehow survived, along with their rivalries. Divisions along these lines survive to this day, as do certain connections. New ones spring up. The result is a culture of many parts that is different to the British-style culture as well as those of other Aboriginal communities to which it bears the greatest similarities. They are not, it must be said, the same. They were never the same. And the differences are still a matter of some pride. Language, for example, varied from district to district. Although most of those languages have been lost, enough words survive to point to the distinguishing characteristics. Language still divides many. When I had to speak to a gathering of the full membership of a coastal land council I was asked some very intelligent, searching questions. In answer to one, I was saying something like, 'If this happens then, maybe that, or on the other hand ...'

Suddenly one of the delegates smashed his fist onto the table and said, 'Listen here ya fucken cunt, speak to us in blackfellas' language willya!'

Many thoughts ran through my head, nonetheless a fragment of remembered history jumped into my mind. A settler had commented that the old tribes learned English very quickly, the only problem was that they learned the very worst of it, and as GA Robinson said, 'The Omeo blacks make use of very foul and blasphemous language taught them by depraved whites.' Much as I might have been insulted or upset by the confrontational nature of his words, I knew he was asking for language with stronger points of emphasis. I changed my delivery to a more rhythmic form, as if I were hitting my fist on the table regularly to keep a beat that emphasised my main points. And they were with me. They understood it all, and yet I took away a sense of something else, as though I'd been granted insights. We had found ourselves talking in a language rich with symbol, metaphor and emblem that goes simply and directly to the heart of things without the clutter and jargon of modernity.[26]

Howitt described friction between groups from certain clan and tribal territories. In some circumstances that still holds today, even though they have lived together on the mission stations for generations. Decision-making on a community level does not correspond to the European manner. Knowledge is not monolithic in the sense that one person might be expert on everything; that person will only know what he or she should. A man's knowledge is different to a woman's, which differs again in relation to where they're from. It's like a jigsaw puzzle of knowledge pieces and it can drive the authorities crazy when they are only asking for a simple, clear opinion for guidance. And in no sense will, say, local government ever receive a list of all the places that are culturally sensitive in a certain district. It may take a number of authoritative Elders to give a big opinion, even Elders in a circle. There are no chiefs or kings, or even professors. Sometimes a particular clan will have authority but that does not necessarily grant them respect. Some are passionately for or against the land council system of ownership and management. Land rights have been a blessing and yet it seems to me that the great disservice of current native title laws to the Aboriginal people is to set neighbour against neighbour in untoward battles for pre-eminence, as if one might 'own' land to the exclusion of others. Traditional 'ownership', as against 'custodianship', is a difficult concept for the region. So many claims, I wonder whether a new form of commonality can be found.

In the 1970s as clear-fell logging reached up the slopes of Mumbulla Mountain, overlooking Bega, the conservationists raised a mighty clamour. Public meetings were held. Motions passed. Public figures spoke passionately about what would be lost. In 1975 the issue of the logging's effect on climate was raised. It seemed nothing would prevail against the bulldozers, not until the quavering tones of Guboo Ted Thomas entered the debate. A Yuin Elder of Wallaga Lake, Guboo spoke fearlessly of his people's regard for the mountain. He said it was sacred, and logging was delayed while investigations tried to figure out what to do next. This led in January 1979 to the minister for conservation, ARL Gordon, expressing outrage that 'logging was being disrupted for a rather obscure reason'.[27]

The following week the *Bega Times* reported that the president of the logging contractors had in disbelief said, 'Some people want a ban on timber being removed from the whole mountain.'[28]

This was big news to the local media, alarm spread. What next? Numerous dignitaries and politicians flooded down to take stock of the situation. But at Wallaga, Ted Thomas was not happy with the politicians' approach to the issue. In March he wrote to the premier, saying:

> Our people here at Wallaga Lake are very angry about the way in which politicians such as Mr Walker, Mr Gordon, Mr Britt and Mr Brereton ... come down here and go up Mumbulla Mountain looking for Aboriginal sacred sites, yet never come and ask us, the experts on such matters ... It is hard to imagine anything more stupid, arrogant and bad-mannered. What do they expect to see – stained glass windows and statues of angels?

In February 1978 logging was stopped for 6 months while a report was prepared by anthropologist, Brian Egloff, who worked furiously to complete his report by June. The time constraints coupled with an increasing public agitation made all sides to the debate more pessimistic that the report would finally settle the issue. Passions rose.

Old-timers were having their say, because they believed they knew better than anyone. Their families had been in the district since settlement and expressed their bafflement. Local farmer Jack Moloney wrote to the newspaper:

> I spent most of my 73 years living on properties adjoining the mountain and during those years I walked many many times over all the areas mentioned above ... to round up our cattle which used to winter in those areas. I state I never saw any indication of any Aboriginals ever being in the areas. To those suffering imagination and who say

> there are sacred sites in those areas in my opinion is a lot
> of trash. I would say, let them come along and point them
> out. From what I have heard of the Aboriginals in the days
> before white man came they frequented, and lived where
> their food was available around the shores of lakes and
> rivers. I ask just what food was there ever in the Mumbulla
> Mountain that would entice them up there?[29]

Other factors beyond conservation and sacred places were raising the heat of the debate. The Kooris were – and remain – a substantially disadvantaged section of the community. At about the time the Eden woodchip mill was established, there was a nasty ruckus in Bega to stop Aboriginal families being housed in the town. Many relied upon seasonal work, such as bean-picking to get by. But this kind of work was drying up and changing. The camps where Kooris used to stay following well-established seasonal patterns were closed down by local councils. Similarly, where many used to work in the forests and saw mills, the increasing mechanisation of operations and clearfelling for the woodchips squeezed out Aboriginal workers first. Ossie Cruse led a number of Aboriginal families to Eden in hopes of better living conditions and work but there would be no promised land for the Kooris. The poor white principle came into play as well: when some of the poor whites saw the poor Kooris about to get some kind of advantage in stopping the logging, they attacked ferociously. In April 1979, perhaps troubled by the accusations that were flying hard and fast, the Kooris decided to respond. Answering many of the concerns expressed on radio and in the press as best he could, Merv Penrith wrote on behalf of the Wallaga lake community:[30]

> Sir, I Wish to take issue with the point of view your paper
> has taken on the Issue of Aboriginal Sacred Sites. Why
> does Mr Gordon, NSW Minister for Conservation and

Cultural matters

> Mr Walker, NSW Attorney General doubt our Tribal Elder, Mr Ted Thomas, when he talks about our culture and sacred sites on Mumbulla Mountain which has been handed down to our people for 40 000 years? ... May I point out to you something the white people overlook? Where do white people build their places of worship? I find that the biggest majority of churches are built on a hill – so did our ancestors have places of worship and they climbed mountains to do their worshipping and initiation and Mumbulla Mountain is one of them.[31]

Not long afterwards it was found necessary for Guboo Ted Thomas to broadcast news that a petition with 142 Aboriginal signatures, the entire adult population of Wallaga Lake, supporting the sacred sites had been sent to the then New South Wales premier Neville Wran.[32]

Many Bega townspeople were shocked by this turn of events. The Aboriginal people often worked in the mills and as loggers out in the bush, they were friends of many farmers and forestry workers. His claims didn't sound right to the conservative communities who became convinced Guboo had 'been put up to it by the Greenies'.

But other Aboriginal people spoke out in his support regardless of the old alliances. Other highly respected Elders like Percy Mumbler and Jack Campbell joined him and put their name on a petition. The battle was not won until archaeologist Brian Egloff showed that special ceremonies were indeed held on the mountain. His evidence of oral histories was backed by the field journals of Howitt, who actually attended the ceremonies held there in 1883 and kept notes of some major stages of what happened on the mountain. The knowledge of the local people that had been passed down from mouth to mouth was confirmed by the scientific writings of Australia's first and arguably greatest anthropologist, and so the mountain was set aside from logging as an

Aboriginal Place, now incorporated in Biamanga National Park under leaseback and management of 'traditional owners'.[33]

On the first day of spring, 1980, at a meeting on Mumbulla Mountain, the people agreed on the special qualities of the place and that they would no longer express the knowledge held by some senior people. From then on, the sharing of knowledge would be 'restricted to the Aboriginal community and developed along gender lines'. This way has not always been for the best. In the Aboriginal community sometimes disputes occur over who actually owns certain special 'information' and little agreement on 'the most respected Elders'. Many of the broad family are close friends and relatives, and yet the problem is exacerbated when issues of privilege or compensation arise.[34]

There is also the matter of, as they say, 'We don't want whitefellas knowing all our stuff. Next thing, there'll be whitefella experts saying they know us better than we know ourselves. Where would that leave us?' Fair enough, I say. I believe that the Aboriginal families with connections to Country should keep their own knowledge and express it only when they believe the time is right. This form of cultural knowledge would not become part of the shared history.

The respected Elder Merv Penrith did not register as a 'traditional owner' because, as he told me at Wallaga Lake in 2007, 'Everybody knows who I am. I don't need a dog-tag round my neck saying the whitefellas acknowledge me.'

Soon after the Mumbulla decision, Gulaga (Mount Dromedary) was also shown to have great Aboriginal significance and the process began that eventually saw both mountains handed back to the Aboriginal people on 6 May 2006 and leased back to National Parks for management in cooperation with the new owners. The minister for environment, Bob Debus, in formally handing back the mountains, spoke of taking repossession and how Gulaga was 'the first place named by Captain James Cook on the Australian continent. He sailed by on 22 January 1770 and named it Mount Dromedary.' Debus closed by quoting the words of Guboo Ted Thomas, who many years before told a Parliamentary Committee, 'Why we are interested in this land ... is that they are sacred sites, they are part of us. You have your cathedrals in Sydney where you worship. It is the same for Aboriginal people ... We do not want to lose our culture.'

On that same occasion Jimmy Little, the renowned Aboriginal singer who spent years at Wallaga Lake as a child, spoke passionately of the families of old Wallaga Lake. As he named the families, and sang about them, the emotions of the mostly Aboriginal audience were palpable. Not only was their connection to the land being recognised, but also that most vital issue of their culture: kinship.

The Man

Now comes a diversion. That's how things go sometimes, you get off the straight and narrow. Sometimes more can be learned from the diversion than from barrelling directly onwards. So please bear with me. This is as good a place as any to note that the route I'm walking is, like other routes of antiquity and the Dreamtime, made of many shorter legs. On the very easiest parts, through a gentle valley or across a flat plain, any walkers might wend their way. Just wander. Chase the butterflies. There is not one pathway. But as soon as things get complicated, the various wendings coalesce. They come together to avoid the difficulties and follow the best through route. This often goes by way of a ridge or leads to a mountain pass. I well understand that I'm facing difficult country and my main purpose is to search out whether there is an old way through. The logic of the landscape.

From the Pinch junction with the Snowy, or where the Moyangul meets Nurudj Djurung, the old travellers could turn north to the Tongaroo (Jacobs River) and go up via one of several ladders (or long ridges) that lead to Ingebyra and the tablelands in the direction of Jindabyne, Dalgety and Cooma. Turning south, as apparently most travellers and surveyor TS Townsend did, leads to another route through the heart of Byadbo. Someone in the lands office has penciled a question mark when that route 'to Cooma' heads off in the opposite direction. Something compels me to go northwards, explore this maddeningly wild, unruly bit of strangeness. And so, from the Pinch, I turn left to make my way northwards towards the Jacobs Ladder. It's hopeless beside the river, really hard going due to the extreme ruggedness. The road would have been easier.

From a rocky ridge the view upriver to the east is a daunting prospect, the once-mighty Snowy is hemmed in by raw-looking and extremely rugged peaks of the Byadbo Wilderness, the country from which many say the original Man from Snowy River rode into legend. Maybe the myth is a little too good to be true. Maybe I need to find out for myself. But then, in the face of such steepness, the easiest way to go would be on horseback.

Dense mounds of blackberry complicate crossing at the foot of Jacobs Ladder, one traditional route, maybe not the easiest, to Ingebyra and the tablelands. It was here, for example, that cattleman George Fead described how 500 head under eight or nine drivers came 'stumbling and sliding much against their will. At the foot a blackfellow, with three gins, offered their services to help us through the rocks and we found them very useful.' He paid them, of course, with tobacco and whitefella rations.[35]

The Tongaroo is bracing to my bare feet. They are still numb as I stride out easterly along an old track which, allowing that there was no vehicle access to this region before the Barry Way was put through in 1961, was most likely graded between that date and when national parks took over in 1971; it is now trafficable only by foot. I ignore the ladder to head easterly upriver. The walking is easier above the river. Soon I come into a special place: a chapel of impressively tall yellow box, white cypress, bundy and white box, where the ground is covered with Australian bluebells, and then I rest at Bark Camp Creek, where the cypress are huge. Some were logged many years ago, perhaps by a spot mill, at about the time the track was last used. Their stumps survive because the cypress resins make them resistant to termites. The ridge here rises northwards up to Jimmys Stairs, perhaps the easiest route to the northern Monaro according to the maps.

I cross over and keep on upriver to Biddi, now without pasture. I wonder how cattle survived here. The first parish map shows a hut above the river about which cattle might once have prospered. A bridle or brumby track leads further north along the river for a few kilometres to the flats at the junction with Slaughterhouse Creek. Many Aboriginal artefact sites show how much even this section, leading towards the gorge, was once used.

There is a flat space for my tent, and an alleyway to the river where I swim in the company of thousands of water striders. The water's sluggish – brown and murky – and not much cooler than the air. Once settled and rested, I find a spot to meditate on the thin moon, while the platypus come out for their evening frolics. It's not the most beautiful place on earth but it starts to grow on you.

Craggy ridges on both sides of the river are dotted with the blue-grey cypress which disconcert me somehow, perhaps because they look too much like Christmas trees and picture-postcards from another continent. This is their only significant occurrence east of the Great Divide. Plenty of silver wattles grow nearer the river with masses of seaberry saltbush as groundcover.

On my way up the fire trail next morning, headed for the top of the range, some red, stony cliffs smile from where the stone has – in a more recent epoch – broken away, exposing the fresh colours that are otherwise camouflaged by lichens and weathering. In geological terms this sharp rise marks the change from the orogenic granites of the Kosciuszko batholith to the much older Byadbo beds of volcanics and sediments that date from the late Ordovician some 400 million years ago. Also along this range are caves and cracks and crevices where the bogong moths gather in summer. Cypress-pines grow out of the bare stone that comes in so many different forms: rose quartz, yellow ochre colours punctuate many shades of red. Incongruities abound. The white box is a colourless kind of tree, usually well-formed, slow to grow, with a very hard, dense wood and bark that is grey, fibrous and scaly. Where so often mistletoes mimic their host, here they stand out from the silvery sheen of the box foliage by their bright orange leaves and pendulous habit and flowers; at a little distance what stands out are the vivid dot paintings of mistletoe.

Near the top I veer a kilometre or two down to the Slaughterhouse Hut, a miserable place still used by horsemen. On my way upwards along the trail again, there's plenty to interest me and yet I ponder what I'm doing. I've lost connection. I walk on automatically. My lips are cracking. This strange, difficult country must somehow fit into the jigsaw puzzle. In various places I can see the large ink-blots they call the Black Scrubs, which are in fact a dry rainforest comprised of a dense acacia canopy of up to 20 metres with an understorey of wax-flower, daisy-bush and hop-bush. They stand out like dark, sharply delimited birthmarks on precipitous slopes among the lighter coloured grassy woodland with their long-leaved box and mealy bundy. Research shows some of the patches are more than 100 years old and can be related to particular wildfires, although none that I know of can be dated to before the coming of the white man. The whole patch would be killed only by the hottest of fires and will regenerate as a closely growing, even-aged stand which, in the driest times, is likely to be favoured as a refuge by wildlife such as the wallaby, antechinus and such.[36]

Eventually, before the sun is directly overhead, I reach the top and the spot from which I can cut down the other side to the much spoken of Edbo Flats, the site where a hut once stood among a grove of plums now gone wild. These grasslands, attractive, lush and green along the drainage lines, in the midst of the bone-dry Byadbo Wilderness comprise country the horsemen still regard with an awe that verges on the mystical. It's another kind of Shangri-la in the midst of dry ruggedness; it even has a pool of murky water in the dry creekbed. This can't be permanent, surely? Above the knoll where the hut stood I find a scatter of very beautiful stone artefacts: one, sharp as a razor, sits so well between my forefinger and thumb as to suggest it might have been an ideal tool for cleaning possum skins. The 1845 returns for this area show the licence holder as Patrick McGuigan of Stockyard Flat. He had two huts, one set of stockyards, 6 acres under wheat and nine persons in residence. It was carrying 235 head of cattle, 17 horses but no sheep and produced, surprisingly, 500 pounds of butter. In 1848 the Stockyard Flat had an estimated area of 7000 acres and a carrying capacity of 600 cattle. Patrick McGuigan died at Stockyard Flat on 27 December 1862 aged 50 years. The death certificate states that he was born in Belfast, Ireland, and had been 33 years in the colonies.[37]

It was the luck of the Irish to find themselves stuck with the hardest lands. Time and time again I note the early Irish settlers on the rougher, difficult margins, always dependent on labouring for the wealthier squatters to survive. The grassy flats at an elevation of about 900 metres would have presented the perfect oasis for travellers on their way from the Snowy to the easier climate of the Monaro. From here, the route I propose following at a later date is a well-used way leading eastwards to the Byadbo Gap and the old Merambego station site. Then a little-used country road follows the ideal walking route through Corrowong to Delegate and beyond.

The Man

As evening colours the wispy clouds I'm headed back in a loop towards the Snowy and make camp at what I call the Impossible Flat, known to the cattlemen as The Lookout, elevation about 1200 metres. The temperature has quickly gone from very hot to very cold. The flat seems an impossibly good earthy perch this high on the ridge overlooking the deep wilderness canyons of Byadbo. It's a great place to camp, and as I hunt for the best sleeping spot I wonder how this remarkable place connects. Can there be a way forward? All I can see are sheer drops of several hundred metres. It's scarily beautiful. The sun's going down as I finalise camp. All day it's been so dry I haven't had enough fluid to take a piss. The horting, snorting and growling of possums barely disturbs my exhaustion. In the morning as if to demonstrate my height above it all, mist hangs over the snaking bends of the Snowy from the wilds below farmland near Paupong and Jimenbuen all the way past Biddi and Willis as far as I can see towards Orbost. It's disturbingly beautiful, for above that cloudy whiteness, the air is as clear as can be. Distance has its true colours rather than fading to blue. Places like the Cobberas and the high country are clear. I joke with myself that it's idiocy to trust 150-year-old maps, but push on confident this is the way to go.

From the flat my way drops quickly as though into the wild blue yonder, and yet there is always one comfortable step after another as I come down onto the gap between Sheep Station and Right Hand creeks. The dry creeklines far below form deep erosion scars, often overgrown with briar. These coarse granite soils drain immediately and wash away easily. Before too long I am on top of the ridge that leads me ever downwards. This is such a beautiful way, with bizarre colouring in the desiccated vistas of the valley bowls on either side. Creeks on the far side are like chasms cut deep into the slate and quartzite of the Black Range. My path through the white cypress–white box woodland is punctuated with the strange cranberry heath and the food plants, native cherry and kurrajong. The cherries are most common along major pathways. They're parasitic, not at all a tree that can be cultivated. Discussing this with a botanist one day we considered a likelihood the seeds may take best after passing through the human digestive system.

Hundreds of wanderer butterflies.

On my left, far below at the bottom end of the Sheep Station flatlands, lies the site of the long-gone McCoy's Hut and above that Reed's cattleyards. How many cattle could you run here today during our ever on-going drought? Maybe the national parks have done the cattlemen a service by pushing them out. George Reed senior took over the leases for this area in the 1920s until 1953 when Pat Ryan and the Reeds formed a partnership that leased 'about 58 663 acres of Crown Land which embraces the whole of the Parishes of Biddi, Tangaroo and Mount Trooper, and part of the Parish of Byadbo' for the annual sum of £48.10s. Clive Cottrell of Wallendibby told me that in 1957 on behalf of four different owners he helped them bring out 300 head of fat cattle, ones ready to go to the saleyards. This is something that could not happen today. He assures me that their practice at the time was to light slow burns in spring as they took the cattle out in order to produce grass for the next winter's grazing. Nonetheless, this country could not support the stock numbers of old, so they kept dwindling. He blames the rabbits.[38]

This route again has me excited and happy about progress, I sense I'm back on track. It's like a highway of nature that no motor vehicle has ever used. It leads me down to the Sheep Station just before its junction with Joe Davis Creek where the high, pine-clad ridges converge. Steep rockiness everywhere is dramatic. Among boulders at lowest points of the stone bed, quite miraculously, I find pools of water. They'd be close to a kilometre below the place where I spent last night.

As I pause in the shade, I consider how it's usually the big owners who are recognised in our histories, whereas the main players were more often their employees and contractors. Many local Aboriginal men, such as Harry Bradshaw, became brilliant horse-riders and sought-after stockmen both sides of the border, while others like Bill Mundy were known for their work with the brumbies.[39]

This is 'The Man from Snowy River' country. What other poem has had not one, but two movies inspired by it? The ethos it evokes is of someone prepared to break away from the mob and follow his own heart and instincts, of knowing the country better than anybody else, of being more at one with nature than the rest. It's the story of the little man triumphing against the odds. But, then again, it's one hard act to maintain. I would like to think I can look beyond the legend to the reality. This was also bushranger country. Rolf Boldrewood brings his hero of *Robbery under Arms* this way and remarks how good a hide-out it would make. But when you get to talking seriously, everyone I've met with connection to Byadbo seems to get round to the subject of the Joker sooner or later. He would be more renowned in the district than our fabled man from Snowy River, he's even dignified in the papers of the Bombala Historical Society:

> George James Howitt Patterson Johnson, always known as Joker not only worked for and with the McKays but one of his three wives was Lucy McKay, sister of DH and Mac McKay. Joker was married three times and often stated that one was for love, once for money and once for comfort. Joker was born at Sale, Victoria, and died at Delegate in 1943 aged 71 years. Magnificent horseman, superb bushman, intuitive worker of stock, Joker became a legendary figure of the northern Gippsland and southern Monaro country and many stories, not always complementary, are told of his feats. It is said that just as nature abhors a vacuum, Joker abhorred seeing anything,

animate or inanimate, without an apparent owner, and would immediately act to remedy the situation.[40]

Local grazier Pat Ryan fleshed out one story for me, saying, 'McKays bought the Slaughterhouse run of 66 000 acres from Haydens round the end of the first War. They were supposed to muster 1200 head but got only 800,' he says with the wry smile that speaks for Aussie humour. He pauses, long and meaningful, then nods. 'Joker.'[41]

The route from the creek junction takes some pondering. The mountainsides appear to rise in cliffs too abruptly from the creeks: crumbling granite soils make clambering too difficult and so, needing to go south, I choose to head towards the gap to Sandy Creek via the mountain on my left. A brumby trail points the way at first but soon peters out, as they do so often. Most brumbies clearly migrate across the Snowy to the high green flats closer to Kosciuszko when things are so dry. Then I spot two greenhood orchids in flower, and a boomerang wattle. In the heat, the clamber up the crumbling slope is demanding.

The big spreading cypresses are certainly the oldest. Some have been dated to over 200 years ago. When GA Robinson came through in 1844 during his quest to find the Aboriginal people, he described even bigger trees with dense grasses and rich dark soils, but things are very different today. The soils are unstable, crumbling, gouged into stony gullies by erosion; they lack the grasscover and the stabilising effect of surface lichens and fungi, so that the rich layers of the topsoils have gone and generally the oldest trees seem perched on their root systems a hand-span above ground level. In recent times every 5 or 10 years a fire will pass through to consume what little grass and shrub layer has remained after the trampling by cattle and horses, the devastation wrought by plagues of hares and then rabbits. As a child visiting the Monaro during holidays, before the myxomatosis came, I witnessed entire hillsides turn brown with a carpeting of live rabbits. The damage done to the countryside is, now, almost unimaginable; what remains are only the after-effects. But now, with rabbits still present in a thinly spread population, they are always threatening to increase again. It is an ever-changing equation, as the rabbit numbers fall and pasture begins to return, the brumbies increase.

At the crest of the ridge, eventually, round 3 pm, I come onto the fire trail, and walk towards the river. But the signs of fire are only part of what made the countryside. On my way to the river crossing I note many Aboriginal places; so many along the Lower Snowy they suggest it was more than the winter refuge adopted by cattlemen. Its far richer environment in early times must have been used intensely. At one large flat I stop for a closer look because it is so rich with artefacts. It may well have been used for thousands of years. Ancient white gums nearby still bear the scars where canoes were cut from their bark. My mind charts the connection with a carved tree a little downriver – its representation of the jagged mountaintops and circles – and the vision I had earlier in the day of a mystic arrangement of large stones. On one of the higher parts of the walk my mind only slowly began to comprehend how the rocks all round were arranged into patterns at first hard to discern due to weeds and patches of scrub. I'm used to finding stone circles that take many forms, in similarly elevated places, but the shapes the stones take confound me this time. The realisation slowly dawns on me: it is not an arrangement, but simply one of those few-and far-between magic places.

With all its dryness the country round Byadbo and along the Lower Snowy stays much warmer in winter than the high country or even the tablelands, and was hence much sought after by the cattlemen for winter grazing. The landscape is dramatic enough to figure in the national mythology. Banjo Paterson's setting for the poem does in fact bear more than a passing resemblance to the Byadbo area:

> ... And down by Kosciusko, where the pine-clad ridges raise
> Their torn and rugged battlements on high,
> Where the air is clear as crystal, and the white stars fairly blaze
> At midnight in the cold and frosty sky,
> And where around the Overflow the reed-beds sweep and sway
> To the breezes, and the rolling plains are wide,
> The Man from Snowy River is a household word today,
> And the stockmen tell the story of his ride.[42]

Maybe Joker was The Man. Maybe he was just a typical character. Maybe The Man stands for individual human spirit triumphing over a hostile environment. But then again, maybe we should rename him the man from the Nurudj Djurung. Aboriginal friends tell me, 'That "Man from Snowy River" feller, he was a Koori. Who else coulda done what he did? Who else woulda known the country that well?'

I'm back at my Moyangul camp before sundown.

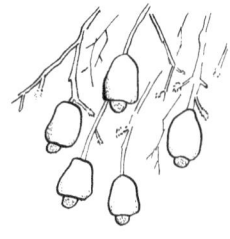

Byadbo trails

A few days by the river are the perfect respite before I head back into Byadbo. As I climb a fire trail beside the very dry Sandy Creek the wildlife becomes scarcer. The slopes of the trail here, like those of the Pinch, are too steep to attack directly. You have to zigzag to keep traction. How the cypress survives on such bone-dry hillsides defies imagination. Maybe it's the difficulty of clinging on that makes it all so appealing.

Some distance up and more than 300 metres above the river, as I come out of the cypress country into the white box woodland where there is a little more grass, I veer off the trail to visit Reed's place, the Sandy Creek Hut, a relatively charming corrugated iron box with several ingenious window arrangements that flip up to let in light. Three empty Icemaster fridges serve for storage, a couple of empty Scotch whisky bottles, an empty pack of Ratsak and an ancient but full bottle of Coke reside there along with a dead rabbit, highly desiccated, in the middle of the earthen floor. The heat of the day is sapping all moisture along with energy and it's a relief to sit under the shade of an iron awning beside the fireplace to eat my lunch. Logs have been cut into tables and chairs, which make primitive but effective comforts. The district is generally dry, grassy woodlands.

As I continue higher I come among the red mudstones that overlap the granite. It's getting hotter and shade is rare. Views direct my eyes back towards the high country, shimmering with heat like a seething blanket of blue haze. Salt crystals form on my skin. I'm glad when things cool towards the end of the day as I'm making camp in the middle of the track. Just on nightfall I hear a whooshing through the forest. I look up in shock that is reciprocated by the huge owl, which baulks in its glide to settle on a branch not far above my head to inspect me for a while. It's an awesome, fully grown powerful owl, almost as big as my backpack. What a vision.

My camp is only a short distance from the well tree, a landmark of the hot, dry ridgetop. It is an old mountain gum with part of its top knocked out and a hollow at ground level where good water accumulates. So far as anyone knows it has never run dry. Many animals know its secret. Well-trampled tracks converge here from all quarters. Softer patches of sand reveal dingo, wombat, macropod, pigeon and possum tracks as well as those of sundry other small mammals that probably include antechinus, bushrat, quoll and even small bats. Perhaps this makes the place a good hunting territory for the owl. At daybreak, all manner of small birds come visiting. I also take my share. It tastes sweet and not at all of the gum resins I expected. At least I still have a few litres of water in my backpack.

The way to Tingaringy by this fire trail follows the crest of the range, unfortunately it's mostly either steeply up or down, hundreds of metres at a time. Without compromise. This is the divide that roughly parallels the state border; the natural border. The forests are now changing from the white box–cypress of the Snowy districts. The changes are sometimes radical, depending on variations in soil and topography. The black scrubs are so sharply delineated they look like ink spots on the hillsides. Here among mountain gums, peppermints are creeping in. My feet are fortified by liberal applications of Goanna Oil and I feel I'll have to walk a long way today. I'm happy to be going before the unnaturally hot autumn sun kicks in again. My thoughts turn to the possibility of tolerance and humour in the wilds. It seems crazy that so many groups want to lay claim to such country as this, even the horsemen with their huts who should know better. They once managed it on their own terms, for better or worse, and now see it as falling apart or 'going to the dogs'. Neighbouring landholders have long plagued the parks to control wild dogs.

Among stringybarks later, I come upon feathers. Then, curiously, the very large beak and head of a night bird (often mistaken for an owl), a tawny frogmouth. Quite a few feathers but not enough. The kill must have been last night. And all that remains is the top of the skull and the horny beak. What creature might have the skills to capture and eat a fully grown frogmouth? Could I say it's a dog-eat-dog world out here? Owl-eat-night bird? The forests are taller, the hills more abruptly steep as the full heatwave strikes and very foolishly I allow myself to drink copiously. Then, there are the small, white-stemmed eucalypts forming ghostly patterns through the scrub. In a patch of shade I wolf down lunch and finish off with the succulent little green fruits of the devil's twine that taste like jelly babies. Then from one hilltop I get a fabulous view of Tingaringy in the afternoon light, its stony ramparts so shiny red and polished they look slimy; a giant slippery slug lying on top of the forests. This precedes a very steep downhill section.

The monotony of taking one step after another, uphill and then down again, is shattered when I arrive at a track junction where I buried a bladder of water some weeks ago. In an old stump-hole I dig through stones, soil and general litter to find the bladder has been punctured and now contains not more than a tablespoon of water. This is serious. I curse my stupidity in trusting it could survive. One corner has been chewed by small teeth, perhaps those of an antechinus or bushrat. I guess water is at such a premium it was eagerly sought. My practice in these places is never to drink more than half the water I'm carrying. So even though I drank heavily earlier, my sips have been getting sparser as the afternoon draws on. Even so, I don't have enough moisture to urinate. My resolve now is to make as much distance as possible in the cooler evening hours. It's more than a day's walk to the next place where I know I'll find water: Corrowong Creek. I search the maps for inspiration so that when a good camp presents itself, my thought is to visit an old grazing lease a few kilometres on the fall to Victoria. Jerry's Flats are not necessarily promising, but they do present the best possibility of finding water sooner rather than later. I stumble down through the stringybarks following a dry creekline that begins to look greener and greener. At last, after a few kilometres, in a rocky section I find a well that's been dug out by kangaroos and used by very many creatures. But the few tablespoons of water are brown and putrid. In such stony soil, digging it deeper would take a very great effort and so I continue in the hope a better waterhole might appear. I note that many of the old Aboriginal wells were covered by large stone to keep the water at its best. Further along, green flats have tussocks over a metre high and falling down wire fences. A few more of the wells present only water too disgusting for me to drink even in my present condition of thirst and despite the fact I know ways of filtering it. There might be better water further downhill but my condition won't allow further exploration.

Back at camp I don't think about how peaceful it is here until noisy neighbours in the form of sulphur-crested cockatoos begin their evening call and response and partying. As the cockatoos fade in the dark, the possums begin their squabbling. The extremely low humidity here is due to a rainshadow from the high country.

The trees are now taller and the forest grassier. From one mountaintop Tingaringy, at closer range, looks as threatening as a hunk of rock can be. Scientists investigating the wildlife of those relatively treeless cliffs abseiled down to set up movement-triggered cameras to see what creatures might visit a small cave. Among the usual suspects, one shot showed a koala visiting the cave. What strange country this is. There are some very old brownbarrel, one as twisted and wrinkled as an ancient woman. Then, way down in the lowlands, I spy the very beautiful property called Ambyne, a place friends suggested I visit. Aha. Before too many kilometres I come into the Ambyne Gap where I leave my pack behind and turn downhill towards the station through magnificent open tall grassy forest of pale-stemmed mountain and ribbony gum, the sort of place that gives me the strength to continue regardless. It is more like a mythical forest: how things used to be. I realise there's a chance I'm hallucinating, so I take photographs just to prove to myself such a forest still exists. There is little understorey, a few paper daisies and small silver wattles, leaving only the soaring trees whose height and separation is reduced by perspective so that a clear view of over 100 metres appears crowded with trees. And so I can walk steadily towards the fences with no impediment. The low grasses grow all the way to the tree trunks. Kangaroos, wombats and emus are clearly in their element here, although koalas are extremely hard to discern as the canopy is simply too far away. Once I pass the fenceline into sheep paddocks, the granitic soils are eroded into terrifying erosion gulches.

Approaching the rambling old weatherboard homestead, I see a bent figure and call to him. The man is deeply shocked. How long must it have been since he's had a visitor on foot come from the south? I introduce myself, saying, 'I've come for two reasons. I understand you're one of the few traditional farms left in the area and I wouldn't mind a drink.'

'Traditional?' he says.

'In the sense it has passed on down through the family.'

'Ah,' he says softly as he sizes me up. 'Well, first off, you look as if I better get you a drink.' Norman Stewart has a way of understatement. He leads me towards a rainwater tank where I manage to glug down a few litres more than you should drink at one time.

'Excuse the house,' he says to me before we go inside; 'but it's a bachelor's house.' He shows me a painting of how it used to be 80 years ago, the classic homestead with formal flower gardens all about, where today the surrounds are much less genteel, being little more than a house paddock with scattered fruit trees. It is nevertheless a big house that sits on the property handsomely. Then we sit at a little table in a cool corner with a water jug and tell our stories. He says how Robert Campbell, the first white settler to come across the Monaro from near where Canberra stands today, squatted on all this country. Campbell made his station at Delegate, claiming all the vast lands of the southern Monaro. 'After the Selection Acts, which let in the small farmers, my grandfather dummied up here. He used to carry the mail between here and Delegate and Bombala. My father was born in 1898. All that country out the back is where they used to run thousands of head of cattle but it's all scrubbing up now. The bushfires started that. We used to go out to Willis on the Snowy chasing brumbies but all that's scrubbing up too and you can't get through nowadays ... There's a permanent creek at the bottom of Jerry's Flat which runs into Ambyne Creek, which comes out on the Deddick in Vic near the swinging bridge.' On the subject of the forest that so impressed me, he tells me that over the years they had only ever taken a few trees for their own purposes, such as fence posts, and there's never been any logs taken out for milling. In more recent times before Parks bought Merambego, Pat Ryan used to run cattle out there in the Edbo Flats and Jerry's Flat, both freeholds that went to Parks with the purchase. The country out towards the Snowy and Willis was wintertime grazing as it's too dry and too hot the rest of the year. It's the opposite of the high country where they had to get the stock out during the cold weather when Willis is as warm as anything.

Now in his 80s, he's still a horse rider, he says, especially as this has been beautiful country to ride in. He helped build the hut at Sandy Creek. The one at Slaughterhouse Creek was built by Gordon Walker who had the grazing leases there many years ago. McKays owned all the Wollondibby country and they had a couple of outlaws working for them including Joker Johnson who was a pretty smart fella. Haydens sold McKays their brand for £2000 but McKays didn't get the numbers they were expecting. Joker Johnson and his mates had cattle planted out there on Haydens' behalf, and they doubled their money when they drove out the planted cattle. Everything that had a brand on it was McKays, the rest were Haydens. 'It's outlaw country,' he tells me and continues:

> They done it hard. It's been 10 years since I've ridden in the Edbo because now it's wilderness you can't ride there any more ... Haydens used to live at the stonehouse on the other side of Merambego, and they used to run their blood stallions up by Edbo. There used to be a hut on the way in from the gap at the Stockyard Flats: Ffolkes's Hut. You could only sleep one in it. They were digging for gold there, you can see their mineshaft. In the paddock at Edbo there's graves, about five. They used to be able to take the wagon in from Merambego. There was a hut at Jerry's Flat too. We get better rain here than Bombala because we're in a gap beside the mountain. Ours is 30 inches but looking down on the plain they only get 20. The soil here really washes out. In the old times all the family had was a single furrow plough and, when they ploughed the flat clearings, it started the erosion washouts.

He seems to be enjoying himself. As he talks, I glug down his rainwater as if it's the finest wine.

The cross-country walk back to my pack confirms why his grandfather took up the land in the saddle on the edge of the tall forests. The slopes below look out across the Monaro, command it magisterially. You can see the patterns of the land and its vegetation beyond the foreground vista of white sallees forming woodland with all too many clearings that were formed naturally or fostered by the fires of its Aboriginal inhabitants.

Tingaringy and the Howitt country

Very much more fortified and rehydrated, I take another route back to my pack. My plan is to camp on top of Tingaringy tonight even though clouds have come over and showers fall. Just as Norman Stewart fatefully told me, this is a good rainfall district with tall red stringybark and ribbony gums. Good koala country. For the first time in weeks it's so humid I'm sweating profusely. I take a short-cut cross-country, the direct walk from Norman's is 8 kilometres and a climb of 500 metres. Changes in the geology bring a succession of plants and demand exploration. As I walk upwards, commanding views of the region take away my aches and pains. In stony heathlands on ledges along the way up come a profusion of wildflowers: *Gompholobium, Dillwynia, Oxylobium, Kunzea, Hibbertia, Phebalium.* The sheer beauty lifts my mood on par with the mountain. Patches of forest and white sallee woodland interweave. A New South Wales–Victoria border cairn stands near the summit, a neatly squared pile that speaks of greater importance than the rougher heap at Forest Hill. There's an extraordinary range of plants as I climb towards the peak at 1450 metres, including the khaki-stemmed mallee known as Tingaringy gum. It's one of those eucalypts that have adapted to the harshest places and taken a delightful form in the process. It varies from place to place, here being low-growing but in other places further away in Victoria such as Mount Erica it can top 40 metres. A very similar eucalypt, Suggan Buggan mallee, also takes a many-stemmed form on the hard ridges overlooking the Snowy. It's as though the country demands specially adapted forms from its vegetation. And can it be that its people and their fires have worked with the countryside to produce such diverse wildlife? This variability is what makes the route so exciting. AW Howitt found a similar thrill and wrote about it in his long 1890 paper, 'The eucalypts of Victoria'.[43]

As I look south and westwards where the rivers run southwards through Gippsland to Bass Strait, I realise I am looking over the Howitt country. It's an area where he has manifold connections, for when I come to consider the question of fire and this landscape I must turn to his family.

While I was very young I learned the extreme emotions that bushfires can bring. It's one of my first strong memories. In 1952 my family was camping on the south coast of New South Wales at North Durras as the Black Friday fires approached. They had been burning for months in the mountainous back country after a farmer's burn-off escaped. Then, nor'-westerlies blew in from the deserts to drive fire fronts at the drought-stricken settled areas all along the coast and into Gippsland. The smoke was stifling. Burnt leaves fell everywhere. As the sun set, the air took on a frightening orange pallor, and we moved the car and all our things into the lake shallows. Darkness never really came that night. The glow of the fire lit the sky more brightly as time passed. There came a distant roar. When the entire western horizon was illuminated by leaping flames my senses were gripped by an excitement I remember vividly to this day. It was a conflict: I felt terror we might be hurt and lose everything, that all would change, but also I was struck by the beauty of a vision that seemed savage, unnatural, unforgettable in its power.

Fire is part of the Australian ethos. Beside a campfire, looking deep into the coals, is the best place to tell its stories. There is an inevitability that Judith Wright raised in her poem, 'The Two Fires', a spectre of the return of the ancient kingdom of fire.[44]

The history of fire in Australia appears to tell the same story over and over, whether of the firestorms of 1939's Black Friday or 1983's Ash Wednesday. Is it that enough years pass between the most extreme conditions for the memories of the terror to fade? An all-but forgotten chapter of Australian fire history was written by Englishman William Howitt, and published in London by Cassell's *Illustrated Family Paper* on 4 February 1854. Other parts followed in subsequent issues. The detail suggests that the 1851 fires were worse than any that have followed, even though the rise in population could make today's big fires more calamitous in terms of the loss of property and human life.

His intense curiosity brought William Howitt and his two sons to Melbourne in 1852. The gold rushes also played a part. He was the renowned author of works that included *The Rural Life of England* (1838). His literary circle included Charles Dickens, Alfred Tennyson, Robert and Elizabeth Browning and the Wordsworths. His brother, Godfrey, a much-respected doctor who lived on a Melbourne acreage that spread from Collins Street to Flinders Lane, with a formidable garden fronting Spring Street, was also a celebrated entomologist and botanist. In fact, Godfrey was the Howitt rewarded by Baron Sir Ferdinand von Mueller with the native plant genus name of *Howittia*. Their family inclination was to see nature with a scientific eye, that reason and faith could co-exist, even guide our understanding of God and nature. His pedigree meant William was welcomed by Melbourne's gentry and granted access to society and the institutions that might be helpful to him.

He soon found there were signs to be noted in the bushland that came to the doors of Melbourne. No observer could miss them. Even 18 months after the event, the Black Thursday fires were still a topic of conversation. They had affected all aspects of life. The costs were substantial, not only in economic terms. Wherever he went William Howitt witnessed the appalling evidence. 'Why?' he asked. 'How could such a calamity happen? Might it come again?' In his methodical way he set out to document the fire, its causes and consequences.

In those days of limited communications few could give an overview of what happened, for the inferno had swept away so many of its witnesses. Howitt saw the extent of the calamity, how

> No one could possibly imagine it. That the country was actually one blaze for thousands of square miles, that the conflagration extended ... 300 miles in one direction, and of, at least, half that distance in the other. It extended eastward to the Dandenong Hills, to Western Port, and right away into Gippsland. Who could suppose that over all this vast expanse this annihilating incandescence had passed in one day?[45]

Coming only 15 years after the beginnings of European settlement, the countryside was still subject to the traditions of Aboriginal burning. Howitt makes it clear fires were being lit all the time, even 'during the summer. They arise from various causes, and are, in many instances, originated purposefully, both by natives and colonists, from ideas of utility.'[46]

The fires of 1851 did not come only as a consequence of European practises if Aboriginal low-intensity mosaic burning was still taking place; but perhaps the traditions were discontinuous by this time, although a mere 15 years should not have made much difference. Nonetheless it has to be emphasised that the fires came regardless of very extensive burning. He made careful distinctions, for example, differentiating the more common dry eucalypt forests from the ash forests and their ferny, misty gullies that can sustain fire only in the worst droughts, usually sparked by lightning.[47]

Howitt saw the factors that can turn a bushfire into a firestorm: a blowtorch combination of wind and temperatures in the mid-40s that vaporise flammable eucalyptus oils. His descriptions of 'cattle in vast herds ... careering madly before the fires,' and 'troops of horses, wild from the bush ... Flocks of kangaroos, and of smaller animals ... hosts of birds swept blindly on ...' provided the inspiration for composition on a grand scale in the well-known 1864 painting by William Strutt, *Black Thursday, February 6th, 1851*.[48]

Howitt wanted to strike it rich on the goldfields but, ever the writer, few observations from his travels went undocumented, undoubtedly to the detriment of his prospecting. In the preface to his 1854 *A Boy's Adventures in the Wilds of Australia*, he says the boy's adventures and experiences in the Australian bush were written amid the scenes and characters it describes, which is patently true for it is written from the point of view of his son. Descriptions of conversations, landscape and all that happens from day-to-day abound. There are also detailed descriptions of their life in the bush and on the goldfields in his more considered *Land, Labor and Gold; or, Two Years in Victoria* (1855), which forms its tale through letters to his wife. He describes the post-fire forests on the road to the Ovens goldfields in terms that might as easily have been applied to any of the old Aboriginal pathways:

> The road, or rather track, continued for some miles dry and good; and we seemed to be journeying through a pleasant park. If there were a bad place in the road, we could turn out – there were no fences; and we found many such winding tracks, all leading back again into the main road. As there was no underwood, and the trees were only thinly scattered, we had a clear view of our way before us. All was green and grassy beneath. So far we have no dense woods, such as the beech-woods of Germany or the oak-woods of England, where the tree-tops make a continual shade – in the former country often for scores of miles – and all below is brown, bare earth, scattered with leaves. Here the eucalypti are so thinly scattered, and their foliage is so thin, that they afford little or no shade in sunshine, or shelter in rain. Everywhere the traces of fire in these parts are universal.[49]

And although today many understand the interdependence between fire, forest and people in scientific terms, it is something else for us to be able to admit the consequences in human terms. Conundrums spring, like the issue of fire-caused 'scrub'. Oversimplifications abound. Many seek to blame other people when the truth lies in the nature of the forests, for there is a considerable variety of them, and all take fire differently. Howitt documents many consequences including, often in fine, gruesome detail, the cost in human life: 'The bodies had been placed on the dray in the same positions in which they were found, and had their faces to the ground. Four of the bodies were quite charred, and of those two of the children were far from complete ...'[50]

The memory of fires can haunt, even scar; those fires of my childhood are indelibly fixed in my mind. But my family was fortunate for at some point in the middle of the night the flames stopped. At the edge of the nearby escarpment, perhaps propelled by wind furies of their own making, they leapt towards the ocean to pass over the strip where we sheltered. Next morning, beyond our still-green oasis, the countryside was changed. Blackened, smoking, drained of colour, little remained of the works of man bar heaps of twisted corrugated iron and standing chimneys. Perhaps my memories have a positive side insofar as they taught me early that there are forces beyond the reach of humans, beyond control. We are drawn to the intensity of infernos but at the same time it is as though we must look away, for fear of damnation and consignment to a flaming hell.

William brought his tale towards conclusion by describing what he found in his travels over the desolated region. From Mount Disappointment he saw the ranges covered with leafless trees which had perished, whole dead forests. At the last moment, however, he averted his eyes from visions of the thundering tide of fire blown to whiteness by the super-heated wind, perhaps to avoid looking into the abyss.

Fire is part of the Australian countryside, and always will be. Firestorms, that most extreme form of bushfire, are possible no matter what manner of precautionary burning has taken place. So much is beyond the control of man. The natural forces that Howitt described are now threatening more often. His account shows that we had an understanding even then, in the 1850s, of what it was all about.

Within days of their arrival in the colony, William Howitt's 22-year-old son, Alfred, already well-schooled in the natural sciences and clarity of observation, was writing to his mother of parrots and lories screeching in old gum trees by the Yarra bridge, while noting the creeping native plants and their flowers. The young man demonstrated the value of consulting others. He would continue his father's observations of humans, fire and the countryside and, better known as AW Howitt, become the renowned bushman, explorer and pioneering anthropologist who documented the nature of south-east Australia as well as its Aboriginal people and, himself, become a guide to later generations.

From Tingaringy, I can see directly over the gap of the Playgrounds, south of the Cobberas, towards Omeo where AW Howitt spent many years as gold commissioner and, beyond that, the Ovens goldfields where the bookish young man was introduced to the wilder Australian bush in the company of his father and 14-year-old brother.

His writings are an invaluable guide precisely because not only did he have a curiosity about the region, he actually got up from his desk and went out into the bush. On the theme of fire in this region he noted his observations of the effects of Aboriginal burning on the countryside at the same time as he supplied not only the Aboriginal names for the trees, but also the dialect and districts in which they applied. His investigations took him all through Gippsland and into New South Wales.

He was a frequent visitor to this district. I can make out fences of the Tubbut station which abuts Tingaringy, where his great friends the Whittakers settled in 1850 after 4 years at Tombong. His daughter married their son. The connections go on.

Much and all as Howitt wrote about the trees and the geology and particular places, his deepest interests came to be focussed upon the Aboriginal people, especially those of the region. He wrote eloquently of the Kurnai, the people of his country in Gippsland, but also the related neighbouring tribes: the Yaitmathang from near Omeo, the Ngarigo from the Manero, the Biduelli from the valleys and forests south of the tableland, the Krautungalung, a clan of the Kurnai tribe from the coast between the 90 mile beach and Cape Everard and the Yuin of the coast and coastal plains north of Cape Howe. His thinking changed over time. His opinions were often inaccurate, and sometimes out of sync with modern knowledge. But his attempts to describe the traditional cultures of the Aboriginal people were sufficiently systematic they made a foundation that could be built upon and provide invaluable insights into a way of things that has been all-but forgotten. Much has been made of his dealings with sacred objects, one suggestion has been that much of the information he gleaned was arrived at falsely because he misled Elders into thinking he had been initiated. That is, to my thinking, underestimating the Elders he was supposed to have tricked. My strong suspicion is that they well knew Howitt's position, his level of understanding and his empathy regarding what they let him record. They chose to honour his standing in their community and include him in certain ceremonies, as an honorary or whitefella wise man, but did not necessarily give him everything. They kept back what was most important for them to retain. If, in the Aboriginal culture there is no single holder of all the knowledge, the closest you can get to an 'expert' view of the men's culture is to have all the wise men or knowledge holders sitting in a circle to give their judgement, which he seldom had. Then again there is the women's knowledge, which Howitt did not record. Wisdom lies with the Elders, not Howitt. He could record, without practising, how the gommera has the magic wisdom. No one knows it all. The moral is, respect the knowledge of the Elders. I would add that, notwithstanding his flaws, we should also respect the knowledge of AW Howitt. His *Native Tribes of South-East Australia* is a monumental work that deserves respect. It is of value to me to understand that the knowledge of the local people passed down from mouth to mouth can still coincide with the 'scientific' writings of Australia's first great anthropologist.[51]

That Howitt was interested and took the traditions seriously was fundamental to the maintenance of the culture at a time when the authorities were doing their damnedest to end it. When he attempted to revive a Kurnai Jeraeil ceremony in 1884–85 he incurred the wrath of the missionaries who were concerned about the return of paganism. The Ramahyuck mission superintendent, Reverend AH Hagenauer, wrote in protest to the Board for Protection of the Aborigines that, 'it seems as if Mr Howitt is becoming a Black brother himself'. The mission stations of the time throughout the south-east were places where Aboriginal people were to be contained, under threat, regardless of tribal ties or connections to country. In the hopeful prayer they might be trained to find gainful pursuits, any distraction such as the revival of 'paganism' was ruthlessly quashed. Missionaries railed against Howitt's proposed 'corroborees' to the board and the government as disruptive of mission life. Howitt nevertheless continued to promote activities such as his ethnomusicology:

> To most people they are unmeaning or barbarous chaunts, and to the missionaries, who have some knowledge of them, they savour of heathendom, and must, therefore, be altogether pushed into oblivion and be forgotten. Thus it is that before long all these songs ... will be lost. As it is, a source of simple and innocent amusement is cut off from the Aborigines by, no doubt, well-meaning but very narrow minded men.[52]

Alfred William Howitt was a man whose dedicated attempts to come to terms with this countryside were regarded as falling only a little short of madness within a society that demanded conformity. His 'eccentricities' were tolerated only due to his position in society. In the course of his attempts at better understanding he realised great and distinct lasting beauty in his sketches of the bush and its people. And so I'm happy to have him along as one of my guides. He was a man of his times, certainly, and he was often quite wrong. He missed a lot. Nonetheless as I go along, I argue with him. We dispute. We tell our own stories. We sit round the campfire at night and try to get down to what's important. The distance between us is not so great.

Tingaringy and the Howitt country

Tingaringy is a name I love for its tintinnabulation. It has been spelled variously over the years including Dingoringy, Tzingeringy. It gives a clear view west (as well as north and south) and hence allows me to trace my route from the Ramsheads while the winds start howling and storms appear. I watch wild showers falling on the Pinch and then go over the core of Byadbo! Rain there!! On Willis and Sheep Station? I can hardly believe what I'm seeing. Dark storm fronts appear everywhere as I sip my mug of tea, towards Orbost and the mouth of the Snowy then across the Monaro all the way to Canberra. I imagine that nowhere else in Australia could anyone find such a panoramic view of the Great Divide. The weather gets wilder by the moment. I am more excited as a lightning storm brews up with jags here and there at first, followed by sheet lightning. After one nearby strike a fire appears in the forest near Corrowong. When the rain comes I retire to my tent, certain it will extinguish the bushfire, and sleep soundly regardless of the buffeting and showers.

In the morning worse weather threatens on the far horizons and so I take off as soon as I can. My route is easterly through the tall forests to Corrowong Creek. The walk is refreshing for its cool and dampness, so I guess my body is still recovering from the dry. I love the blackwoods and shapely banyalla that overlook the extremely tall alpine ash forests which grow on the more-protected, southerly side of the ridge. They are big enough, perhaps, to be the survivors of the 1851 fires which brought about the death and regeneration of many such stands of the ash species. These eucalypts have developed as specialists in sustaining and surviving the very worst of firestorm conditions. While we have the ferny gullies and tall ash forests, we will continue to suffer the firestorms; such is one more fact of nature in the forests of Australia. They are a very different proposition to the mighty trees on the drier side of the ridge. Emus run ahead of me, indignantly shaking their tail feathers.

Glimpses come of the paddocks further ahead. Sometimes the ridgetop is rock and sometimes I find joyously grassy flats overlooked by the Christmas tree shapes of black olive-berry.

Among huge brownbarrels I come off the mountain and make my way to a truly great campsite near the creek crossing, arriving at lunchtime. There's more water than I've seen for a long time. In no time I peel off my disgusting clothes to splash about in a pool. What joy! When I finally get dressed storms unleash heavy rain. And I have the chance to reflect on how all the way from Geehi I have been walking in Kosciuszko National Park. Now, a few hundred metres along the track, I reach its eastern boundary.

During the night comes one of those miraculous events. I am sound asleep when a dingo nearby begins howling, soon to be joined by its mate. Their sounds are amplified by the mountainsides containing this forest, as though they come from the choristry of a great cathedral, their chorale rising and falling, the echoes sustained for an impossible time. That would have been magnificent enough, but soon more dingoes respond from further downstream. My hair stands on-end. I dare not move. Then two more dingoes on the mountain take up their part, before even more upstream also give voice. I have my little tape recorder with me in the tent but dare not move in case I interrupt the ceremony. The clouds have cleared and the moon is high when even more dingoes join in. At one point I count at least 30 dogs in the performance. Soon their voices are counterpointed by flying foxes cackling and squabbling in blossom high above.

Over the next few days I lay out my maps and research. It's the perfect place for me to come to grips with the Monaro's early days and the fact that my recent walk is off track.

Through the Stockyard

Walking Byadbo has to be one of the region's most extreme, unique and thrillingly beautiful undertakings. Realistically I have to admit I almost killed myself in recent days. The problem was water and heat. I didn't carry enough fluids. In the autumn weather of mid-March, usually great, cool walking weather and despite wide hat protection, I was sunburnt under my nose and chin by the sun's reflection from the crystals on the ground. Snakes are plentiful: tigers, browns, blacks and copperheads. Spiders of many species manage to survive the sometimes desertlike conditions. The nearest house at any stage is a very long distance away. The management trails I followed go for over 50 extremely hard kilometres without guarantee of water. Do you need to be mad to go there? No, I simply went the wrong way. Nonetheless, Byadbo is probably the most rewarding place I've ever walked. I'm well aware now of the preparations that are necessary. And so I immediately prepare to walk there again.

Ultimately, I figure, the old-timers will be able to point me in the right direction for travelling Byadbo. With some understanding of how intensely the area was used in the past, I go out of my way to speak with as many of the horseriders who knew it before it became a national park. The Reeds, Ryans, Guthries, Stewarts, Walkers, Prestons, Cottrells and others have spectacular stories reaching back to the early days of settlement that bring the area to life and point the way it was used over the years. Graeme Worboys, a ranger in the early days of Kosciuszko National Park, rode horseback through the area and kindly lends me maps of his routes. Chris Griffiths, a local Aboriginal ranger who wandered the area in his youth, tells me some of his stories of the greater district. For an area that appeared to be inhospitable, these people speak of it with such great affection and intensity I am better equipped for the trek as I begin walking again from Moyangul and along the Sandy Creek trail.

I understand how it is a climb through various steps, each like a bowl separated by ranges that run north to south. Nurudj Djurung lies at about 220 metres, the Sheep Station then sits at about 500 metres, further up across the Black Range at Byadbo it is 900 metres, then the Stockyard at 800 metres and over the Merambego Ridge to Merambego at 800 metres. The relatively fertile flats and grasslands of each have been protected by rocky gorges that choke the flow of the streams and maintain upstream silt deposits.

TS Townsend's long detour south by the river from Moyangul would be inexplicable if the terrain was not so much easier this way. You don't find those precipitous ridges – that complicate the shorter northern route – rising directly from the water. He used a traditional crossing point at the Sandy Creek ford, about 8 kilometres south of Moyangul. Above the crossing here I find a number of scarred trees and survey markers. I assume he left one of his marks here in 1842 because going back a mile at a time more trees appear to bear his marking. This crossing must have been the safest one when the river roared and bubbled its swollen course after the snow melt. Also, the route he marked is now followed by the fire trail until it crests the ridge dividing the Sandy and Sheep Station Creek catchments. At this point the ancient route goes directly down into the Sheep Station. It runs beside a true curiosity, a very old fence most likely constructed, I am told, during the 1840s. It consists of Y-shaped posts set in the ground with sturdy cypress poles topping them, the whole constructed without need of nail or wire, runs directly all the way down the hill. It has survived because the wood is resistant to termites. At the creek the route heads north following a remarkably well-defined pathway that crisscrosses the stream all the way to Joe Davis Creek, where Townsend deviated up the creek towards what they now call Pinch Gap and the head of Willis-Biddi Creek and then across the Snowy to the northern Monaro.

A few water holes can be found under granite boulders along the lower creek, but these might disappear in the driest weather. Any moisture quickly drains away deep into the granite sands. It might not be a desert but it feels like one. The steepness means a hard day's walk to get to the head of the creek and I push myself that extra bit to reach the crest of the range.

The route through the Sheep Station is a delight to follow, not only because of its unusually open wild and scenic qualities but because it is engrossing. The ancient route to the southern Monaro continues a little further beside the Sheep Station Creek and then climbs gradually out onto the rim of the bowl to follow its northerly divide all the way to the top of the Black Range, as some refer to it, onto the hill marked with an elevation of 1219 metres and on down the south-easterly ridge to Byadbo Flat. In general the horsemen agree with this route, although some also regularly used a lower route along Slippery Hole Creek. Throughout the Sheep Station, perhaps due to its very little grass or scrub, the signs of its prior use are most evident. Foreign metal objects here, from the cattlemen, artefacts there. On one flat, all stones had been moved to form rings around the old white box tree trunks, as though to make a playground for children. Horsemen assure me they'd never bother with such an exercise. The quantity of artefacts along the route confirm how the cattlemen simply followed the old Aboriginal pathway. Despite being so wild and uninhabited I appreciate the dark humour of it being named a *sheep station*.

Questions of fire are like my constant companions. Here in Byadbo they were considered by park scientist, Ian Pulsford, in his 1991 thesis on disturbance history. He followed dendrochronological researcher John Banks in dividing the influence of human use into eras of the Aboriginal, pre-1840 – when a sequence of events within a decade of the cessation of mosaic burning by Aboriginal people saw woodlands become more dense, and fires less frequent but more severe – and the European, from 1834 to the present, which has five periods:

1| 1834–70: large numbers of cattle grazed freely and graziers increasingly used fire to promote green shoots for the cattle. There was a significant difference between these fires, typically started in the heat of summer, and those of the Aboriginal people. Severe erosion, more scrub, and loss of old trees were common outcomes of the grazier fires.

2| 1870–1900: good rainfall years brought wheatfield regeneration of white cypress and lower erosion.

3| 1900–40: rabbits arrived bringing lower productivity and more erosion. Fewer fires were more severe and more destructive. Severe droughts in 1935–45 aggravated stress on the oldest trees and caused the loss of many.

4| 1940–61: decline of grazing. Little regeneration of the

cypress. Myxoma virus wiped out most rabbits after 1952, but no massive regeneration of trees occurred, perhaps due to loss of topsoil and its stores of organic matter and nutrients.

5| 1961–present: grazing was prohibited but continued illegally and feral horses had their fill. Grasses began to return, but recovery was extremely slow due to depleted ground conditions, which continue.[53]

Today, there's barely enough vegetation at ground level to sustain a fire. But after I cross the Black Range the flats round Byadbo Creek have a very different quality. The mountains are topped with more varied forests, which give way to clearings and grasslands on the flat country. But intense wildfires of recent years have produced a scrubby acacia/eucalypt regrowth that is taking over the tussocky grasslands.

From the Edbo Flats I stride out downstream beside Byadbo Creek, through grassy flats with plenty of khaki-trunked black sallees. At the junction with O'Hares Creek, the first major junction, the track runs directly uphill to follow the crest of the Stockyard Ridge northerly and parallel to the creek which here forms a very difficult gorge. The way eventually tilts back towards the creek and peters out where it rejoins the stream at a place of pleasantly grassy flats. At a crossing near their centre the track becomes more obvious. Bulbine lilies, an Aboriginal food plant, cluster on richer parts. Kangaroos and wildflowers are plentiful, as are brumbies, unfortunately. The Stockyard has ancient quarries and partly-worked hatchet or axe blanks are common. Volcanic activity and intense folding has resulted in useful varieties of stone, including shales that have metamorphosed into intensely hard rocks that come away in ideal, ready-to-work sizes. The resulting dark grey to black hatchet or axe heads can be found all along the ancient route.

The higher country

My route passes the long-deserted Ffolkes' mine, located in a hairpin bend in the creek, which is also called Little River. The excitement of following this way with its quick changes and delights has been growing as the track becomes distinct, I'm certainly back on track. It's more like a route used since ancient times, along which carts could have been hauled more recently. Then, passing through woodlands and low forest and wildfire generated silver wattle scrubs, it leads by a simple, direct route to the Byadbo Gap, overlooking the grasslands of Merambego. Of all my walks, I treasure this one the most. It beats the fire trails on every score. Reaching, at last, the crest of the Merambego Ridge is a triumph.

PART 2
THE MONARO

We wish to walk with you, we don't wish to walk alone.

Pastor Doug Nicholls, 2010[1]

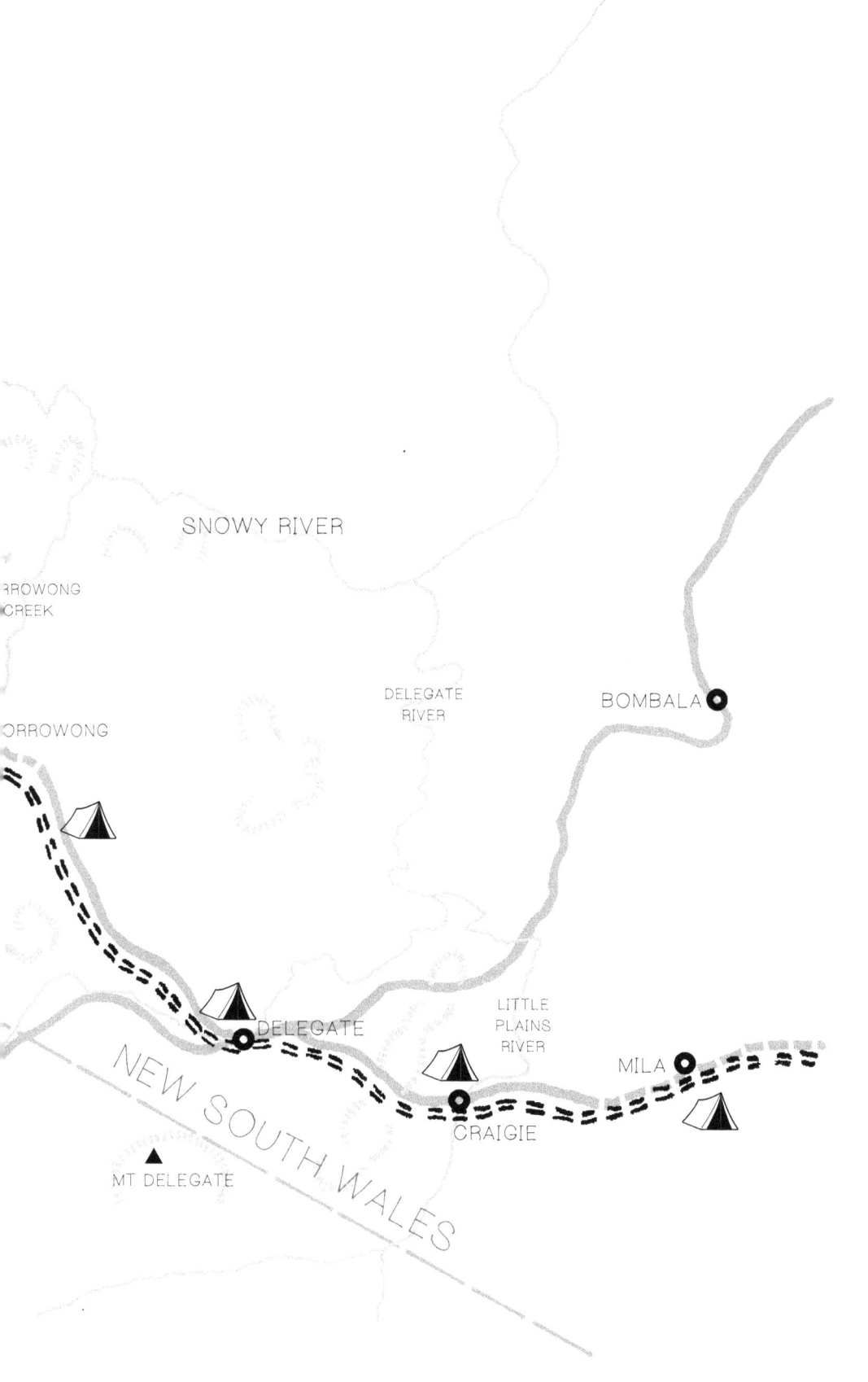

Merambego

Merambego is a grassy valley of various moods. Now part of Kosciuszko National Park it displays its Aboriginal and grazing history as easily as you might read it in a book. My understanding has developed since my thirst-quenching meeting with Norman Stewart. Now I find a landscape with people, not ghosts. And from here the country brings a different challenge to the wilds of Byadbo. To begin with there's a road; it must lead towards civilisation. Suddenly I have to consider others, and their conceptions of a world. Things are different here. I feel a need to make sense of what's happened in this distinctive countryside.

As I come over the hill towards the site of the Merambego homestead 30-odd emus run away in a cloud of dust. This is a serious drought; hardly any grass is to be seen. The scene strikes my heart so that I feel not lost, but out of the way of things. A sense of desperate isolation overtakes me. The emus pause, looking back at me until I move again; they quickly disappear into the dusty mirage. Back in the wilds, it was only me and nature. But here other people figure. It's so out of the way it's like being on the outer rim of civilisation, a Mad Max sort of place. The sense of desolation is deepened by my knowledge that these now gone-wild places were once well populated, by the old Maneroo and then by the settlers who had few expectations other than to observe the seasonal conditions for a sufficiency in the abundance of the time. *What now?* I wonder. I look down along the pot-holed dirt track that must lead me through scrubby pastures back towards the 21st century and a town that's seen better days. The way has brought me to the extensive grasslands of Merambego Creek's catchment. This is where the many forests meet, the far edge of the barely-recognisable Monaro.

Merambego was purchased in 1953 by Pat Ryan. All that's left are the flies and scattered debris where his old home was demolished. It would be a source of anguish to him that the paddocks he kept clear with fire are now scrubbing up with teatree, silver wattle and dogweed. A dam provides water for the emus and great mobs of kangaroos. So far as I can find, some springs apart, no streams have running water. Ongoing droughts seem to indicate changing climate has hit the district hard. It must be a blessing that Ryan doesn't have to make a living off this land any more.

But that was what I found on my first visit. Yet first impressions do not always capture the place adequately. Now I have been back through Merambego many times and each visit brings new visions, my appreciations have greater depth. Whenever I come over the ridge it's like the beginning of a new adventure. On one occasion, a few square hectares around the homestead are painted a surreal purple. (The Pattersons curse sprayed by parks, is no longer evident.) On other occasions the place is crowded with thousands of kangaroos, all too numerous brumbies, tiger quolls. One springtime, the lateral branches of young gumtrees have all been bent and broken by the weight of heavy snowfall during the winter. But always the mighty wedge-tailed eagles soar over the grasslands or high in the thermals overhead.

A rough 4WD trail runs through Merambego's centre with a few spurs heading off in different directions. From McGuigans Gap in the east, a pass between valleys, it generally runs beside the creek, through various discrete flats and clearings until about 7 kilometres in you find the Darrewarra camp under mighty ribbony gums and a deviation through a swampy creek crossing before the main paddocks and homestead area. From here vistas of the hilly grasslands run in all directions. Then, another 10 kilometres along the trail is a freehold block at the junction of Little River and Merambego Creek. A ruined stone hut and clearings stand amid spectacular mountain views and white box and white cypress.

But for all its drought-time desolation, the native grasslands only need rain to transform. At Darrewarra, the day before rain, I witness one of the little miracles of the ribbony gums, also known as manna gums. A white substance resembling snowflakes drifts to the ground in copious quantities. Extremely sweet, I gather it and roll it into balls; far superior to any lolly I've tasted. A few days after the rain those bare hills are painted bright green with fresh growth, the kangaroos and emus grazing the grasses down to lawn. Yam plants like early nancy, vanilla lily and *Diuris* or donkey orchid proliferate, along with other food plants and their seeds. Some koalas survive but brushtail possums are present in remarkable numbers.

Pat Ryan lives in Delegate. A tall, wiry man who looks as though he could only have been a horseman, in 1971 he was obliged to sell his Merambego run after the New South Wales government cancelled all grazing leaseholds to incorporate land into the Kosciuszko National Park. He remains the dislocated, taciturn bushman despite years of living in town. His old friend Barrie

Merambego

Reed, who ran cattle with his family in the Sandy Creek Hut area, joins us to help jog Pat's memories. A hint of bitterness sharpens Pat's voice as he speaks of places that still mean much to him.

He took over Merambego in the early 1950s and ran cattle through Byadbo in partnership with the Reeds. He describes graves at Stockyard Flat, and others at Edbo, adding that many people, especially kids, are buried in the bush throughout the region. (The name of the region is Byadbo but old-timers said Edbo for short.) He ran sheep and cattle at Merambego, cattle up in the back blocks and the sheep closer home. He lost a few head in his first year so he decided to do something about the dingoes. There were no doggers then. You did it all yourself, and received £4 bounty a scalp. He got 23 dogs that first year from a line of traps that stretched from home to Edbo and over to Jerry's Flat: it was a 3-day job to run them.

Ffolkes had the mine below Stockyard Flat for molybdenum, he said. But then I've also been told it was for copper or manganese oxides which were also found locally. But most likely I suspect it was for gold, as Stewart told me. Nobody let on where gold was involved, it was always a secret. There's a diamond prospect not far away across the hills towards the Kangaroo Grounds. Whichever, none of the prospects made anybody rich.

With a hint of scorn for my water shortage, he says that there's water if you know where to look: check Spring Creek and beside the Monument Trail junction.

When we come to talk about fires, he impresses on me the need to burn often to keep the scrub down. His daughter laughs. 'Burn,' she says. 'He sure knew how to burn. In fact any day he'd been out in the bush, Mum would hold off putting on the tea until she knew he was coming close enough to home. You see, he'd be riding along on his horse flicking matches into any patch of grass that would catch fire, so she only had to watch out for the smoke.'

The Monaro

Despite Ryan's vaguely simmering resentment of his 1971 loss, Merambego is a valuable part of the park, as a buffer for the Byadbo Wilderness, and because it represents the edge of the grassy forests and woodlands that were so common about the edges of the Monaro. Not a lot of the once-extensive native grasslands are represented in the park system. Here, their value is to show how things were before settlement as the subsequent interventions such as clearing are evident.

Merambego was once part of McGuigan's Stockyard Flat run. My walking makes me wonder about the seasonal harshness of life in days gone by, and how well people can adapt. Heavy snowfalls in winter, blistering heat in summer, it's a place of extremes.

Certain features stand out – ones that stick in your mind, characterise the country, and demand explanation – and beside the track where it dips close to the creek you find extraordinary, ancient signs of erosion in the high bank. In this canyon mysterious internal workings of the land are revealed. Here koalas were once regularly reported. ribbony gums grow pale and tall. A spring rises nearby. This could have been a gathering place, special in one of the great Dreaming stories of the Maneroo. Part of the saga of Dyillagamberra in connection with the Tuross River, which rises in the north-eastern extremes of the tableland about as far away as you can get from here without falling off the Monaro's edge. A 1904 note by the surveyor and early anthropologist RH Mathews relates the story of a mystic person named Dyillagamberra who travelled the region, 'and at short intervals he dug holes or springs, some on the sides of hills and others on the tops. This was to secure a supply of water for his people, and the waterholes still remain.'[2]

Aboriginal people have more detailed Dyillagamberra stories than were provided to Mathews. The lore continues from the Tuross and across the Monaro and beyond. In one sense it maps connections to the swamps and springs that were such valuable resources, bringing well-being and plenty across the country. Rod Mason, Indigenous education and community liaison officer at Kosciuszko National Park says:

> In the southern part of the Snowy Mountains, the Monaro and associated south coast, the local Rainmaker is Dyillagamberra. He is part of local Creation, part of Darama (a local word for 'Dreaming' and associated law). All families are in some way associated with the Rainmaker through water animals and water plants. Everything needs water and we believe that Dyillagamberra provides it. Dyillagamberra's main camp is at Blue Lake in the alpine area. He is present in the landscape in Dyillagamberra Mountain near the upper reaches of the Tuross River … Dyillagamberra has three sons who are responsible for specific parts of this country. They unite the country from the mountains to the sea.[3]

Thoughts of the stories resonate in my mind as I walk the dusty track. Perhaps it is no wonder such dryness has been visited upon the land.

The number of artefacts show the once most-favoured places. A number of Aboriginal families, particularly the Hayes and Hammonds, have a particular connection to the Merambego area. The Solomons were often mentioned in nearby country. They must have often looked eastwards.

The way to Delegate

Leaving Merambego, at McGuigans Gap, near the crest of the scrubby range that divides Merambego from Wallendibby, I witness one of the strange traditions of the Monaro. A number of dingoes – in various stages of decomposition – are strung up by their hind legs from the branches of a tree. Maybe this is a pagan ritual meant to warn other dingoes to keep out of the grazing land, or maybe it's a sign the trappers and landholders are doing their job. The trappers and responsible authorities say they are only catching wild dogs, that even the dingoes that look like dingoes nowadays don't have pure genes and are cross-bred with feral dogs that roam the wilder country. These ones sure look like dingoes to me. Some say, especially those who have seen the damage a few dogs can do to a flock of sheep, that all the wild dogs, dingoes included, should be exterminated. It's a position I cannot countenance. But national parks are blamed for every sheep death because they supposedly harbour the dogs. The mauled carcasses are paraded and dumped on office doorsteps. Complaints echo throughout the local press. And the process of wiping out the wild dog, especially through baiting, continues.

The way to Delegate

On top of the stony McGuigans Gap I take in views back to the snow-patched mountains and forwards towards the Coolangubra at the far edge of the Monaro. In both directions, the ranges line up north to south with neat geological folds. In between the valleys present their unlikely grasslands. From the gap it's easy walking. As the track winds through an open forest of pale gums beside the spring-fed Wollondibby Creek to the Wallendibby station, there's still a mad wildness to the countryside; it's one of the oldest runs, far richer in rain, soils and grasses than either the Merambego or Stockyard Flat runs. It continues easterly following an ideal walking alignment, always compromising between the shortest, the boggiest and the steepest until the country flattens and opens up more. Sheep form into lines as they follow trails on their way back from water in search of pick. There's so little grass I wonder what they subsist upon. This property was originally part of Corrowong — spelt, of course, in its numerous ways over the years — which was taken up around 1833 by James and Duncan McFarlane. In his records for 29 November 1839, Maneroo lands commissioner John Lambie found: James McFarlane licensee at Carawang with superintendent Alexander Gow, and on its 100 square miles there were 16 residents, one barn, one stockyard, 1300 cattle, 11 horses, 3600 sheep and 45 acres of wheat; it was granite — good sound land bounded by the Snowy River and creeks with open forest. It was from McFarlane's station that, in 1837, another Highlands Scot, George MacKillop, set out along the old pathways with directions from the local Aboriginal people, to begin the expansion of Highlander settlement into the rich Omeo district. A few years later Angus McMillan gathered the ill-fated Jemmy Gibber to guide him southwards from Corrowong and further extend the Scottish annexation of the less drought-prone Gippsland pastures. This journey would bring land, riches and fame only to McMillan. By the economic slump of the early 1840s the industrious McFarlanes had apparently extended their empire too far. Corrowong was purchased by James O'Hare, an Irishman from County Clare, in 1846. The western parts of their run, named Wallendibby, were sold or given in lieu of wages to Gow. An experienced Maneroo hand, he had earlier been overseer at Burnima. But, in turn, he had to sell to the MacKay family in 1855, and it ran the property in various configurations, including forays into Byadbo, until after World War II.

The clan connections were valuable; climatic conditions were more significant. Closer to the tall forests you get better rainfall, and as you move through the woodlands to the grasslands, water becomes more problematic. Rainfall has been a major factor in keeping the Treeless Plains treeless. So, for example, the tall forests get better rain and misty dampness. Up the hill Norman Stewart's gets better rainfall than down on the neighbouring woodlands of Wallendibby, just as the Coolangubra forests east of Delegate get more reliable rain. Farmers – stuck with a homestead that might only be habitable in certain seasons – have been at the mercy of rainfall and geology no less than the Aboriginal people who had, in the times before European settlement, adopted more flexible ways to inhabit their country.

We sometimes need reminding that the coming of grazing changed the structure of streams and their chains of ponds that held water back. In more recent times the coming of mechanisation meant dams could be constructed to provide more consistent supplies of water, and better drought-proof the land.

It is hard country nonetheless. Clive Cottrell, who looked after Wallendibby for 42 years and has the drought-grizzled skin to prove it, told me that they never fed sheep there before 1979; since then, the feeding has been on-going. In fact, he assures me that once, if you had 1000 acres (405 hectares) you could afford to keep your son at home to help keep the place, but now you can't do it with 5000.

The way to Delegate

As I walk I meditate on nature and the land and recite its stories, relate them. The old ones seem to resonate best. A good camping site presents itself at Sandy Creek on an old Travelling Stock Reserve, ironically an old Aboriginal camping place. Later, at Corrowong Creek, the way crosses the stream that rises in the tall forests of Tingaringy to flow generally northwards through various clearings and grasslands, then on through rockier country and over the Corrowong Falls to the Snowy as it is entering its deep gorge section. At the creek lies a junction, a crossroads, where a north–south pathway from Cooma and Dalgety on its way to Delicknora, Tubbut and Wulgulmerang, crossed the east–west pathway to Delegate and the coast.

Corrowong is rich country indeed. It takes in the most southerly of the Monaro's Treeless Plains with their basalt-derived soils, but the one-time vision of its place in untamed nature is fading. At about the time when the pastoral industry of the region had reached its height, in 1872, a visiting journalist published verbal snapshots of the region. Here, he found plains and lightly timbered country.

> Corrowang is the station of James O'Hare, Esq, a resident of twenty-six years standing. The station is about twenty miles long and six miles wide, and carries about 20 000 sheep and 700 head of cattle. Corrowang is a somewhat different soil or climate to that nearer Bombala, for it has proved a capital wheat-growing country. Mr O'Hare himself has over seventy acres under cultivation this season, and his shepherds had various quantities up to twenty acres each under wheat. The crop looked splendid, and oats, and barley, were also growing vigorously. The view from the comfortable residence of the proprietor was very fine; hills to the right and well grassed plains away before the door for miles. One in particular I am informed is seven miles long and three or four miles wide.[4]

A few years later the view was much less verdant. Out of desperation to save his flocks during severe drought in December 1877, O'Hare sent 1000 sheep beyond his already ravaged yards on the Snowy near Biddi to the high country near Kosciuszko to see whether the snow country grasses might save them. They were close to death at Corrowong, and may as well die elsewhere was the reasoning. He secured the necessary leases of country, and dispatched them with shepherds via the Nine Mile Pinch to see what would happen. He never expected to see any again, and yet in less than 4 months 900 returned in good condition. After that the high country was seen as a summertime paradise and he was joined by a flood of graziers who looked to salvation in the snowgrasses – at least, until the dire consequences of grazing there were fully realised in the 1950s – and saw them as giving relief to the Monaro pastures which were already suffering severe degradation from over-stocking. By 1878, every spare inch of grass was being utilised. The ancient pathways had become stock routes.[5]

Although the original 60 000-acre Corrowong grazing run has gradually been whittled down by processes of free selection, subdivision and soldier settlement ballots to a fraction of its former size, it nonetheless remains a vast and impressive sight. It is classic Monaro landscape which to me has never felt mad and wild. But that is a deception. The land is less extreme in its topography and the absence of trees makes it feel tamed, agricultural, broken. In fact, many of the views I'm now finding are very much of the land as it was before the settlers came.

In 1848, the secretary of state for the colonies responded to a report by GA Robinson on the rights, or absence of rights, of natives on pastoral properties, by confirming 'the Leases are not intended to deprive the natives of their former right to hunt over these districts or to wander over them in search of subsistence'.[6]

And it would be fair to say that the right to belong as before and the treatment of the Aboriginal people varied from one station to another. But on this part of the Monaro they fared better than on many others. Furthermore, the relationship between some settlers and the Aboriginal people was tolerant and respectful. A particular brotherhood often grew also between the Aboriginal people, the Highlander shepherds and the Chinese gold diggers. But it was in the Corrowong area that the old traditions remained longest.

AW Howitt recorded one of his earliest meetings with Aboriginal people in 1854, but in 1874 after offering information from Australia to Charles Darwin, a reply came exhorting him

> to keep full & accurate notes of the mental powers ... etc etc of the Australians. Also of their quasi religious beliefs, – their curious marriage laws; & all other such points. With your means of obtaining information, & with your scientific habits of thought, you could certainly write a very valuable memoir or book ...[7]

His anthropological interests grew apace and he sent out questionnaires seeking information on a uniform set of topics about the local Aboriginal people from correspondents across the country. After his collaboration with Lorimer Fison on their classic *Kamilaroi and Kurnai* of 1880,[8] and working towards his *Native Tribes of South-East Australia*, he began to deluge his informants with circulars as part of an increasingly desperate quest for ever more information. But his requests weren't by any means easy to answer, given the difficulties of communication with many of the Aboriginal informants. Among Howitt's copious papers are the actual replies from many correspondents. Although only the European correspondents are acknowledged in the published edition of *The Native Tribes of South-East Australia*, it is clear that without the local information from respected men like Old Munday, Murray Jack, King Charley and others, the correspondents would have been able to provide little but hearsay.

In the present context the process of searching for answers is what's illuminating. It shows a level of trust, even respect, between many of the old people and the settlers, and how interrelated things were between people and their places. Also, as time passes, with the need to survive in the landscape, sharing knowledge of predicaments results in a generally unacknowledged common understanding, a shared history comes into being.

Even though systems of Aboriginal knowledge did not conform to a European paradigm, clearly each informant would have their own stories. Some are local, others more general. And if Howitt's informants give apparently contradictory or complementary information, which he smoothes from his own accumulated experience, it shows the problem with an overly literal reliance on ethnography. The truth exists, but it's hedged in unsatisfactory words, it's disguised, comes with red herrings and misunderstandings. Sometimes there are no answers to the questions Howitt asks, let alone any knowledge of how his correspondents framed them. Often the answers are cagey, especially where the informant does not want to say anything he knows should be kept secret or that was not his place to say. All players take the exercise with due seriousness. Where necessary, efforts are made to get the best-informed person to answer the questions. The results are more like a snapshot of the times and yet they are interesting in many, many ways beyond the strictly literal sense.

On 5 December 1881, from Wallendibby, C Clive responded to Howitt that he had obtained answers from the Currawong Aborigines, noting, 'The accompanying answers are exactly as I received them without any addition from me. Munday and Murray Jack show no reticence with me, particularly the former who is a very old acquaintance and to whom I have always shown kindness.' He responded again on 22 December 1881, with more answers, describing the tribe as Ngarego but adding, 'They also call themselves Mur-ring to distinguish themselves

The way to Delegate

from other tribes.' The answers were detailed and complex but not exactly what Howitt had requested. As he had to leave Wallendibby for the Christmas holidays it is possible he was a teacher or tutor.[9]

Another correspondent was Frank James, police officer at Bendoc, a man who commanded respect, who did what duty required, and received grudging cooperation. He was situated about 15 kilometres south of Delegate and 25 from Corrowong, just across the border in Bidwell country, a tribe he named 'Maap'.

> Jemmy Lawson was the informant. His father (Wothango) married Loah and their children were (f) Maak (m.) Maathung (m.) Jemmy Lawson, all three unmarried (?). Informant states that the Maap tribe has a sub-division called Maapkoolong and that the territory of both divisions occupies the whole of the Snowy River watershed (eastern side only) from the Little Plain River (NSW) to the coast in Victoria ... 1876[10]

During preparation of the drafts of *Native Tribes of South-East Australia*, Howitt noted Munday's assistance, as well as that of King Charley (with him Neddy Rourke) who described people from Manero and some Biduelli sharing initiation ceremonies, with John Ginau and Murray Jack also in attendance.

Another informant was Mickey,

> born at Mutong near Buckley's Crossing [Dalgety] – it is his country.

> His language is called Ngarego ... Of the classes all he knows is that he is Tchuleba, rabbit rat. His father and mother were Nadjatejan [bat] and his children would be Nadjatejan. He also says that Old Nukong was Nadjatejan

> and that Charley Nukong is Tchuleba. When they played at Ball – made of opossum skin – Tchuleba played on one side and Nadjatejan on the other. Sometimes when there were not many people there, women and children of the proper names joined. They also send the ball as a friendly greeting. String of possum fur is called Kumil.

John O'Rourke of Wulgulmerang, the tableland above the Snowy a little south of the border, wrote to Howitt saying how he talked with 'a Monaro Blackfellow but I am sorry to say that he is not sufficiently educated in their language to give me all the information that you require. But he tells me that Old Munday is gone to Cooma to get his Blankets and then he is coming down.' A few days later in June 1881, when Old Munday had completed his walk back from Cooma, O'Hare lent him a horse so he could ride the 60-odd kilometres over to Wulgulmerang to speak with O'Rourke on behalf of Howitt. He was unwilling to stay at Wulgulmerang overnight and in explanation said, 'Too many blackfellows have died here.' This was the same reason he gave for not going down to Lake Tyers. Obviously O'Rourke and Old Munday had a strong affinity and they spoke at length on subjects like initiation, the making of boys into men, and marriage; but even so Old Munday was reluctant to elaborate on some topics:

> I could not induce him to make the message stick or to tell me much about it as he seemed to have some superstition about it, it being something that was in use by his ancestors it was with much reluctance that he spoke about it at all. He told me that there was such a thing.[11]

After the turnoff to Corrowong station, the small O'Hare Catholic Church and graveyard stand at the roadside, and then near a stately two-storied O'Hare residence with wide verandahs and cast-iron lace, the dirt track gives way to bitumen for the very pretty way through rolling woodlands and grasslands to the next important stream and Delegate. Somehow, as I walk, I am haunted by visions of those old inhabitants. I imagine the Aboriginal people with their numerous campsites tucked along the creek in the sunniest places not too far away from wood and game. The country was so rich that for many years they could share to mutual advantage. I can even see the rabbit rats, which perhaps were bandicoots or some other hopping marsupial like the rufous bettong (kangaroo-rat), now extinct in the area.

This isn't hard walking country, the rounded hills come at regular intervals. The white of summer-bleached grasses stands ready to give way to green after the next rains. For the most part it is sheep country, grassy woodland, with tall rounded ribbony gums spaced well apart. Travelling Stock Reserves (TSR) mark places where the old Aboriginal people used to stop over, good places near water and firewood, that lie about 10 or 12 kilometres apart. So it is with the Union TSR, at a comfortable day's walking distance from Sandy Creek. This would seem to make a good walk each day, especially for an extended family travelling with children of various ages and old people. And they still make the best places to camp along the way to Delegate, and what a destination it would have been. Then it was the place of abundance, where you gathered and met up with everyone. And so it is today. Lying halfway along the route, it's the only town between Targangal and Bilgalera with a full range of facilities. My pace picks up as I savour the prospect of a real bed and fresh food. But, perhaps more importantly, it is the place where the themes of the Bundian Way come together and it illustrates the circumstances that changed the Monaro forever.

The Maneroo

The first contact between Europeans and the Aboriginal people of far south-eastern Australia came about in 1797 after the wreck of a trading vessel, the *Sydney Cove*, on its way from East India to sell its products at great profit to the hungry, very much isolated European residents of their only outpost on the continent at Sydney Cove. When some starving survivors from the also wrecked longboat passed by on their long walk to Sydney, they were offered very considerable hospitality and guidance by the clan they met at the mouth of the Nadgee River, not far north of Cape Howe. Apparently speakers of the Thaua language, the Aboriginal people quickly made friends, fed them and helped the 17 walkers along the more difficult stretches of the coastline to beyond the Pambula River. Only three from the expedition would eventually make it to Sydney, which was then essentially an inward looking outpost that was attempting to survive by applying the land use methods of the old country. The walkers' stories of the abundant riches beyond the limits of settlement caused a sensation and awakened a spirit of adventure in the name of exploitation and entrepreneurship.

The Maneroo

It was as though at last the doors had opened to the possibilities of the continent. William Clark, a leader of the survivors, had been supercargo (superintendent of the cargo) of the vessel which carried over 7000 gallons of grog and he was the nephew of a partner in the Calcutta trading and agency firm, Campbell and Clark. Like most of the East India traders, the business was run by Scots who called upon family and trusted home connections as their trade grew. Clark delivered his tales of coal seams, whales, seals and bounteous grasslands to the thirsty colony, then took the first opportunity to retreat home to Calcutta where he revealed the new trading opportunities to his family and countrymen. Perhaps deeply scarred by the privations of his long trek through countryside hitherto untrodden by Europeans, he would never return. He was, it seems to me, suffering from poisoning caused by eating untreated Aboriginal food plants en route.

Campbell and Clark did send another trading vessel which arrived in Sydney Cove on 10 June 1798. It carried their very canny representative, Robert Campbell, the 29-year-old younger brother of the firm's senior partner. He quickly sized up the opportunities, starting sealing operations and, within a few years, established a base at Circular Quay in Sydney Cove which included house, warehouses and deep water dock.

The merchant Campbell would have heard the stories from Captain Mark Currie who led the first official expedition south of Lake George and the Limestone Plains, which at the time were disputably beyond the Limits of Location where settlement was permitted. On 3 June 1823 Currie came within sight of 'a long chain of down country'. The next day, after a sharp frost, his party with the assistance of their Aboriginal guide made contact with the native people, from whom he 'learned that the clear country before us was called Monaroo, which they described as very extensive ...' At first they had fled, but were induced to come nearer and nearer, until 'we ultimately became good friends'. He reported how they were more frightened by the horses. By 8 June, with their food resources running low, he resolved to return and on the way back approached two natives who 'fled like deer the instant they saw us, and being pursued on horseback, ran with great agility to the tops of trees, whence it required no small degree of persuasion to remove them; but succeeding at last in getting them down, we compelled one of them to go with us to show us the way to Lake Bathurst, they being invariably well acquainted with the best passes in the hills'.[12]

Whilst Currie believed he was the first white they had seen, they had probably heard of white people at the regular gatherings; they had been told, for example, favourable stories of the party who walked by along the coast. They would have gotten wind of the settlers to the north. But Currie's actions in forcibly taking a guide would have provided the modus operandi: do as we want, or else. It is only a small step for settlers to use extreme violence to enforce their will.

Robert Campbell sent his superintendent James Ainslie to head southwards with sheep looking for those downs. He had taken up a site on the slopes above the Molonglo River overlooking the Limestone Plains, now occupied by the city of Canberra. In 1825 Campbell applied for and received his grant, naming it 'Duntroon' after the family castle, Duntrune Castle on Loch Crinan in Argyll, Scotland.

Once that grant was secured Ainslie was sent to look further afield in the south, in those fabled downs of Monaroo. With Aboriginal guides it would have taken not much more than a few days heading generally southwards through woodlands and the Treeless Plains before they came to the southerly limit of the better grazing country near Delegate Hill, beyond which everything changes. They promptly established a camp on what became the site of the first station, there on the rich grasslands of Delegate, a desirable location with permanent water. The new owner would have been able to say, as he gestured towards Duntroon, 120 miles to the north, 'All that lies between is Campbell's!'[13]

The spread of settlement came rapidly after Campbell's claim on the wide open spaces of the Monaro. Labour was the problem in maintaining large squattages. His workers had to focus on a few areas while he adopted a novel means to overcome the labour shortage. By 1839 he had over 70 Scottish Highland families living at different parts of his empire that included Duntroon, Mount Cooper and Delegate. The joke was, the wags said, that you couldn't work for Campbell unless you spoke the Gaelic. The wife of a Cameron from Argyll who settled nearby spoke nothing but the Gaelic all her life. Anyone who had survived the hardships of the north and west of Scotland during these times made an ideal candidate for dealing with isolation in the harsh Monaro climate and the Campbells encouraged their immigration. Their routine was in the Highlander manner. By day the shepherds would roam with their flocks of about 500 sheep and bring them back at night to a place with water and shelter. Gradually, huts were built at these bases, which became out-stations with folds for accommodating the sheep. The first fences were branches dragged from areas being cleared, and piled up on top of one another. These were replaced by post and rail, and eventually by wire fencing, but it wasn't until the 1870s that broad scale paddocks were being fenced. The main problem was finding labour. In his memoirs, Frederick Campbell, a grandson of Robert Campbell, and the first child to be born in Duntroon House, wrote that:

> In 1825 the only procurable labour was Government men [the convicts], until the immigrants gradually began to find their way into the country. From 1830 onwards there was a small but steady immigration, which was scarcely stopped by the record drought of 1837-8-9. After the recovery from these three years of drought, livestock in the forties

increased so rapidly that there was no means of realizing cattle and sheep, and Australia saw its worst days. There were two banks in Sydney and one of them failed.[14]

After Campbell's death in 1846, his daughter, Sophia, inherited Delegate station, becoming the first woman landowner of the colony. In 1872, during his visit to the goldfields, a journalist reported a general country store and post office, and:

> Within sight of the bank of the Delegate River, is the Delegate Station ... The Home Station and buildings connected therewith are very comfortable. The extent of the station is about 10 by 5 miles, and it carries about 8000 sheep. Fine paddocks well grassed and watered ... are about the house, and all the way ... the traveller passes the meadows through which flows a beautifully clear creek, resembling the trout streams in the old country.[15]

It is an impression that continues today. Upon Sophia's death, the station passed to her sister, Sarah, who had married a Jeffreys. It has remained with the family since. Their home overlooks the campsite, just above that junction of creek and river where the native blackfish still run.

That first building on the Monaro, a tiny rude slab construction, has now been restored on its original site and serves as a tourist attraction. When the survey crew look at the site we find artefacts all about the location. Not only that, we find a number of Bimbola shells, a thick-shelled bivalve only harvested to my knowledge by the Aboriginal people in coastal places. These shellfish were probably brought up from Twofold Bay. The location's shared history stretches well before European settlement.

During the years that followed settlement, one way for the Aboriginal people to avoid the brutality was for individuals or families to attach themselves to a particular station, where they came under a protective umbrella. Another was to be herded onto a mission station or reserve. Both happened at Delegate.

Perhaps the influence of the Highlanders made the district tolerant of an Aboriginal presence; as if they understood each other's wandering habits and paid due respect. There were probably many reasons, but Aboriginal people from other parts were attracted to the Delegate district. It had always been regarded as a good meeting place.[16]

Economy of the Maneroo

So many things that had considerable consequences for the countryside and its Aboriginal inhabitants were a long way beyond their control. The irony is that the people, like their landscapes, were in no position to complain. Stoic resignation in the face of dramatic change, perhaps necessarily, is a characteristic of the region's people, black and white. Perhaps it has to do with life in a climate that has considerable fluctuations. Too many of the changes became permanent, but few understood this until too late.

While the first whites were arriving on the southern-most parts of the tablelands – by then known as the Maneroo – its inhabitants who also went by that name had been wracked by diseases including influenza and smallpox. Historian WK Hancock, in his gentlemanly, pioneering book on the Monaro, wrote that 'the white men took the land, and some white men took the women; but there, as almost nowhere else, resistance and retaliation did not ensue. Quietly, the Aborigines submitted.'[17]

But this was questioned by Mark McKenna in his work on the region, *Looking for Blackfellas' Point*. Indeed, as Hancock himself forecast, much that he wrote needs re-examination and McKenna effectively did that, showing that often a violent struggle for land ensued. Hancock's clearly reasoned voice speaks of a recognisable Monaro, and yet when I turn to *Discovering Monaro* for guidance I find too much missing. It doesn't feel right. And even though I appreciate Hancock's ambitions as much as I enjoy his prose, it seems I must do my own discovering, that I have no option but consider my own picture of the Monaro and how economic issues affected its peoples through the years of grossly changing circumstance.

For settlers who were faced with difficulties they regarded as life and death, their common approach in the early days if the 'blacks were troublesome', was to deal with the difficulty by 'punitive expeditions', whereby 'they were shot first and not even tried afterwards'.[18]

Even by the time GA Robinson passed on 9 September 1844, the practise for dealing with resistance or competition for resources was harsh. He quotes a much-respected squatter, John Cosgrove of Bililingera, as saying the Maneroo blacks were fine, well-behaved and never troublesome, but 'the Yass blacks were dreadful, settlers used to shoot them whenever they met them. Parties went out [and] purposefully shot men, women and children.'[19]

Given such treatment, it is only a wonder that so many of the Maneroo survived; afterall how could riflemen know the difference between a Maneroo and a Yass black? And many other such instances exist, some of which I will consider later.

But life was not always so brutal. Some people of the Maneroo survived then, as they do today. The fact is that in the early days they were not necessarily visible to the new settlers who, once their stations were established, had to look inwards to the economics of their own farming activities to ensure their survival. The places the regularly-travelling Maneroo camped were not always where the settlers thought of going. But on certain occasions their interests overlapped. Some interactions meant that the smart farmers received help to find new pastures. How many others received a similar invitation to Robinson's on Sunday 25 August 1844? 'One Biggah asked me if I had seen his country, "good place budgery place by and by you see", another said his country was a cubboin. Monday entered head of Biggah called Mumbuller or Mumbeller, belonging to Yow.e.ge, says it is his farm.' Pride in his country is one thing but most settlers would, if it was not already settled, have regarded it as an invitation to settle there. Perhaps something more was going on in these 'invitations'.[20]

Surveyor Stewart Ryrie passed through what he called Dilliget on 20 March 1840, and made several attempts to head directly south, only to be repulsed by 'thick scrub'. On 31 March 1840, he had to wait at Corrowong 'for the purpose of getting a Black to accompany me to the coast'. He needed guidance to find the pathways to the south, experience had already showed him what happens when you find yourself off track in the wild country. He was led through the valley south of 'Dingayringo', to 'Calantaba' and on through 'Buckan' to the mouth of the Snowy.[21]

Maneroo lands commissioner John Lambie reported to his commissioner in Sydney on 14 January 1842 that 'The Aborigines of the District, with the exception of the Coast tribes, may be said to be almost in their primitive State.' But many went to Twofold Bay for the whale season. 'The Blacks were stationed on the opposite side of the Bay to the other Fishermen, and they adopted the same habits as the Whites. They lived in Huts, slept in Beds, used utensils in cooking, and made the flour into bread; but, as soon as the fishing Season was over, they all returned to their tribes in the Bush.' He added that 'the tribes to the westward of the Coast range are very little employed by the Stockowners, except a few occasionally in washing sheep; they preserve their original habits of hunting, and are constantly moving from place to place.'[22]

The 3 or 4 months of the season would have suited the whalers. Above all, the Maneroo were traders. They had well established trade routes and times of the year when they would gather for social, trading and ceremonial reasons. Each group had a 'Country' to which they belonged. In those very first days of settlement could they simply be giving land away to the new settlers? Or did its Aboriginal owners see an advantage in the settler moving onto particular land? If its owners could imagine the land being taken away from them, why would they invite the settlers with their flocks and herds? Might the owners believe their Country would be enhanced by the new animals, and that they had a certain ownership of the new animals that would come to graze on their Country? After all, these newcomers had no greater right to the land than its Aboriginal inhabitants. Maybe those Aboriginal people saw their ownership more as custodianship of the land, bearing responsibilities that might be shared? Indeed the newcomers were squatters who could claim only vague rights to run their stock on the lands they occupied. Why shouldn't the Aboriginal people envisage a mutually profitable co-existence? Many fraught years would pass before the squatters could effectively exclude the Kooris, even though was it never envisaged in the first place (see the secretary of state for the colonies' statement that pastoral leases do not take away the Aboriginal right to hunt or wander there gathering food).[23]

In 1848 Henry Haygarth described one typical exchange of the time:

> The stock-keeper was one day taxing a black with having speared some of the cattle under his charge, and as the accused failed to exonerate himself, he was called, in conclusion, a 'cabonn' (ie great) rascal. This roused him to a defence of his conduct, and after a hot argument and a good deal of excitement, he proved pretty forcibly that, in the natural course of things, he was not the aggressor, and

that his tribe, the first occupiers of the district, had as much right to help themselves to a piece of beef, as the white man, by his intrusion and presence, to drive away the emus and kangaroos, which the black denominated his cattle.[24]

These matters were a trade. Although perceptions of rights to land have changed with the times, there are still calls for the exchange to be completed. And too many of the old deals remain open. Dues should be paid. Fair's fair.

At the time of first settlement, the country of the Maneroo was a place of abundant resources. Numerous large freshwater lakes, some more ephemeral than others, served people, wildfowl and game as well as livestock, not to mention the countless ponds where the watercourses trickled from one to the other. Springs were common and well maintained by the Maneroo. All about the land rolled, covered with grasses that softened the hardness to a rather human appearance while towards the edges and on some hills there were trees, but the bounties of the land varied from season to season. You chose well where to stop, where the best resources would be available. Its food sources were so plentiful, to begin with they included kangaroos, wallabies, emus, wombats, echidnas, and all manner of small macropods like the potoroos, pademelons, kangaroo rats and bandicoots. Koalas were aplenty, sometimes wandering the grassy plains and in other places as many as four to a tree. The possums were numerous also, in fact the Maneroo deliberately made fires to hollow out trees and make them more suitable for nesting by possums, of which there were numerous species that included greater gliders, yellow-bellied gliders, brushtails, mountain brushtails, ringtails and sugar gliders. Forests in the Coolangubra were found during the 1980s to have the highest level of arboreal mammals in the world. The fur of the greater gliders was much sought-after for making cloaks. Yabbies inhabited the many ponds, waterholes and swampy areas along the creeks and still may be found in some of the swampiest country. During droughts, trampling by settlers' stock compacted the dried mud and this meant many potential foods – including the frogs and eels and lizards and snakes, not to mention the edible plants – could not survive. Bustards or wild turkeys were very common. Emancipated convict Joseph Lingard, during travels across the region, reported how 'the river was covered with all kinds of water-fowl. I could take my gun in a morning and shoot as many as I liked.' The food plants included many forms of yam and tuber, leafy stems, fruit and seeds of innumerable species.[25]

Charles Harpur was born in the colony in the early days of settlement. He came to be the first native-born writer to sign himself 'An Australian'. He set his eye to record Australian scenes and the local ways, and ended his days reflectively at Euroma station, near Nerrigundah, reflecting on the nature of the original countryside as he knew it, as it had once been. Notes for his long poem, 'The Kangaroo Hunt', observed

> In the unbroken skirts of the forest lying about new
> settlements, there is always a greater prevalence of saplings
> than anywhere else; for no sooner are the old trees
> thinned away for building purposes and firewood, than a
> superabundant growth of slim pole-like young ones is sure
> to replace them, even to the extent of making a perfect
> brush of what was originally open woodland.[26]

He observed significant changes taking place in the bush, lamenting the extinction of many creatures, including a satin bird whose 'back, including the wings, is of a bright red or scarlet'. He saw factors in settlement that might as readily have been expressed in any district, such as how, as a boy, he commonly used to see four species of bird that had since become extinct. He blamed the unchecked increase of goannas, which ate eggs and chicks, following the extinction of Aboriginals in the district, adding 'it is a pity that we Colonists do not esteem [the gwanas] as great a table delicacy as our sable forerunners – the former lords of the soil – undoubtedly did'.[27]

Other observers of the time saw to the dire consequences of losing the Aboriginal land management practices. The colonial 'sciences' were directed towards increasing the land's carrying capacity for the animals and crops introduced by the settlers, whereas the Aboriginal methods provided for continuing sustenance from what was already there. Yam sticks loosened the soil in places. Fire was only one of the tools used, but it helped focus kangaroos into burnt areas to make hunting predictable. It also brought on the right grass seeds and the yam plants. The various patches of woodland, white sallee and peppermint for example, still have discreet clear areas where the old people likely used fire to manage their land. These clearings a few kilometres apart are where, after the hunt here today, the kangaroos could be found at the next patch tomorrow. The squatters and settlers arrived, assuming the country they found was the way it had always been and would be forever. As their husbandry intensified, the lasting impacts would slowly become apparent.

During the difficult financial times of the late 1840s, when effects of ovine catarrh and scab compounded the settlers' difficulties with drought, they very often gave the Maneroo work and protection by providing for them on the stations. Squatters, who generally knew the country and the Koori forebears, were quite sympathetic to elements of the traditional lifestyle whereby, for example, they might not always be available for labour. Ceremonial obligations overrode 'work' obligations. Nonetheless, when they were available the squatters employed the women in the house, men as stockmen, and in tailing, fencing, barking, and as firewood gatherers, message carriers and so forth. For example, William Whittakers, the friend of Howitt, had first settled at Tombong between Corrowong and Delegate in a slab hut with a bark roof and dirt floor and no glass in the windows. In the Whittakers' day books, before their move to Tubbut, they wrote of day-to-day matters on their cattle run that would have been typical for that time:

> 1847 Sept 20th – ... blacks came 21st – ... blacks stripped 40 sheets of bark 22nd – ... blacks got 45 sheets of bark. 23rd – ... Micky at hurdles, Smith &: Riley splitting. Blacks left. Oct 29th – Sent a blackfellow to Mr Gow's for 5lbs of tea. 1848 March 15th – Raining. Sent the blacks to Forest for Wallabys – brought home three. March 16th – Out with blacks – very heavy rain. Cut up cow. March 17th – Out in the forest for wallabys – killed several. August 1st – Killed a blackfellow's dog ... one lamb very badly bitten. September 21st – Out with Stokes and Black Harry to the run for a beast ... September 25th – Black gins shepherding ewes. September 26th – Harry shepherding ... October 3rd – Harry shepherding – Jemmy the (Pig?) here October 4th – Jemmy went away ... 1849 Sunday 30th November – Harry and Big Lip fought – Blacks went.[28]

When WB Clarke passed through the Delegate district in January–March 1852 during his geological survey, his reports were sent directly to Sydney and released to the public straight away by the newspapers. He told locals of his discoveries beforehand, so that in no time gold strikes were being worked on Campbell's property at Delegate. By 1854, further new strikes brought excitement and the roads were crowded with pedestrians, horsemen and drays. The gold rushes of the 1850s had massive consequences in that many workers deserted the countryside for the distant goldfields. A previously unimaginable number of people would arrive at local diggings when hints of a strike circulated. Prospectors quested in every corner of the region for the elusive metal. There is not one elbow in a ridge of the region that has not apparently been fossicked and probed in the search for that mythical reef.

With the end of indentured labour and the convict system, the squatters had no recourse to the cheap labour that was necessary to manage their vast estates. Then the labour they still had vanished overnight to the fields, where instant wealth beckoned. But also it meant their produce was worth very much more, especially when they could supply the richer diggings in places like the Ovens, Omeo and Kiandra. Lesser rushes occurred after alluvial deposits were found at Corrowong, Mila, Craigie and Little Plain. Mines were established at Bendoc and Corrowong. And, of course, very great changes came to the relationship between the Maneroo and the squatters. After the dispersals, by 1854 there was a 'coming in':

> In the coast portion of my district the relations between the Europeans and the Aborigines are most friendly, and the advantages mutual. During the recent excessive scarcity of labor many settlers were mainly dependent on the natives for the means of carrying on their operations. I know of several instances in which the blackfellow's assistance has saved the Europeans from severe loss. Thousands of sheep have been tended, and large herds of cattle entirely watched by the natives, who some few years ago even in these parts were regarded as unteachable and useless, and whose presence even created alarm and was too often the signal for treachery and ill usage.[29]

But just as a peaceful accord appeared to have settled on the land, when the rushes tailed off and gold was no longer seen as the way to instant riches, came the rush for land. On the Monaro many unhappy gold diggers returned from Kiandra (often driven by the cold) looking for a more solid employment, something that offered a reward for individual initiative, and what else proffered but the land? The squatters had often done better out of the rushes than the diggers. The proof was there for all to see, but the land was locked in a lease system. The survey departments were unable to cope with the new demands. Demand grew for reform of the land laws to enable sale of Crown lands at a reasonable price and terms. As in America, the cork had to come out of the bottle. The *Robertson Land Acts* of 1861 allowed free selection to unlock the large runs or leaseholds in favour of small farmers. As with the land at Tingaringy, it was very often the biggest squatters, like the Campbells, who actually bought the best of the land, often using dummy selectors to lend their name to purchases of the prime lots. Nonetheless, it was those back corners of the big squatters' runs that made up land where the Kooris had been able to sustain themselves and a semblance of their traditional lifestyle. But now many selectors, fresh from their failure on the goldfields, arrived to grab every last corner of available land, without survey.

By 1872 Alfred McFarland, a judge of the District Court, could still describe an anything but degraded people when he found a camp of about 30 men, women, and children at Monderragen on the junction of the Bombala and Delegate rivers.

> An old fellow was engaged in the light pursuit of 'boomerang' making; and several of the children were rolling on the sand, as naked as the hour they were born. The costumes of the rest of the tribe were rather varied in material, color and cut, but loose and flowing; and hats, caps, and bonnets were not wanting. In the afternoon I met their chief huntsman, or provendore, as he returned from the 'field'. Over one shoulder (flapping on his breast) there hung the skins of three opossums, and a bear; dangling against his back were the bodies of the same; and upon the other shoulder he carried a quantity of honey in the comb, resting on a strip of bark. He was accompanied by a couple

of dogs, and bore in his belt a good-sized tomahawk, with
which he had knocked his 'game' on the head – when he or
the dogs caught it – and he had cut the honey from some
tree, or branch, in which the wood bees had deposited it.
Half an hour later, the entire posse were enjoying the game
of ball-throwing and catching it from hand to hand.[30]

If the times had become more peaceful for the Kooris, in a sense also they became a golden age for the squatters as they improved their breeds and pastures. But changes to the structure of soil and the way it held water were becoming apparent even though nobody could be sure what this would mean. And eventually hard times arrived again with the terrible 1888 drought, when those suffering soils became desert-like, only to be followed by the economic downturn of 1890. A run of bad seasons followed; hare plagues, droughts, metal and wool prices falling. Shearers' strikes hit the wool industry. Unemployed city folk flocked to the bush. The Depression of 1892 hit the pastoralists too. But the worst hit were the Aboriginal people, their former lands were fenced with barbed wire; they could no longer be where they'd always been, go where they'd always gone. Squatters and selectors alike were hard-pressed to provide for their own families. Few pastoralists would keep their links to the old Kooris when an abundance of skilled and willing white workers became available. Pearly Gunnang, an Aboriginal woman, however came to do housework for Delegate station and remained there for many years, almost as a member of the family. On a bend upriver from the station lay what came to be known as Gunnang's orchard. Finally, the Maneroo were pushed off their traditional Country into the towns, finding themselves at the mercy of townspeople who were not always noted for their acts of tolerance.[31]

Economy of the Maneroo

The rain shadow influence of the high country spreads across the Monaro and can make the region susceptible to severe drought. Native pastures, the kangaroo and wallaby grasses, the poas and such, can fail leaving bare paddocks without feed for stock, let alone the native animals whose survivors were remorselessly hunted by all.

The old Maneroo had no conception of the legal 'ownership' of land or stock. They had to change their ways, and adapt. Their struggle was not for a fair wage, it was to find sustenance, for survival. The pressures of livestock took their toll on the Aboriginal landscape and the effects became more pronounced, especially when the droughts came on with unerring regularity. Fencing that hemmed in too much stock in too small an area also excluded the people from their waterholes and most productive places. And as the once wide-ranging clans were obliged to leave their traditional country, they found themselves crowded into places where they did not belong. New pressures applied to the places that now had to be shared. Conflicts grew. Those who were once amicable friends and neighbours became enemies in the hunt for scant resources when their families starved. Some attached themselves to the settlements in the name of survival, places where there was also grog and tobacco and flour and all the other persuaders of society.

Corrowong Creek, along its length from the tall forests of Tingaringy, through the woodlands and treeless plains to the gorge of the Snowy would have been an extremely rich place for its original inhabitants. Long after settlement came, the people from Corrowong survived on their country and somehow kept their special identity longer than those from other parts of the Monaro; their names ring down through the years. Some came from other parts of the Monaro, Gippsland and coastal districts. Also, there was the dictate that all Aboriginal people should marry the right person from as far away as possible. Nonetheless their numbers dropped rapidly. One cause might well have been the issue of blankets, but there were many factors.

During the earliest years of settlement on the Monaro the political response to the 'Aboriginal problem' was not focussed, often driven by missionary impulses, until the Aborigines Protection Society lobbied Westminster for an Aboriginal Protectorate. In 1839, a pious Methodist with limited education, George Augustus Robinson, already known for his work rounding up the Tasmanian Aboriginal people, was appointed chief protector of Aborigines in the Port Phillip district, which at the time was still part of New South Wales. In each of four protectorates under his charge, a tract of land was set aside to serve as a station on which Aboriginal people would be encouraged to stay. The intention was that, by providing food rations and a refuge, the Aborigines would stop interfering with the settlers and their sheep, and consequentially be protected from punitive actions. Well-meaning enough, his administration failed because of incompetent assistants and the long journeys he made into the bush as a result of which he lost contact with authorities and Governor Sir George Gipps, who advised that Robinson was at least 'efficient so far as his own mode of holding intercourse with the Blacks is concerned'. Although his protectorate was to be abolished in 1849, it was the course of his duties that brought Robinson and his notebook to the Monaro in 1844. Without the detail of his notes we would have a much impoverished picture of the way things were.[32]

In 1860 a Board for the Protection of Aborigines was established in Victoria primarily to give attention to affairs at the state's staffed Aboriginal station at Lake Tyers. Here housing, rations of a kind and some medical attention were dispensed to people who had come from many places in both New South Wales and Victoria. It was not until 1883 that a Board for the Protection of Aborigines was established in New South Wales along the lines of the one operating in Victoria. The board, through its managers, administered a number of stations while police supervised unstaffed reserves such as the one at Delegate. Finally, in 1890 the Wallaga Lake Reserve was formally dedicated, formalising an old camping site and school established in 1887, with some resistance among its inhabitants to regulation, especially to being 'missionised'.[33]

But the people who had once lived free, who had found an abundance all across the Monaro and in the forests beyond its limits, who travelled regularly to refresh their world-views, who had never been restricted, were finally contained at the Delegate Reserve, all the bounties of civilisation were visited upon them. One old Aboriginal woman told the story of how, when her family from the rugged valleys of the Bidawal Country, first met white men at Delegate they were so very shy, they hid their heads in their rugs so the men couldn't see them. The whitefellas gave them grog and tobacco and they soon grew sick and rolled about on the ground, crying, 'This country running away. Trees jumping about.'[34]

NSW Aborigines Protection Board 1884–1942

One of my first contacts with Delegate is a phone conversation; I explain how I'm looking at the old Aboriginal pathways of the region, and receive the response: 'But there were never any Aborigines round here.' That's not a response, I believe, I will ever hear again. Delegate now takes pride in its connections with Aboriginality. But the episode is a reminder of how quickly we can forget.

Delegate is a strange and lovely little place located just north of the Victoria–New South Wales border, about 80 kilometres as the crow flies from Twofold Bay in the east and from Orbost and Marlo, at the mouth of the Snowy River, southwards. As I walk into town on my way from Merambego and Corrowong, I don't see a single person until I enter the general store, where I'm warmly welcomed. The hamburger I order is without doubt one of the highlights of my life. Several cups of tea strengthen me for a walk through the town. This is the oasis, I think. This is the only town on the way to the coast with a range of amenities.

The architecture of the main street is a mixed bag, dominated by a pub that was probably fronted with bricks in the 1920s. Weatherboard rooms out the back hail from much earlier days. It has everything you'd look for in a country town: hotel, bank building, post office, generous school of arts, primary school, police station, two petrol stations, RSL club, hospital, churches, op shop and several general stores. Most of the buildings however hark back to better days. It has the feel of the goldrush days and cowboy movies due to old facades and shops that haven't traded since before World War I. Like the archetypal Australian country town, it's almost a museum-piece. And as I walk the back streets checking the old route of the Bundian Way, which simply crosses the main street and continues easterly, anyone I see has a good wave and a smile. The main street runs parallel to its river, its dominant features: the freestanding Mount Delegate at 1308 metres a few kilometres to the south and to the north, on the hilltop across the river, massive rock formations in evocatively rounded granite. Both, of course have deep significance in the town's Aboriginal story. One of its sorriest chapters is woven through the Annual Reports of the New South Wales Aborigines Protection Board between 1884 and 1942.

The 1885–86 report stated that 26 Aborigines were settled in the district, generally employed on stations as labourers and stockmen. None were in need of aid from the government. Six children of school age did not receive any instruction. Their parents, from Gippsland, Victoria, were always going from one colony to another, never remaining in one place. The majority were very temperate. They were very seldom ill, but when they were, their employers purchased medicine for them.[35]

By 1891, owing to arrivals from Victoria, the population increased by 41 although 'the greater number have now returned to their proper homes ... Some of the reserves, and more particularly those in the pastoral districts, are simply used as camping grounds, the men being generally employed in various kinds of labour on sheep-stations, or in rabbiting, marsupial hunting, etcetera.' In May a second blanket was permitted to each Aboriginal due to the severe climate, while investigations were made regarding their means of livelihood and state of destitution. And by August, Donald Campbell, recommended the reservation of an area of land at Delegate for them, and also the issue of tents, rations, and clothing. As drought and economic conditions worsened police reported that an area of 10 acres would be sufficient for a reserve. In March, a tender for rations from Cheesman Bros of Delegate was accepted for: flour 3d, tea 1/9 and sugar 3 and a half pence. Later in the year tenders for fencing with a 2-rail fence and the erection of two 2-roomed slab huts with iron roofs went ahead.[36]

In 1892 the board built 'comfortable dwellings' for Delegate's old and infirm Aborigines. In later years complaints were made about the difficulty of taking census due to 'the wandering habits of the race, more especially in the remote districts; and the border tribes crossing into the other Colonies'. After 1897 'all youths and girls should, after receiving instruction, and when of an age fit to work for a livelihood, be placed in suitable service or induced to accept it' amid general efforts 'to raise their moral and physical state'.[37]

In 1904, the concern was that the children 'are in some instances absolutely prohibited from attending the public schools' owing to the objections of a few parents of European children, although 'there is nothing to which exception can be taken either in their habits or behaviour, and the board are ever ready to see that they are decently clad'.[38]

In 1905, a radical change took place in board policies when its chairman of 21 years, EW Fosbery, resigned. The board took over distribution of blankets and concerned itself 'that a large number of children who are almost white are growing up at the various stations and camps, and consider that, for ... the good of the community, it would be desirable to remove them from their present associations'. An extra hut was built in Delegate in 1908, with materials provided for tanks, guttering, and such for three huts. During 1911 a 'home-finder' was appointed to visit 'stations and camps, with a view of inducing the parents to allow their children to be apprenticed out'. The duties were carried out mercilessly. The young girls were sent to Cootamundra Domestic Training Home to undergo a course of training to fit them for menial work.[39]

World War I brought changes to Aboriginal welfare. Many of the young men joined up to fight. Work was scarce. But the board would only assist those 'deserving', although acknowledging that large numbers of Aborigines would be thrown out of employment due to the hard times. The board resolved to assist, until better times returned, only those deserving men and their families who had been able to wholly or partially support themselves. Its letter of 26 March 1914 decreed that 'boys of 15 years of age, and upwards, be compelled to leave the Board's Stations, which are under Managers, and seek employment, or consent to apprenticeship'.

Legislation was passed that gave the Board very considerable powers, and in 1918, 'Aborigine' was defined to include full-bloods and half-castes, and to give the board power to deal with any person apparently having an admixture of blood in his or her veins. The aim was to keep the reserves free of girls and boys above 14 years of age, and of neglected children, with numbers regularly being transferred to the board's homes, or to domestic service where circumstances permitted.

In the Cootamundra Home 'a moderate standard of education is aimed at while manual work is made a feature. It is found that the Aborigines prove adaptable to the latter, and some very good samples of basketware, carpentry, net making and raffia work, may be seen ... The process of gradually eliminating quadroons and octoroons is being quietly carried on ... the children are rescued from camp life ... A continuation of this policy of disassociating the children from camp life must eventually solve the Aboriginal problem.'[40]

By the 1922 report the noose had tightened with a 'considerable diminution of the numbers of Aborigines residing on Aboriginal Stations and Reserves'. Although some feared that many who left the reserves 'would have been better off had they remained, in view of the fact that in leaving they forfeited the benefits of good housing accommodation, regular supplies of food and clothing and schooling for their children, to which they were properly entitled'. The board however cautiously sought a legal discretion to prohibit people from leaving a reserve.

Young men from the region were often sent a long distance away to the notorious Kinchela Home on the north coast's Macleay River where, in 1926, 'neglected Aboriginal boys' received, in addition to their ordinary education, 'a sound training in cultivation and gardening'. By 1930 the board took over 'administration of all moneys payable in respect of persons having an admixture of Aboriginal blood'. The system adopted by the board provided that parents no longer had responsibility for 'food, clothing, bedding, optical, dental, and, in short, anything which is for the direct or indirect benefit of the children'.[41]

The Great Depression brought further hardships. Many Kooris who had found it preferable to control their own destiny were thrown out of work and had no option but to go to Wallaga Lake, which was under the control of a missionary teacher–manager, assisted by his wife who acted as matron. Its 1932 report sought powers to 'enable it to, among other things, concentrate on its Reserves, persons of Aboriginal blood, who are now living on stock routes and alongside of towns, and maintain a definite control over them, so that they will not be at liberty to leave without permission'.[42]

The issue of 'resident supervision' meant the Aboriginal residents at Delegate were forced to leave for places like Wallaga Lake during the 1920s. The 'supervision' was to keep things under strict control and aimed towards the extinguishment of Aboriginal culture. Travellers could no longer stop off at Delegate for a while. The ancient traditions of meeting by the river were prohibited.

When I was a child a favourite expression of my parents' generation, when you asked for too much, was, 'What do you think this is? Bush week ...? And I'm the sap?' With some dismay I found there really was a 'Bush Week', held in February 1919. For the occasion the secretary of the board – seeking to make it grander and more memorable after the World War I austerities – wrote to the stations requesting the participation of 100 'full bloods and very dark half castes' to pose on the back of lorries, thence to participate in a corroboree and boomerang throwing competitions. Appearances, of course, were everything.[43]

The blankets of Delegate

The ranges overlooking Delegate were home to the greater gliders. These were the most prized of the possums for their fine fur, the warmth of which – when stitched together to form a blanket – was a blessing in a climate that could bring such extremely bitter cold that the trees of the plain were killed by snow storms. The largesse of the Crown in giving the blankets to Aboriginal people has been as problematic as the issue of sit-down money or welfare to Aboriginal communities today. Their presentation to Aboriginal people commenced under Governor Lachlan Macquarie in 1820s and soon took on a symbolic role, whereby each Aboriginal would demand their own blanket. It was as if issuing one each year was the appropriate acknowledgement of their dispossession, and so came to be regarded as each person's right, 'an emblem of civilisation'. Although the practice had its ups and downs through the years, economies were a continuing factor so that a limited quantity only might be sent by the government in any year; at the same time misappropriation of them happened frequently enough. By the 1890s it was acknowledged that

The blankets of Delegate

> The result of the gift of the blanket was, that the natives who received them ceased to clothe themselves with the skins of the kangaroo, the bear [koala], or opossum. The rugs which they had been used to make for themselves would keep out the rain, and in them they could pass the wettest night or day in their miamias, warm and dry. But the blankets we kindly gave them by way of saving our souls were manufactured for the colonial market, and would no more resist the rain than an old clothes-basket ... Mr Tyers [commissioner for Crown Lands in Gippsland and police magistrate] was of the opinion that more blacks were killed by the blankets than by rum and bullets.[44]

But of course, once the giving had started, it had to be continued on humanitarian grounds, and individuals were more than affronted if they missed out on their due. The symbolism of receiving or not-receiving the token blanket took on a new ritualistic significance and became part of the new order. According to historian Michael Smithson

> A possum-skin rug among Aboriginal groups was not the anonymous manufacture of a factory, but involved a complex set of interactions within the Aboriginal group. Hunting possums was a male occupation. Not all males, however could make use of possums: newly initiated youths and some Aboriginal groups were forbidden by traditional law from eating possum. Dressing the skins was a task for the women, but sewing the skins into rugs and decorating them was the role of the men. Rugs were thus distributed by men to women and children and other men, along kinship lines or through gift exchange.

This complex system was changed utterly by the annual issue of blankets. Aborigines saw the blankets as an acknowledgement or exchange for their loss of lands, but Europeans figured the Aborigines valued woollen blankets for their superior utility. Smithson added, 'It was paradoxical therefore that woollen blankets should have played a part in the destruction of Aboriginal society.'[45]

And yet, of course, many Aboriginal families did survive in the Delegate district. Even as early as 1877 some local clans led by Yibai Malian, also called Murray Jack, considered settling at Lake Tyers Aboriginal station and visited the place but decided not to stay. In 1881 Murray Jack, Munday (Mundy) and others offered to meet Howitt at Delegate. Old Mundy was probably the first to formally move onto the Delegate Aboriginal Reserve after its gazettal. He came out of the range near Craigie, as did Maggie Tungai.[46]

Various parts along the Delegate River had provided gathering places where people from many tribal groups – from as far afield as Omeo, Gippsland, Nungatta, Cann River, Monaro and the coast – could come together regularly. Once formalised, the reserve became the main place to meet up. Several Aboriginal families were based there by 1892 but the numbers kept changing. For example, the Moffatt and Hayes families soon moved to Lake Tyers. Other names associated with the reserve include Lassie, Newcong (Nuking) and Thompson but those most closely associated are Brindle, Booth, McLeod, Mundy, Rutherford, Morris, Solomon and Tungai.[47] According to the New South Wales Police Salary Registers 1882–1916, Gobiam alias Billy Hayes worked as a tracker at Delegate in the late 19th and early 20th centuries. Brindle, Rutherford and McLeod were listed as trackers with police at Delegate and Cooma and a member of the Solomon family worked as an assistant to a Monaro land surveyor in 1886 according to the Diary of Duty and Occurrences at Jindabyne Police Station 1885–88. Historically, the Brindle family had connections with Nungatta station while the McLeod/Booth families were associated with

The blankets of Delegate

the non-Aboriginal McLeods, landholders who employed many Aboriginal men from different families and regions, where all of those without a European name already were obliged to take on the name McLeod. Some came from Gippsland and others from the coast. In 1964 Arthur McLeod, who was born in Delegate when the Kooris still lived off the land, described the exodus from Delegate of the McLeod and Solomon families:

> When the families at Delegate heard of the Kooris down at Eden whaling, many of the men went down there to join the whaling crews. They often visited Wallaga, Lake Tyers and Orbost. Things were getting difficult at Delegate, the tribe went to look at other areas. They all dispersed until only Arthur's family was left, [and] the Solomons. They finally went to Orbost. Some people went to Lake Tyers, others to Wallaga Lake. From Orbost Arthur's family went to Bermagui. The older people went in a horse and sulky, the children walked. Some people went into the mountains at Cann River and lived in bark humpies. They lived on hunting and they sold rabbits to feed themselves.[48]

Celia Bond, Arthur McLeod's older sister, was born in Delegate in 1910, and, at age 14, was sent by the welfare board to work as a bonded servant on Litchfields' sheep station near Cooma. Four years later at the end of her bond she returned to Delegate to find her family gone. Everyone else on the reserve had been obliged to go to the coastal reserves. She joined them finally, leaving the Monaro to live on the coast as the Depression worsened. In an interview, she told Brian Egloff that she remembered when there were three huts at the reserve and 'Reserve residents caught eels, trout and blackfish and a Chinese gardener gave them vegetables.' She had to walk 5 miles to school and back each day. But many of the young boys were taken away to Kinchela Boys Home. In 1986 talks with Sue Norman, during a visit to the old reserve, she pointed out the nearby Aboriginal cemetery and a scarred tree. A Chinese family lived just north of the reserve where they sluiced a bit of gold and ran market gardens, all the time maintaining a close friendship with the Kooris. 'Celia had language, and she never said anything she didn't know to be true,' says Norman.[49]

BJ's father, Ossie Cruse, spent some of his boyhood in the region. His grandmother was Nellie Bungel, who came from between Bombala and Delegate. He tells me how the Delegate reserve did not have a resident manager. The place housed permanent residents, most of them related to his mother and father, but it was also a wayside to the people who travelled between New South Wales and Victoria. Because it was the old way to walk, because there weren't any deep rivers to cross, it was the natural way to and from the Orbost area. It was a place where many of his people lived temporarily or permanently

> because ... it was open for all of us to use. If you look around there, do a deeper search of that region, you'd find there were lots of other places that were campsites equal to Delegate. That's what I'm saying about it ... The painful side came when we had to move elsewhere, it separated us. We couldn't share those old camping places any more, meet up how we'd always done. We were pulled apart and it hurt us because we'd never been that separated before.[50]

Just as they did before the reserve was formally declared, Aboriginal people continued to camp on the land after the reserve was closed. But eventually they were persuaded to move on and not come back. Ossie well remembers the times before World War II when his people were loving and caring. 'We went and lived with other families and they grew us up to a certain point. The kinship was strong ... There were a lot of families associated with Delegate. But they had to move, so there are none living in the district any more, and they're scattered everywhere now.'

Ossie is a pillar of the Eden community: quiet, firm, resilient, dogged and a champion of his people regardless of the circumstances. From time to time he has served as chairperson of the Eden Local Aboriginal Land Council whose territory includes Delegate. He gave up alcohol and other drugs as a young man when he realised their dire consequences and what they were doing to him, and went on to become a pastor in the Aboriginal Evangelical Church. Like many other Kooris who had Delegate as their old stamping ground, he hasn't been back in many years. But things are changing.

On the way out of Delegate the winding road soon changes from bitumen to gravel and climbs towards the crest of the Irondoon Range. Views back and to the south reveal the richness of the plains laid out towards the foot of Mount Delegate. The best grazing country of those plains remains relatively treeless, just as it was when surveyor Stewart Ryrie passed on 20 March 1840. He found open downs of good soil and covered with a thick sward, the 'greatest part of the timber about the plain is dead, which the Blacks ascribe to a heavy fall of snow some years ago'. By an odd twist of fate, the Delegate/Bombala district, always a meeting place where many pathways came together, was a strong contender to become the national capital of Australia with Eden as its port. Politics and large trading houses defeated the proposal, to the eternal chagrin of the local populace.[51]

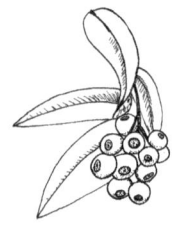

Across the Little Plains

My way winds into the range and presents glimpses of little plains tucked among rolling hills in all directions. Travelling between Delegate and Craigie in 1872, a journalist with a mission to describe the new districts crossed an extensive plain towards a sharp range of hills. He followed what was then known as the Chinaman's track and saw a number of Chinese 'trudging along the narrow track in Indian file, some leading packhorses, and others again mounted on the tops of the packs'.[52]

The diggers were actually following the traditional walking route. Today, it is a little country road that winds over the straggly, grassy peppermint forests of a line of hills, 'rather barren and stony in some parts' according to Stewart Ryrie in 1840. The Irondoon Range, a pretty, wildflower paradise, separates the Delegate and Little Plains rivers. Signs of the hand-made 'Chinese' road persist near the newer route. And why should it be that all manner of travellers have chosen to follow this particular route? The reasons become very clear when you explore the country around it. Southwards, not much more than 10 kilometres away, lie all manner of bogs and fens. Across the Victorian border in the very tall forests of the Errinundra Plateau, where mountain ash and shining gum reach extraordinary heights, there grow very thick, damp scrubs. It is extremely difficult terrain. The ranges tilt a few hundred metres upwards at the ragged southern end of the Monaro, then fall away in a most perilous descent. The country here was described by Ryrie in his unsuccessful 1840 attempts to head southwards to the ocean from Delegate where he climbed the range hoping to find a direct route to the coast, but after going a short way he found 'the scrub became so very thick and so much fallen timber amongst it that the horses could not proceed further'. He left them and fought on foot to the top of the range where he found an impenetrably 'thick scrub full of fern trees, stinging nettles and fallen timber of immense size'.[53]

Logged areas apart, little has changed when I attempt walking the Errinundra. While making his discoveries of gold in the region, WB Clarke also painted a picture of the country south of Delegate where the headwaters of the Bendoc River 'accumulate in swamps and bogs extremely difficult to pass, and in places quite impassable, being deep both in water and mud, surrounded on all sides by frequently impervious gum scrubs and cotton plants and fern jungles'. Clarke suggests 'the chief cause of the prevalence of these scrubs is the occurrence of fires once in about every 3 years, so that the saplings of the scrubs cannot attain a large growth'. Perhaps the fires were lit by settlers to send hot burns at the edges of the forests to clear them, where I would expect just such a consequence. Aboriginal burning would have different ambitions. The tall forests south of Bendoc are misty and wet, interlaced with rainforest-type scrubs comprised of plants like the tree waratah, blanketleaf, *Pomaderris* and lillipilli that cannot survive frequent burning or sustain fire other than under the worst drought conditions.[54]

Out in the more open country however the old Aboriginal fires might not have been regular, but targeted to produce the concentration of game in certain clearings. It is unlikely large acreages of the Monaro's grasslands were deliberately burnt at the one time as this would scatter the game rather than concentrate it where you wanted. The concept of firestick farming has now passed through so many hands that it means something altogether different from what archaeologist Rhys Jones proposed in the 1960s. On the tablelands burning can be as much a subtle tool as a sledgehammer. Nowadays, with burning strictly controlled for the general public good, fire has come to be regarded as a threat. Sure, if you start a fire in the dry midsummer and let it go down-wind, you're in trouble. By choosing carefully the time to light a fire, you can more or less easily control it, such as burning downhill, towards a river or rainforest or previously burnt patch, when there is little or no wind, when conditions are damp or on a day when the dampness will come in the late afternoon. Or, as one landholder said to me, 'If in the old days you saw smoke somewhere in the summer, you didn't worry. You always knew there had been other patches burnt recently enough that would bring it to a stop. But nowadays if you see a fire heading in your direction, you start packing.' This is one way to describe the benefits of the old mosaic burning.

The views today across the country are absolutely charming and little changed from 1884 when a travel writer from Bega reported leaving Delegate for Craigie and crossing 'the pretty plains which surround that rising town to pass over the arid but apparently auriferous range which divides them from Chinatown. A few years ago Chinamen could be counted here by the hundred and they contributed in a very great degree to the commercial prosperity of the places around. Now they are very few indeed and are mostly employed in fencing and other works ...' There were two joss houses in Craigie. Along the way easterly towards Bondi he passed 'over hills of gravely soil on which vegetation is very scant ...', the stony woodland hills and the swampy dales.[55]

The way passes from the Irondoon down a route that has changed to accommodate vehicles and then along the river among the goldfields of Craigie. Wedge-tailed eagles soar over the little plains. Blue wrens dance across the gravel road, oblivious to any danger. When the alluvial gold seemed to peter out, the field was left to the Chinese who had their own ways of finding the metal, and it became Chinatown. Few signs remain today apart from pock-marked river flats. A cluster of houses with a pine-plantation back-drop and a public hall that is a good place to stay overnight. There is a reserve at the riverside and a travelling stock reserve. Many platypus gather and frolic in the fast-running, clear water here. I see them easily from the bridge around dawn and dusk. This is Platypus country. The Little Plains River continues on through the hilly country where the plains are truly, if not ironically, little.

An upper tributary is named the Bendoc. Attempting to confirm the name in 1840 for his survey, Ryrie noted that 'I could never learn from the Blacks that they continued the same name to a stream along the whole of its course, but when asked the name they always give it the same name as the place through which it flows.'[56]

A story of the Newton family illustrates the routes and needs of travelling on the Monaro. As the result of a trading association with the Campbells, John Newton came to take up 640 acres on the Little Plains near the junction of the Little Plains and Delegate rivers by Conditional Purchase in 1875. This land was not far from the site where, as legend goes, there was a massacre of Aboriginal people in earlier days. His brother William, born in 1844, married the daughter of John Nicholson, their neighbour who owned the extensive Little Plains Run, and they settled at Orange View station with lands fronting permanent water at Jacksons Bog. This is gorgeous country, rich, green and bountiful in the best seasons, but during drought I have seen the grasses blown out of the ground and piled so high you couldn't see the fences, the soil as bare as in a desert. It is the effect of the rain shadow but another factor was the appearance of hares, which were introduced for coursing and became a pest during the 1880s. During the 1890s they were in plague proportions, and hare drives were organised when reports show that as many as 700 were taken in a day. When foxes and rabbits were introduced in the 1900s, hare numbers plummeted.[57]

Graziers who were over-stocked after a few good years faced exceptional hardships when the inevitable drought arrived. Some, like O'Hare of Corrowong or Brooks of Gegedzerick, as we have seen, had looked towards the Lower Snowy and then the higher country for drought pasture. Yet others took their stock into the grassy forests. Every blade of grass was contested. The consequences of the 1895 drought when barely 15 inches fell across the region would be far-reaching.

At this time the Newtons of Little Plain took a gamble. They looked eastwards. William knew something of the wild coastal country after serving on the Black-Allan survey of the border between New South Wales and Victoria. Perhaps the route was suggested by the Aborigines, who well knew Nadgee (just north of Cape Howe), and their markers showed the way. An Aboriginal credo to move on when the time is right helped the Newtons survive the worst of the drought. William took his brother Wally and their stock and they set out along the track that led past Craigie and south of Mila through the rolling grassy woodlands towards the most prominent landmark of the region, the White Rock of Nalbaugh. Then they followed one of the mountain passes and went along the ridgelines to the place on Imlay Creek which came to be known as Newtons Crossing. They then headed to the coast in Nadgee, where they set up yards and a hut behind the beach now named Wally

Newtons Beach. The drive brought a good enough result; they decided to keep using Nadgee, moving stock backwards and forwards, seasonally grazing the long grassy forest paddock. William obtained a lease of 4030 acres of the complex coastal country on 7 October 1897. But sometimes Nadgee was even harder than the Monaro, and William eventually left for Sydney while Wally stayed on. His little homestead on Newtons Flat was destroyed by fire in 1933 and the remains were washed away later by floods. Wally stayed on until 1939 when his remains were found resting against a tree. The local story goes that they brought him out on a shovel, because it was all that was left after the goannas had finished with him.[58]

The track leads from Craigie along a narrow, winding country road lined with old trees and grasslands through low hills with some remaining patches of the peppermint forest. A delight to walk, it passes places with evocative names like the Pipeclay Ford, Jacksons Bog, Duiguds Bog, past the handsome grassy flats and woodlands of the Mila Travelling Stock Reserve, to the Yellow Waterhole wayside resting place reserve and then on to the Gulgin or Rock Flat. Round the rim of the south-eastern Monaro, where the water is captured from misty rains or bubbles up in the swampy springs, you find tall forests comprised mostly of finely shaped narrow-leaved peppermints, along with some ribbony and mountain gums. Along the lower country and streams and swampier flatlands there are no trees. Elsewhere on hills stand the well-spaced, graceful swamp gum, white sallee and ribbony gum.[59]

My direction is towards the south-eastern corner of the Monaro. Every step is a pleasure as the route neatly continues to avoid the broken country that lies south of the border. At about 800 metres elevation the undulating country hosts patches of open woodlands. The way keeps to the more naturally treeless areas and gracefully skips lower parts with their swamps, fens, bogs and ephemeral wetlands. After a relatively easy day I camp at the Mila reserve, a perfectly sheltered, scenic place. Bondi State Forest to the south is nowadays mostly pine. Prisoners worked at clearing and planting pines from the Bondi Prison Camp between 1927 and 1939.

When we meet on his family property, first known descriptively as Spring Hills, bordering the Bondi State Forest, Gordon Platts shows me a tree scarred by the old Aboriginal men cutting foot marks to help them climb after koalas, plentiful through the region until the early 1900s. His family has owned the property since the 1880s, when Aboriginal men like Johnny Brindle, whose beard had red hairs, visited frequently. Billy Bungel was also a regular. He worked for a long time as stockman and tracker on the nearby Maharatta station and was especially skilled at mustering cattle in the wild country before fences were erected. He died here in the early 1900s sitting under a tree in what is still known as Bungel's paddock, and Gordon has maintained the grave. And, in fact, Gordon knows of the Newtons and says that before we had bulldozers to put dams into the paddocks it was common for the Monaro graziers to take their cattle to the coast after a bad winter, one where there was snow and frost and no rain. He's had to do it himself for months at a time, taking his cattle by roundabout ways to Bega one time and Belowra another. He raises the prospect that before fencing and private ownership of the land, in this kind of gently rolling countryside, there was more than one way to go and not necessarily a single pathway. They might well have walked along the crest of the hills not far south of his property, or via the old Aboriginal campsite at Yellow Waterholes. Although the road I'm following is little used nowadays, it leads somewhere that was a more important destination in the old days.[60]

As I come over a ridge and at last look across the Gulgin Flats they make a bowl so serene and rollingly beautiful that I'm put in mind of an ancient playground where I expect to find all manner of gentle and enticing delights. To the south a hill covered in dwarf she-oak heathland and bare of trees, known as the Bare Hill, Gulgin or Calkin, emphasises the area's qualities. However, in severe contrast to the flats, I'm confronted by a horizon of darkly forest-clad mountains that form a gap-toothed wall along the eastern edge of the Monaro. I stand there for ages taking in the scene, spellbound. I try to make sense of it as the full moon rises between sharp crests. Flamelike, startling, the red breast of a robin dances from fencepost to fencepost. The scene is as memorable as it is troubling. My eyes search the mountainsides for a way through. But in the late afternoon they appear rugged, wild, impenetrable and forbidding. I have no idea where to go from here. The realisation hits me that I have come to the end of the road.

The autumn coolness suggests the coming of winter as I make camp on a reserve in the middle of that scene. It's a flat place, sheltered from the breeze. Fresh water trickles along swampy channels nearby.

Directly eastwards, beyond Pheasants Peak and the Coolangubra Range, is the Bold Granite/Black Range that runs easterly to Balawan (Mount Imlay) and beyond. The various mountain ranges of the region are plaited, or corded together, and might best be described as a cordillera. Their complexity makes me wonder how it was possible for the Newtons to drive their stock all the way to the coast, to Nadgee. How did they go? Could it be the same route the old Aboriginal people followed on their way from here to the coast? And more importantly, is there still a way?

Yamfields

A gang of yellow-tailed black cockatoos have taken over a stray pine tree on the far side of the swamp. They're big birds, loud and raucous, but there is something delicate about them and how they function as a group or extended family. As I wash my face I hear a loud crunching when they rip into the cones with their powerful beaks. They must be after the seeds. Good luck to them, I say, then one flies away carrying a cone in its beak. Friends regard their call as ghoulish but I argue the high-pitched wail is comforting much as though they might be the Neil Youngs or Van Morrisons of the back country. They received the common name of *rainbirds* because they like to fly in formation with the powerful air currents ahead of rainstorms.

While it's not a beautiful place to camp, it's interesting. Springs feed several trickling streams that drain into a large swampy area. In the driest times no water is apparent until you dig a little. The tallest trees are widely spaced swamp gum and ribbony gum with white sallee, blackwood and silver banksia. Parts of the area have been taken over by teatree, giving the locality a scrappy feel. As my attention wanders from the birds

Yamfields

I'm struck by a golden flower. It's dandelion-like in a field of weedy dandelions but it stands out from the others. Right by the water's edge, close inspection reveals the blade-like leaves belong to the *Microseris* genus, the yam daisy or murrnong, narngeg or nyamin. Botanists are in the process of recognising three species where there was a variable one. The Aboriginal people had many names for them, perhaps acknowledeging its many forms. The buds characteristically rise bowed over, like a shepherd's crook, until they open.

That sighting weighs on my mind so much that I am drawn back in the springtime and find more of them. And as I wander about looking for more I spy another golden flower, a doubletail or donkey orchid of the *Diuris* genus. I keep looking, and then there's another *Diuris*, but a different species with brown spots. Later, yet another. These have tasty edible tubers much valued by the old Aboriginal people. The early botanist, RD Fitzgerald, told how the Aboriginal children showed them to the Europeans and in the 1870s he bemoaned that one species was becoming rare around Sydney because the children liked to eat them. This grabs my interest and so I look round more closely and find lilies: a number of vanilla lilies. And then bulbines. These are nutritious and tasty yam species. I mention this to some of the Aboriginal Elders in Eden and soon enough, at the beginning of December, we arrive in convoy and a bus to check out the scene. We hunt high and low but on this occasion the best I can find are two yam daisy plants, one in the water. We dig this one up to find its roots are mostly wiry. There are signs they might thicken into tubers. Perhaps they are the high-country species that doesn't have yams, or perhaps the tubers don't form under water or at this time of year.[61]

When I return a few weeks later I find masses of young vanilla and bulbine lilies all just beginning to show their leaves above ground. Back in Eden I tell the Elders we missed the growth period by a few weeks and they think that's very funny.

Maybe some of the plants became evident when the old people passed by on their summer journey to the high country. This place might have been an important stop-over for them. Other species would show up when they returned later in the season.

The Bundian or Bondi Springs became a wayside resting place in 1872. This traditional campsite also came to be used by travellers and bullockies because it was the best place to stop and camp the night on the very edge of the Monaro tablelands.

There are 'wayside resting place' reservations on the oldest parish maps. Nowadays they are called Travelling Stock Reserves and Travelling Stock and Camping Reserves. Usually located near a good source of water and with signs of long-time Aboriginal occupation, they were originally campsites for the old Kooris. The old bullock team drivers and other passers-by learned from the Kooris what good camping places they were.

Near where the pathway leaves the crest of the tableland, tucked up hard against the dark forestlands and under the influence of the mountain country, lies the family property of Neil Platts (cousin of Gordon Platts) who has described how his grandfather immigrated from South Wingfield in Derbyshire to settle in the district by purchasing the 1173 acres of Mountain Top in 1887. Typically then the country 'was all timber and undergrowth with some open country mainly on the flats. The land was cleared by hand and ploughed by horses till the 1950s'. The trees were big and tall, mostly peppermint or brownbarrel. They ran sheep, which were shepherded by day and yarded at night to protect them from dingoes. 'William Junior was the main shepherd; brush yards were built here and there for yarding at night; younger brothers would take supply to him or whoever was looking after the sheep.'[62]

Mountain Top marks the edge, the far south-eastern corner of the Monaro. Beyond it, to the east and south, the country is steep and rugged. Neil tells me how one track ran down towards the Nalbaugh Falls, and a second Travelling Stock Reserve beside Mountain Top was proclaimed to serve it. I come back to walk this country, exhilarated by its sights, following tracks and trails and obscure directions. I check the swampy places and identify the eucalypts as I go. Some have scars made by the old people.

The place I begin to regard as the yamfields calls me back time and again. Each visit reveals more information, lends weight to the place. I have to note when the plants appear as they come irregularly. Sometimes this is related to weather patterns, wet and dry, hot and cold. When I return with Aboriginal rangers the first thing we find is a beautiful artefact that wombats have dug up only recently during their tunnelling operations. A large, translucent orange quartz cutting tool, so intricately worked it might have been jewellery. Then another, and another. In the trees many birds occupy nesting holes. Soon after that I return with a crew of women rangers. We find yam plants galore and other food plants. On the far side of the swamp with a northerly aspect we find a tree with a scar from which a coolamon was removed. Then a large scatter of artefacts. Presumably nearby was a place for women's business cultivating plants, and here all the family stopped over.

Although my travels along the Bundian Way are blocked for the time being by that mountain range, I keep looking for the mountain passes, for the best way to get through to the coast. But in the meantime the yamfields take more and more of my energies. In my mind they become an emblem of the route. People who live nearby keep adding information. I learn of a stone circle overlooking the site on private property. And grinding tools, mortars and pestles. Then I'm shown another place on condition I don't reveal its precise location. It's an extraordinary grouping of large stones with a pointer stone at its centre. Leaning against it, propping it up is a large stone with a surface used for grinding. On the other side, is a large flat piece of conglomerate with a highly polished surface upon which is pecked a large circle pattern. This is unusual because we are on granite country. All the stones are so large it would take more than two men to move them. The location overlooks the yamfields but also takes in Yarramgun and the Coolangubra Range. The stones point to the central peak. With permission, I bring Aboriginal friends here. First thing they note is a group of dancing circles, Bunan rings, imprinted into the ground nearby at the top of the ridgeline.

Meditating on this, I take consideration of the likelihood that during the last ice age when our highest country was subject to ice and glaciation, the bogong moths might have come here for their summer aestivation. This granite range with its nooks and crannies and vast tumbledown piles of boulders would have been the older moth places. Perhaps I've been looking at the stones used for grinding the bogongs into nutritious cakes for transportation elsewhere. And I begin to suspect that those mountain passes listed by WB Clarke might all point to this locality. I'm going to have to reach back in time to find answers. Can any place be quite as simple as it looks on first sight?

So many stories tell of how the clans regularly walked through, east to west and west to east, but also north and south. The older generations were walkers, as distinct from the current generations who grew up with the motor vehicle. Men like Percy Mumbler didn't just walk to get from one place to another. Time didn't matter. You'd follow many considerations during a walk. Some places had special cultural associations. Guboo Ted Thomas told me how when he was a boy, he walked with the Wallaga Lake Gumleaf Band to play at the Cooma show. That was in the days before they achieved a high profile, leading all comers across at the opening of the Sydney Harbour Bridge in 1932. We registered the route they followed to Cooma, which had little to do with being the shortest route. It looped through the country in a manner that I believe made it the most valuable way to walk, a special route for many reasons. He also told me they once walked from Wallaga Lake to Bairnsdale, a 350 or 400 kilometre feat I couldn't comprehend at the time but which takes on a lot more meaning in light of the old route through the mountains and its spur that runs on to Omeo. Some of the older women have told me how as girls round the time of the Depression they were taken to places in the coastal ranges in the summer to feed on the yams, not only on the daisy yams, but others as well. They were good eating. Some were sweeter than others. Aboriginal people used to camp at the springs in the old times but nowadays these places are half-forgotten. They're not places you think about when you're going to and fro in a car. During my earlier explorations I found this kind of rich swampy grassland at points along the crest of the coastal ranges, places like Killarney Swamp, which is on the same catchment as the yamfields, then headed northwards, Badgerys Swamp, Nunnock Swamp, Bega Swamp, as well as those round the Tuross headwaters. All have significant Aboriginal pathways leading to or past them. They had similar proliferations of plantlife, maybe I simply haven't looked at them closely enough across the months. How many are connected to the Dyillagamberra spring-maker stories?

In my experience this place is the richest yam garden of the Monaro due to its population of significant species including: yam daisy (garngeg, nyamin or murrnong) *Microseris* spp. Many hundreds are still flowering in April/May, seeding May. Also present are numerous other plants with edible tubers or fleshy roots, including orchids (at least three species of double-tail or donkey orchid including golden cowslip, highland golden moth and hornet orchid, ladies tresses, greenhoods) and lilies (masses of both pale vanilla lily and bulbine lily, as well as blue grass lily and paroo lily). Also other Aboriginal food plants, including spiny-head mat-rush, Australian blackwood, golden star, saw-sedges, self-heal and others.

These might have been the perfect flats for yam cultivation. The locality is mostly sandy, with late Devonian sediments and water all year round, comprising grassland, grassy woodlands and swamplands on gravel, sand, clay and probably lignite. It has yabbies, active wombat holes, native bee colonies and tree hollows. The patches of trees are mostly white sallee, ribbony gum and swamp gum, with narrow-leaved peppermint on higher parts. It makes me wonder how extensive such places were before grazing arrived.

The identification of such special Aboriginal places along the route brings the need for special management. This location has not been publicised to-date as drawing attention to it means too many people might come; the problem of souvenir hunters is ever present. Some conservationists want to come and collect seeds. It has live-in populations of rabbits which could become a problem when the area dries out more. Wild pigs, whose favourite tucker is the sweet yam, are increasing in the region and appear to visit reasonably often; the place will require monitoring to ensure they don't take up residence.

Special protections will help keep its values, scientific and cultural, for the future. And it would stand as one of the distinct Aboriginal landscapes of the Bundian Way, a showpiece of how things used to be. An Aboriginal Place nomination is in process so that a culturally based plan for its management can be implemented as soon as possible. Scientific researchers look towards sustainability and increase by loosening the soils and burning. A women's business program is being guided by women Elders. Although there are no obvious economic advantages in the place, higher values come into play. In the future it could be a place of learning for the young, an educational showpiece for women's business, a demonstration site for care of country, such as the value of de-compacting the soil, how and when to dig the yam plants, use Aboriginal fire techniques and so forth. It will help boost the understanding of traditional cultural places and give Aboriginal people the opportunity to participate in scientific research.[63]

Insights into Country seem to make the project grow more demanding with every step.

Generally, the upland swamps, the fens and bogs, were places of abundance, not only for their yamfields that responded to the women's digging sticks but also as the country of the hatchet men and their dutifully managed possums. During scientific research, after fencing an area to assess various land management techniques for the yam plants, the first thing I notice is that grazing by native animals, especially kangaroos, is having major consequences. If it is women's business to look after the yamfields, it is men's business to look after the kangaroos and wombats that are undoubtedly more numerous than at the time of settlement.

The locale is a classic example of the Aboriginal landscape, one which contains not only a good sample of the original flora and fauna, but also a great number of food plants and signs of land use through the ages. Old people remember camping here many years ago. But it's a place where I come to search, and meditate on so many signs in the one location. I wonder what it all means. If I drill down through the many layers of meaning for any place along the route, will I get the same levels of complexity? How many otherwise unobtrusive places have such ancient connections? When I'm here, my mind seems to work differently – it's a contemplative place – and I feel I've risen above all the mundane complications of everyday life. Or that's what I find here, a special kind of inspiration. But maybe this place is just a sample of the way things used to be. Given its floral diversity, were plants brought here from other places? Was it carefully managed, created as an important stop-over during journeys along the Bundian Way? Have we been looking at a garden, deliberately cultivated by the old Aboriginal people? But also perhaps it is a beginning and an end, perched right at the edge of the Monaro tablelands, and so marks the upper limit of the Bundian Pass? It becomes a key place in my walk, that doorway I'm looking for, even though I don't yet understand its fuller meanings, or where I should go from here. And I think about the times when bogongs circled overhead.

Above Mount Kosciuszko and Lake Cootapatamba. My campsite lay below the lake beside the Swampy Plain.

Below (L–R) Ossie Cruse, Bobby Maher and BJ Cruse from Eden Local Aboriginal Land Council overlook the Bundian Way where it leaves the high country. On the horizon, distinctive mountains mark the route: Tingaringy, Delegate Hill and, in the far distance, Nalbaugh.

Above At the end of summer, Arabul (little ravens) flock to the high country's moth places in their hundreds of thousands to feast when it's time for the bogongs to leave.

Below Bogongs cluster in the tumbledown rock crevices and caves of the high country, clinging to the surface of the granite walls to form a thick carpet.

Above Wildflowers paint the slopes below Dead Horse Gap in the springtime.

Below The Thredbo River snakes through the Boggy Plain beside the walking route. After leaving the high country the route crosses the plain, then returns to the crest of the Great Divide.

Above Cascade Hut, constructed from alpine ash slabs and corrugated iron by cattlemen, nestles below the crest in white sallee woodlands.

Below A selection of artefacts, which come in all shapes and sizes, from along the route.

Above The grasslands of Merambego nestle in the mountains of Byadbo and feel a strong Alpine influence. Snow patches can often be seen persisting through summer on the distant peaks. The historic path passes through the heart of this scene on its way from the high country.

Below Merambego grassland emus. Before settlement such places hosted a remarkably rich wildlife.

Above left Some of the yam flowers – early nancy, yam daisy (nyamin) with native bee, golden moths and blue grass lily. *Above right* Marking the halfway point, Delegate Rocks overlook the township in the heart of Monaro grasslands.
Below Boronias thrive amongst grasstrees on top of Balawan.

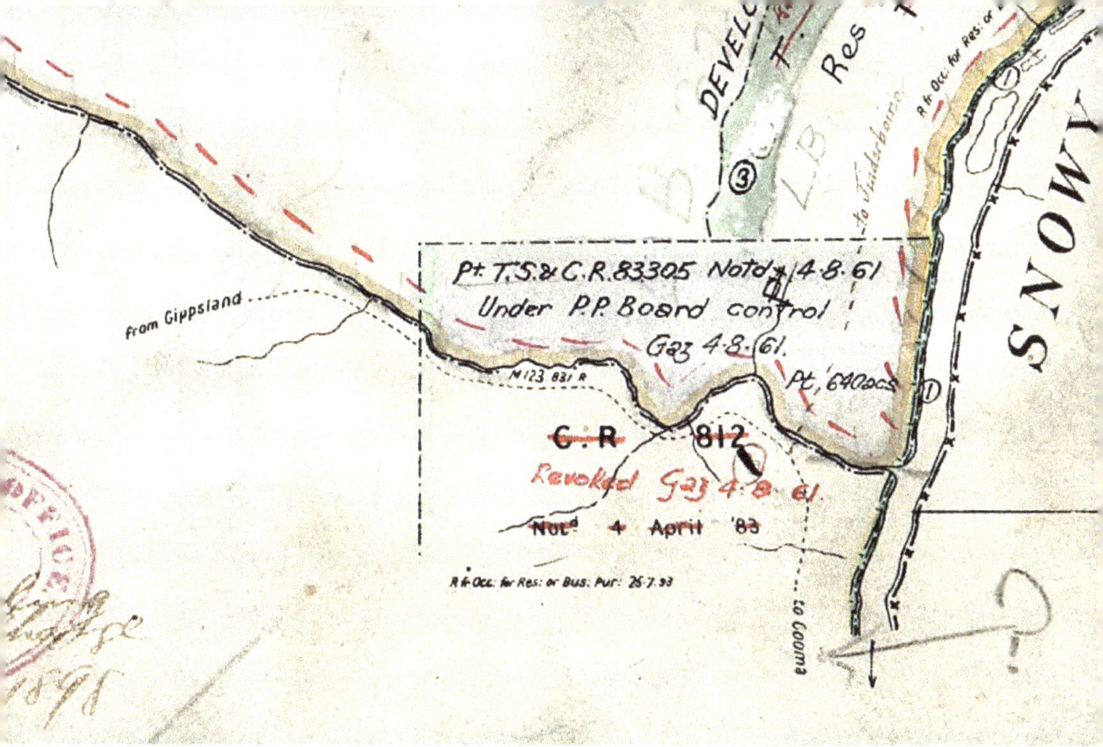

Above Extract from Moyangul parish map, second edition, 1898, showing the old route where it comes down the Nine Mile Pinch to join the Snowy.
Below Extract from Kiah parish map, second edition, 1896. These old maps are often compilations, detail upon detail from the early surveys, that can provide insights into the shared history. SOURCE Land and Property Information [1998]

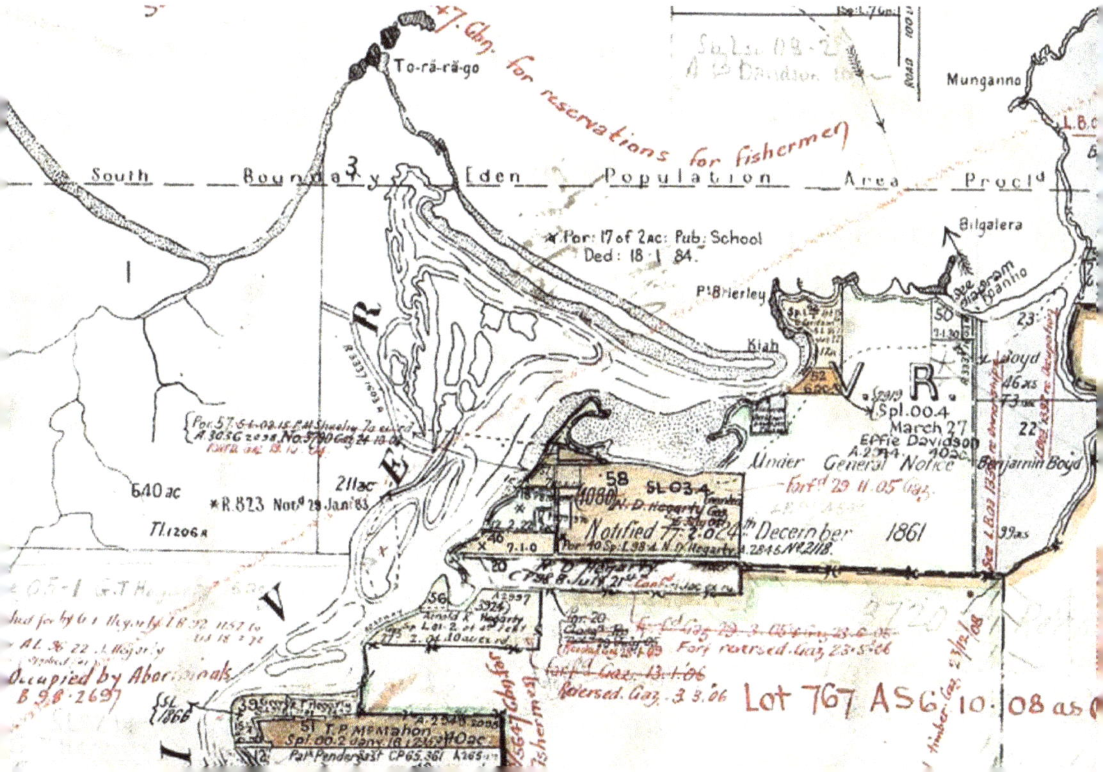

Above The sun sets behind Balawan, overlooking Turamullerer (Southern Twofold Bay), the Whale Beach, Kiah Inlet and the old route to the mountains.

Below Walking the track around the bay.

The Very Reverend WB Clarke

My respect for the Very Reverend WB Clarke has grown over my years on foot in the wild back country. Aged in his early 50s, already bald and portly, a substantial beard growing bushier by the day, he must have appeared like some prophet out of the bush when he approached the stations. At Maharatta, which then had the run of the south-eastern corner of the Monaro, in the shade of the Coolangubra, he found time to baptise a child. No matter what exertions he'd been through, he always had the energy to mount the soapbox and act the preacher, thundering from on high. Similarly, while undertaking his strenuous geological mission, his energies never flagged. He was so driven, it must have appeared he was compelled to turn every stone over, and over again. When he addressed his beloved geology, he wrote as a hungry young man does of his lover.

Even though I imagine he would be great company in the bush, something nonetheless irritates me immensely. For example, he tells me of the old mountain pass in the vicinity, but doesn't write down its precise location. When I attempt to follow in his footsteps, it's hopeless. My first resort is to study his tales of the country as closely as possible.

When he was ready to make for the coast he went to Bundian 'in the hope that I might be able to find an Aboriginal guide through the dense and difficult scrubs that encumber that line of country; various disappointments, however, led to my abandoning the attempt'. He managed to find a good idea of the country but that 'it would be impossible to travel with wheels ... in consequence of the abrupt and difficult cliffs about Nangutta, and the ranges of that vicinity and the dense scrubs, swamps, and hills of blown sand that succeed towards the south-east'. He goes on to list the mountain passes, the ways to get through the mountains, described by the local Kooris, after going to some trouble to obtain the Aboriginal placenames. The first of them:

> The Pass of Bundian is bordered by the defiles collecting the head waters of the Jenoa, of which the northern is guarded by the heights of Coonbulico, Wallagarra, Nangutta, and Ekalun, and the southern by the spur of Diliganea, which precipitates the stream collected to the southward of the Pass, over a wall of granite 67 feet high, and which forms the cataract of Windindingerree. These waters unite a little above the station of Bundian (Bondi), being in vertical descent below the Pass 1173 feet, and falling at the rate of 234 feet per mile; and after reinforcement from the Nangutta ranges, just upon the boundary line, the collected supplies are known as the Jenoa, which passes away to the south-east and meets the salt water at Malagoota ...[64]

But the names he was given by the Aboriginal people do not correspond with the modern names. His enjoyment – some might say childish excitement – at summing up even the slightest of his discoveries is palpable, as though he was born for it. The world opens as he focusses his gaze. It brings him such delight it is hard to see the scientist, whom we might expect to be more dour and circumspect, for he was a man whose first love and training was in the classics at Cambridge, apropos of which he published numerous poems and volumes of verse. His professor of geology would infect him with that passion for the earth and its exploration. In Australia as both clergyman and scientist he would go on to collect a truly amazing range of Australian fossils and minerals, which were acquired by the government on his death, along with his papers that included maps, field note books and journals. All were destroyed in 1882, when, along with his scientific library and many of the colony's most significant documents, fire broke out in the Botanic Garden Palace exhibition building and gutted it. In the few publications and sundry scraps of his papers that remain, the joy he took in his meticulous approach to the science of the colony is more than evident:

> In the creek below Bundian there are numerous drift boulders of a very beautiful porphyry derived from dykes in the granite of the ranges above. Near the Pass, the granite is nodular, distinctly jointed, charged with much hornblende, the chief constituents being white quartz, greyish white felspar, and greenish mica ... and in the quartz between its particles which are prismatic, is abundance of epidote. All these facts point to a period of no great antiquity as the epoch of this granite ... gold should be found in small quantity amidst the detritus of Diliganea ...[65]

His descriptions run on and on, displaying palpable delight in every stone formation, and yet he still identifies how he comes by the information. He would go out of his way to meet up with the local Aboriginal people, eagerly seizing upon what information they could give him. In a postscript he details the care he took in finding the names for places and how he was guided 'by the sounds uttered by the Aboriginals from whom I received them'. He used the spelling 'which appeared most in accordance with the pronunciation of the tribes in the vicinity of those localities'.[66]

What survives is the peripheral part of his writings, not the precise accounts I would have found, had my desperate search for his field journals come to fruition. The parts of his papers that exist today are those he had not earmarked for archiving. They amount more to a series of seemingly unedited, often-repetitious letters and general publications. No maps, journals, or diaries; too few details. Where exactly is this Bundian Pass he describes? I pore over the new maps and the old. It doesn't help that some names have been transplanted, such as what is now known as Pheasants Peak had – in the 1860 county map – once been called Coolangubra, which is now the name for an adjacent but less significant peak while the local chain of mountains is also called The Coolangubra. Many of the beautiful names Clarke found have since lost locality. In fact, it appears to me that he referred to the White Rock as Coolungubbera and the adjacent plateau, now Nalbaugh, as Nelbung. How many other names have been transposed over the years? I suspect Clarke was more meticulous with such things than MacCabe, the surveyor who followed him, whose local field books suggest he was awed into a silence by the very wildness of the country south-east of the Monaro and left no names behind (excepting, most likely, the prissily descriptive 'White Rock' instead of its Aboriginal name).

My walk across the flatlands brings me directly against this abrupt line of mountains that border the Monaro to the east. The district became infamous as the much battled-over Coolangubra during the days of the forest wars when conservationists protested furiously against logging. Its management is now divided between state forest, closer to the farmlands, and national park in the wilder parts. Not quite lost, nonetheless I'm not properly oriented, I don't have the sense of the country and how it adds up. I feel I have come off-track again. It rankles that I can't figure the location of Clarke's Bundian Pass. There is no obvious way forward. What else can I do but look around for a while and explore to find my way again?

The first place I hole up is at Waratah Creek, near the head of the Maharatta run close to where Clarke had made his camp. It lays about 20 kilometres south of present-day Cathcart, where GA Robinson 'ascended over hills (grassy) to Hibbert's Inn, Dollykyo by natives, the tribe is called Pundeang mittong, Bungunggarley alias John Gow is a native of this place at Pandang'. This makes me suspect that all this open forest country along the south-eastern edge of the Monaro where it meets the coastal ranges was regarded as Bundian country and that the Bungels, who were strongly associated with Maharatta, were also Bundian.[67]

The trees here are much bigger than any I have seen since Tingaringy. My aim is to explore the mountain passes listed by Clarke. Three were located round the head of the Towamba River and formed parts of a most important Aboriginal pathway that was readily adopted by the settlers once they were shown the route. Oswald Brierly was led this way in 1842 en route from Twofold Bay to the Monaro. His way up from the head of the river is exceedingly steep, rising over 1000 metres in a kilometre through volcanic geology: not too difficult zig-zagging on foot but an impossible challenge for bullock teams and their hard-wheeled wagons loaded with freight. One route, a 4WD track today, came to be known as the Cowbail. It still has engineering work that dates from the Boyd era. The main all-vehicle track today, the Big Jack Mountain Road, has extensive side-cuts that allow a gradient only modern machinery can provide. Hence the alternatives.

The next route heading south of the head of the river was the Burrimboco Pass, a fascinating walk. The first part of the way down reveals some open, grassy forest and I soon find why Stockyard Creek got its name: there's no way out. It's blocked by a steeply sided granite gorge. The descent is perilous on the lower slopes to above the junction between Stockyard and Myanba Creek, and the route would have led eventually through farmlands to the Towamba River below Rocky Hall. I return along scrubby Myanba, walking up along the ridge beside Myanba Falls, also a most beautiful place. The variations in the tall forests make a dramatic walk along the crest of the range between Myanba Gorge and Waratah Creek.

It is easy for me to find the location of the Wog Wog Pass as it is shown on the old parish maps and follows a very logical route given the local topography. In a kind of exuberance the next day I set off to walk the pass. It starts from the headwaters of Waratah Creek in the shadow of Yarramgun (Pheasants Peak), but unfortunately the upper Wog Wog River catchment, a beautiful bowl of unusual vegetation, was logged by Forestry during the forest wars in the 1980s at the same time as conservationists' claimed the area as wilderness. The forest industry's aim of taking out the eyes of the forests failed, the area is now national park; but today it is not a very pleasant place. Extensive parts were clear-fell bulldozed, the quartzy ground scraped clean as a grave; regeneration is scrappy at best. Some unlogged parts retain their natural magnificence, especially grassy woodlands in the part overlooked by the granite peaks between Yarramgun and Nalbaugh. It would have been a marvellous route, exactly as marked on the parish maps, as followed by local farmer, Gordon Platts; a stock route to the coast.

Many weeks of walking here only make me hungrier to find the Bundian Pass for, although a route is marked on early maps, it could not have been the original footpath that led easily from the tablelands to the coastal plains. The marked path was more

The Very Reverend WB Clarke

a settler route than the shared way of earlier travellers. Europeans preferred to travel between the established stations that supplied hospitality, Bondi and the next outpost at Nangutta station.

The old road to Bondi station is still obvious today as it passes beside the springs and the Bare Hill southwards down the steep slopes into the valley of the upper Genoa, past the one-time Bondi Mill.

This is the route mapped as passing Boondiang station, on the primitive sketch of the region by surveyor Stewart Ryrie, the first government official to come this way. On 7 July 1840 he noted in his journal the country near Gulgin as 'thinly timbered with white gum and well covered with grass, but a great deal of water lying on it'. He then descended southwards through a thick forest of stringybark, 'very gradually, along a leading ridge for about four miles, came to Mr Liscombe's station and camped near it'.[68]

Liscombe's Boondiang (Bundian) station later came to be known as Bondi, pronounced *boondee*, its first syllable as in book. It was not unusual for the first station of the district to be given the name used by its Aboriginal inhabitants, then known generally as the Boondiang-mittong.

At the bottom near Bondi station subsequent maps show a spur turned sharply eastwards to climb steadily to the crest of the range towards the Nangutta station and the old Rockton Road route to Pericoe and Towamba, today replaced by the Imlay Road. The route that continues southwards is today generally followed by the Monaro Highway towards Cann River. Even though it is the ancient route to Cann River, maps and walks tell me it is not the Bundian Pass and the easterly spur merely a settler route from one station to another. Other routes following ridges and creeks through the Bundian district don't feel right either, they don't have the simple logic that fits the country, they're too roundabout. The more I re-read what

The Monaro

Clarke had to say, the more I am convinced I can find the elusive Bundian Pass. I have his map to pore over, but like the County Map of Wellesley of 1860, the pass's location is ambiguous. Clarke's surviving, rather poetic and rambling account does not provide the answers. It entices me with its glimpses of 1852; all I can do is to search harder and more widely. The fragments that remain of his voice insist I have to look more deeply to find the essence of this country. It must all connect. I'm finding hints of the magic. One door might be closed to me for the moment, but I'm finding others.

Shifting 'tribes'

As the first surveyors made their forays across the landscape it was as though, brush-stroke by brush-stroke, they were painting in the shapes and names that would make sense in the British system. At the times when Stewart Ryrie pencilled his 'Boondiang' in 1842, Francis MacCabe passed by with his chain measures in 1846 and Thomas Townsend made his various mapping journeys through the region, these surveyors were legitimising the provinces claimed by squatters, putting them on the map, connecting them with British 'civilisation'. By this process they were painting out the old Aboriginal systems that gave 'Country' its meaning. The old ways only survived in the mind and culture of its Aboriginal people. Settlement brought changes to the land. Culture was tied to the land, sprang from it. The changes continue. Those 19th-century processes of writing down details of the oral culture, were more miss than hit. Gaps create contradictions and misunderstandings. And yet hints remain of those times when everything was enchanted with meanings and names. My attempts to find what I can of the Aboriginal landscape as I search for a route through the Bundian lands demand a re-examination of my often-contradictory sources.

Along with the land, the culture changed, of course, as cultures do. The spelling of names and places changed. The Bundian station, first taken up by Liscombe during the late 1830s, was next purchased, after the hard times arrived, by wealthy rogue, Ben Boyd, and then Captain John Stevenson of Wangarabel. Originally its run took in all of the upper Genoa catchment, complete with narrow river flats and its permanent water supply. The name of the station became the name to the whole district, changing to Bondi. Its pronunciation also changed. Selection saw large chunks taken out of it, so that by the late 1800s, on the parish map, the valley looked like a patchwork quilt. The wilder country in the steep parts was included in the Bondi Forest Reserve in 1884, then various other areas were consolidated to form Bondi State Forest at the end of World War I. As the population of Bondi grew and it achieved its own post office, confusion with the beachside suburb near Sydney saw it renamed Rockton. This grew into something of a village with its own general store/post office, butchery and school to serve the general farming and logging community during the Depression. After World War II people drifted away. Rockton was purchased piece by piece to become part of Bondi State Forest. The store, schools and all were closed. In the bold Depression-time experiment using convicts, it was planted with pinetrees, which present one easy answer to the problem of encroaching scrub: you flatten everything and blanket the area with radiata pine.[69]

So few people live in the district nowadays it seems deserted, as though it doesn't belong in the 21st century. It is one of those remote valleys, perhaps too distant for technology-loving modern families, a place somewhat spoiled by all the pine trees and their harvesting, yet nonetheless pretty enough and even picturesque in parts. The climate would not have been as extreme as the Monaro and it would have been good for those

Shifting 'tribes'

who were prepared to be self-sufficient. It makes a pleasant walk down the Monaro Highway, then turn left at Imlay Road which roughly follows the old way to Nangutta – on the same catchment but on the easterly side of the line of mountains – yet I am more convinced there has to a better, easier way.

The Monaro Highway follows the Genoa due south, until the river turns easterly after the old Bondi station, then it jumps a ridge and continues south beside the Cann River to meet the Princes Highway. This was an old Aboriginal pathway between the East Gippsland Coast and the Monaro.

Monaro identities have told me their grandfathers talked of a time before the coming of the scrubs. It's an interesting conception, the 'coming of the scrubs', as though they were a disease. They have many forms and species, but the consequences for the land are similar. I wonder about the reasons for this, given that I understand there is no single answer.[70]

If the scrubs could 'come' it means they were not necessarily always present. Were they controlled before 1788? And when did they begin to run out of control? I speculate that if they were in control, was it the Aboriginal people who did the controlling? And who were they? Who were the Bundian people? How did they describe their country? Knowledgeable Aboriginal people give me contradictory answers, so before I attempt any further lines of enquiry I check my main historical sources and compare what they said.

Robinson's 'tribes'

Robinson notes his informants (especially Rodney) advising that the 'Cape Howe, Tinnoor [Genoa], Wongererbul, Twofold Bay, and Panbuller all speak the same language; the Bicker is a different language. The tribe at Bane [Bemm] and Karn [Cann River] speak the same language as the Buckun and probably

Gipps Land tribe [Bidawal].' This tells me the Bundian spoke Thaua, and the boundary with the Bidawal ran through the steep-sided mountain range of the Coopracambra and along the divide southwards of the Genoa catchment and the New South Wales–Victoria border, a perfectly natural boundary.[71]

Within this region, during the course of his travels and surveys, he quickly scribbled a note of every conversation and event of any consequence he encountered, simply slapping the details off the top of his head into his journal. He used phonetic spellings that varied enormously, remarkable for their inconsistency, that I'll try to sort in a glossary. But his details do stand as a snapshot of the times. Dates, people, numbers, locations. This is a remarkable legacy.

He made numerous contributions to our understanding of the old clans of the region, including the Bundian. Passing from the tablelands, on his first journey to the coast, he wrote of the Pundeang mittong and Bungunggarley 'a native of this place at Pandang'.[72]

Then he followed up, referring to Davy: 1. Por.er.cow.wel, 2. Tin.yan.gwor, country Pone-di-ang. A Pone.di.ang.mittong.[73]

Later, on board Ben Boyd's *Wanderer* in Twofold Bay, he says how 'Toby furnished me with a number of words of the Twofold Bay language' and refers to 'Bundy: Liscombs station 10 miles north west of Nangutter' and then adds: 'Pandeang Mittong: belong to Lisomb's'.[74]

He is told the people are grouped in various ways, not only by tribe or clan, for example, 'Kud.in.gal is a term applied to all Blacks living on sea coast ... Pyender a term applied to all Blacks living in the woods who live by climbing trees, from "pyen" their word for tommy hauk.'[75]

There is no doubt he meant well in all his wide-ranging activities. He sees the need for change. A frequent refrain in his notes is that in 1840 'large numbers of coast and Maneroo blacks died of influenza'. At Nangutta, Alexander Weatherhead told him the Yass blacks had had the small pox. He notes the vast numbers stricken as a result of their contact with Europeans, how their suffering has been aggravated without corresponding benefit. 'Small pox most destructive, influenza, syphilis, baneful fever and other epidemics,' he asks, 'Now point out any benefit the natives have derived?' But he is powerless to bring about change. All he can do is gather the data.[76]

Clarke's 'tribes'

While he was about Delegate hunting out the traces of gold, WB Clarke ventured into the headwaters of the Bendoc River where, he dutifully reported on how the prevalence of the scrubs 'supply the securest shelter to the eleven miserable and timid Aborigines who now form the remnants that is left of the once more formidable Bidwilli tribe'.[77]

These 'scrubs' and the tall forest began not far south of Delegate, just beyond the hill and the settlement of Bendoc, and form part of the line that might be considered an ecotone or environmental boundary. South of the line, where it gets the mists and rain, the vegetation is different: simpler, cooler and very much damper than the Monaro. The reasons for this are climate, landform, geology, aspect, elevation and so forth. But, very typically, such changes mark different tribal territories throughout Australia. They also mark changes in the management practices relevant to the land.

A clue might be found in those 'Black Thursday' fires of 6 February 1851 that William Howitt described. Although it is known that about 5 million hectares were burnt in the vicinity of Melbourne and westwards, it is possible there were even bigger, more intense fires across the unsettled country of eastern Gippsland which was also under the influence of drought and, in the extreme heat of summer, at danger of lightning strike.

The conditions saw burning leaves fall on ships near Tasmania and New Zealand.

If we look at the sequence of observations on the Bidawal, an interesting change takes place during the 1800s.

Clarke made his remarks on the Bidwelli in 1851, shortly before Howitt arrived in the colony, and a lot had changed before Howitt came to research and write on the subject. For example, if a researcher observed the area after settlement and the ravages of disease and uncontrolled fire, they would see a massive intrusion of young plants into what was otherwise a chain of grassy clearings along rivers like the Bulda or Brodribb (Bidwelli) and the Bemm. The surviving Bidawal would have been displaced by a new growth of scrubby forest. What were once rich clearings within the more open forest would become unproductive, thickly-afforesting areas of scrub that were of little use to man or beast. The land's diversity would be reduced.

Howitt's 'tribes'

In his 1904 book AW Howitt mapped 'approximately' the Biduelli clan of the Kurnai tribe as occupying the upper reach of most Gippsland rivers, including the Genoa. He says the Biduelli tribe's name is 'derived from *brida*, "scrub," and *lle/li*, "dweller"'. His opinion, from the book, has been influential, so I note it at length:

> In that part of Eastern Victoria called Croajingolong there was a small tribe called the Biduelli, who occupied the forest and jungle covered country between the high coast ranges and the immediate coast along which the Kurnai lived ... I have traversed the mountains, swamps, and scrubs of this piece of country three times, before it

was occupied by white settlers, and as compared with the adjacent parts, there was but little animal life. The Biduelli were few in number, inhabiting small open spaces in the dense jungle, and called themselves 'men' (Maap) ... and it seems that their country formed a refuge for what one may term 'broken men' ... [who] find protection from tribal punishment ... I can feel no doubt that the Biduelli country was an Australian 'cave of Adullam'; that the tribe was built up by refugees from tribal justice, or individual vengeance, and that they organised themselves, as far as they could do so, on the old-accustomed lines.[78]

Howitt's comments represent views that have prevailed, perhaps because of the authority given them by publication of his *Native Tribes of South-East Australia*. Many times I have had Aboriginal people say with absolute force of conviction, 'Them Bidawal were all outlaws. They were nothing, not a real tribe.'

But there were other views. Howitt's – perhaps correct to the best of his information – were formed after the Bidawal had suffered severe depredations, including those from influenza, tuberculosis and smallpox. However he did have information that contradicted his published view and appears to correspond with Robinson and Clarke. It came from Mickey of the Ngarego tribe, who was 'born at Mutong, near Buckley's crossing [Dalgety]'. His information was that: 'Cooma blacks = Ngarego mittang, Bega blacks = Waral mittung, Bondi blacks = Bindi mittung, Bendoc blacks = Bidwel mittung, the Tumut blacks = Woradjeri mittung.'[79]

Howitt is widely respected, his works have been one of the main pillars for the re-establishment of Aboriginal culture in the region, and yet he is held in very low regard by many Aboriginal people. 'He tricked those old fellas into thinking he was initiated,' has been told to me by more than one informant, expressing a view not discouraged by his grand-daughter's biography. 'And anyway, he shouldn't have written down all that special stuff where anyone could read it.'

As I walk I think things through. It strikes me that some of Howitt's opinions have clouded the history. Walking in Aboriginal footsteps makes me wonder how we can incorporate a greater sense of the national Aboriginality into the overall Australian culture. How do we begin expressing it? What I see more clearly as I look for the old route is how the Aboriginal Countries hold the clues to understanding Australia. Culture is in the land. My walking is showing me the connections, highlighting elements that let me see the countryside afresh. History continues. Culture is ever-shifting, however we express it. I sense the power of Aboriginal culture at the same time as I understand it varies, sometimes in major respects, from group to group, from district to district, from Country to Country. What I most need to express is the shared history while I heed that decision in 1980 to keep certain knowledge within the Aboriginal community. Respect the different ways of knowledge. If people want to know certain things, I say: go and ask a knowledgeable Aboriginal person.

And to those who criticise Howitt as a trickster and fraud, I say he was a brave and dedicated man whose writings of the region – his gift to the future – have helped us understand how things used to be along the way. But he didn't know everything.

Mathews' 'tribes'

By occupation a surveyor, RH Mathews travelled widely in his quest to record Aboriginal culture as accurately as possible. Although he too was accepted by many Aboriginal people 'as one of the initiated' that is not to say his work agrees with Howitt's. Not at all. He operated in a very different way to Howitt. Where Howitt had the magisterial authority of a superior

Shifting 'tribes'

whitefella, Mathews would pay due respect to the people he was working with. For example, it is told 'that when he got near a camp, he usually lit a small fire and sat at it until invited to join the group. A small thing! but a reciprocal act of courtesy.'[80]

Later in his career Mathews had the knowledge of a man of high degree, of one who knows the secrets, but did he ever go through the ceremonies, or take on 'the usual obligations of secrecy'? Perhaps, like Howitt, his continuing access was more in the manner of an honorary degree granted to a wise and knowledgeable man. Perhaps it was recognised that he too could make a contribution to keeping the culture alive.

In 1907 Mathews published his mapping of the language and country of the Birdhawal tribe, 'prepared from notes taken by myself among the survivors of these people'. Although 'Their hunting grounds were mainly in the extreme eastern corner of the State of Victoria' he believed they also occupied a small strip of country within New South Wales, namely extending inland from the coast to Bonang, Delegete, Craigie, and in the head waters of the 'Bondi and Nungatta creeks'. He proceeded to describe their initiation ceremony, known as the 'Dyerrayal'.[81]

Howitt also described a Kurnai Jeraeil ceremony, noting the similarity to the Yuin Bunan ceremonies, but with differences arising from the Kurnai 'country being shut in by dense scrubs and forests in the west ... The word Jeraeil means leafy, a 'branch' or a 'twig'. It is therefore analogous to the Murring word Kuringal, which may be translated as 'of the forest'. He does however state that the 'ceremonies of the region are the same in principle, even where they vary in practise' and that men attend from many tribes and from far away under a 'ceremonial armistice', and that the neighbours are 'in contact with still more distant tribes, with whom they intermarry'.[82]

Perhaps in contradicting the earlier accounts of those like Robinson who in the 1840s clearly describe the Boondiang-mittong, 50 years later both Howitt and Mathews appeared to ignore their presence. Could something terrible have happened to the whole extended family group or clan? Or were these anthropologists in their individual ways attempting to describe a process by which much-depleted peoples driven from their country for various reasons were attempting to assert new territorial rights? If the Boondiang were gone, there was no reason why the Bidawal should not adopt that land as their own. Perhaps, although the Boondiang belonged to the Thaua language group and were hence regarded as Yuin, it was somehow easy to lump their Country in with that of their close neighbours to the south. Those neighbours are today mostly known as the Bidawal (after mapping published by Norman Tindale and, most recently, on maps widely distributed by the Australian Institute of Aboriginal and Torres Strait Islander Studies), even though the name has been spelt many ways over the years. Numerous people of Bidawal descent live throughout the south-eastern region.[83]

One 1840s drawing by Oswald Brierly shows an inhabitant identified as 'Mur-rowra Esquire Bundyang'. Portrayed as a thorough gentleman, he lies back proudly, a possum-skin cloak tied lightly about his neck, a large boomerang in his hand. The old Bundian resident took his ease with confidence and poise.

BJ and his father Ossie Cruse have told me that Boondi (Bundi) was the popular word for club or nulla nulla, and that it is possible the country of the Bundian people was where a club rather than a hatchet was the most useful tool in hunting, given its plentiful small ground-dwelling animals like wallabies, kangaroo rats, potoroos and pademelons, not to mention the tree dwellers like possums and koalas.

My walk in the heart of those lands leads from the knee-high forests of the Bare Hill into the headwaters of the Genoa and a very strangely formed place, the Bondi Gulf Nature Reserve. I

Shifting 'tribes'

continue downstream along the river, past the Genoa Falls and steep hillsides and paddocks that are all that remain of the station. Teatree, mostly burgan, scrubs have invaded most of the good country along the riverbanks. Thick entanglements make the walking difficult. Soon I am in the national park in dramatic gorge country, a special place, and true wilderness, recognised in the South East Forests National Park of the New South Wales side of the border and the Coopracambra–Kaye National Park on the Victorian side. But the walk convinces me there was no track along the river. It was used by the old people, certainly, there are plenty of signs, but it wasn't a pathway. It's like the difference between a super-highway and a back lane. Things become far too rugged the further south you go, they don't connect.

From Gulgin I look north-west into the country of the Maneroo, the Ngarigo, and south-east into that of the Bundian, the Thaua speaking coastal people, while to the south and west lies the Bidawal. The walking leads me to contemplate the overlap of Country. I note how different the landscape is to the south. Even the plantlife makes it feel different. And yet maybe the answer to my difficulties is that the old Aboriginal people had their own ways to describe Country. Or they didn't need to. They certainly didn't need surveyors. Everybody knew their own Country, they understood, took it for granted, and that's all there is to it. And I understand that my Genoa River walk is off track. The way has to lie in a different direction. I must find different angles, I'll keep walking, but I need more background.

PART 3
THE COAST

The natives gave me quite a different idea of the Australians from that which I had first formed upon seeing the poor creatures in the neighbourhood of Sydney ... At Twofold Bay some of the natives varied strikingly from the rest ...

Oswald Brierly, 1841–43[1]

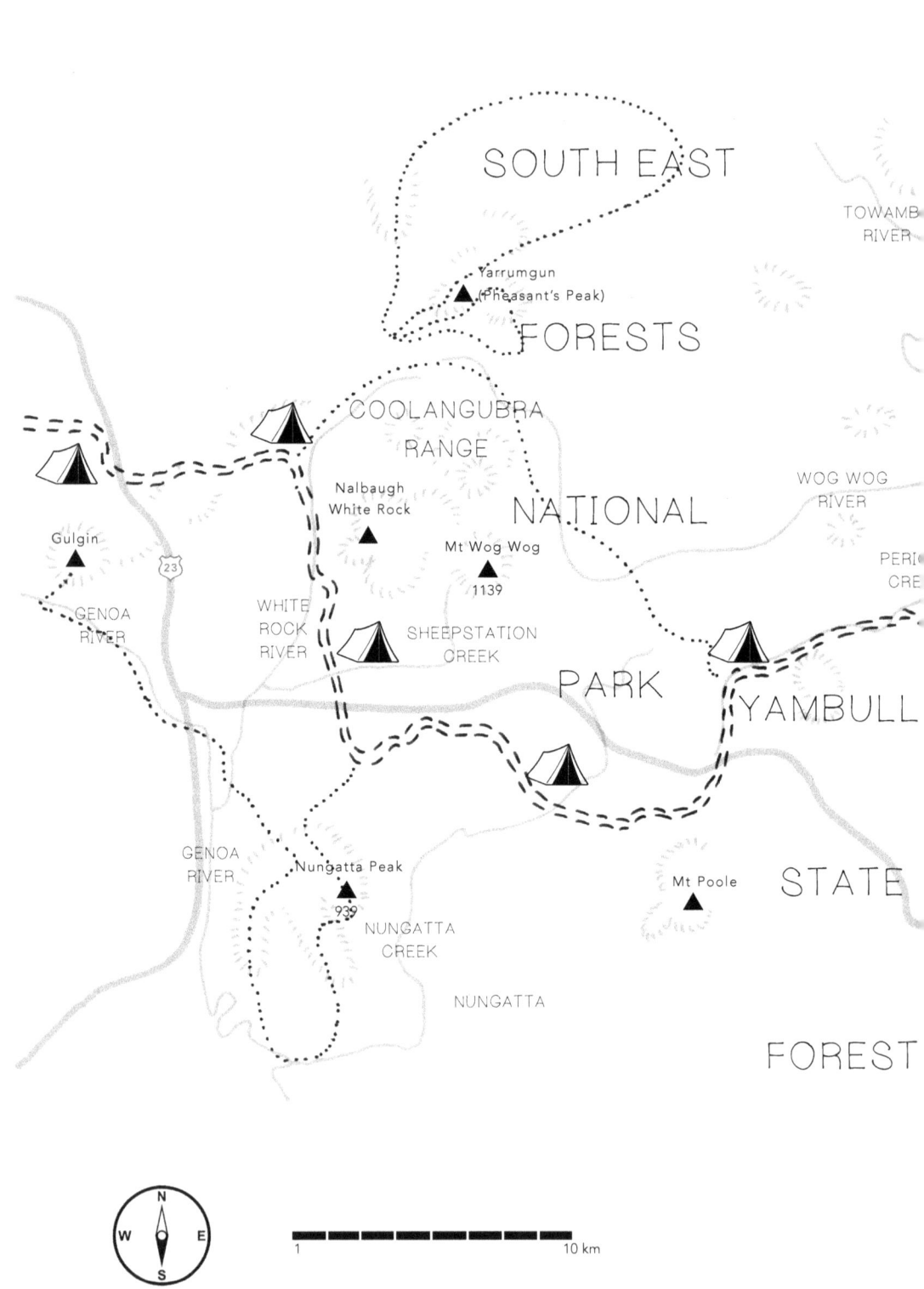

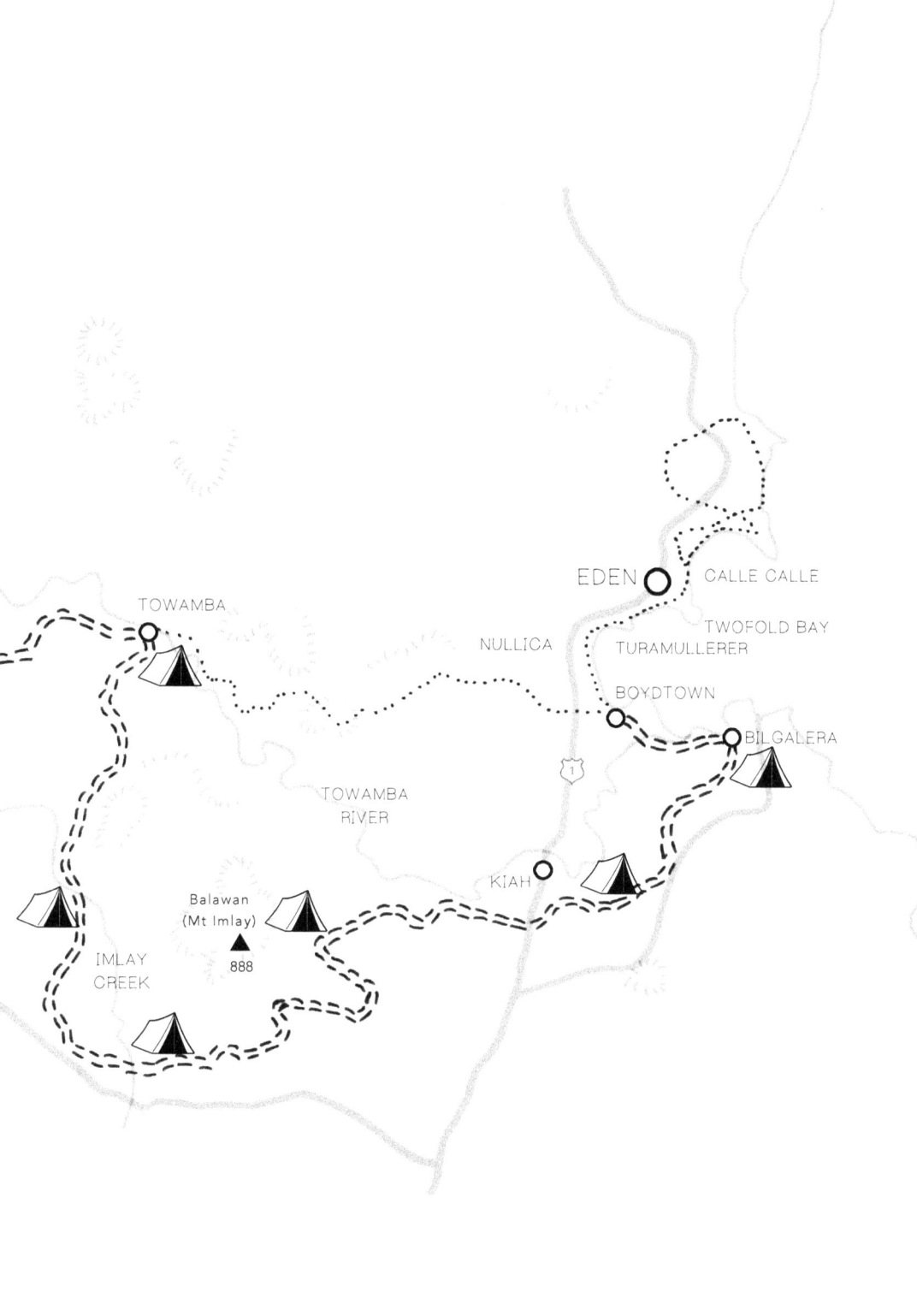

Coming to Twofold Bay

Still puzzled, in between walks I chase down old maps and papers in the libraries of Sydney and Canberra. Maybe the answers to my questions are there in the history of the region. I check yet more and more of the old maps in the state archives. I keep walking. I keep searching. Up on the Monaro it starts to get cold by May, really cold, so I'm only too happy to accept when the National Parks and Wildlife Service (NPWS) offers me the role of caretaking at Davidson Whaling Station, on the Kiah Inlet, Twofold Bay. After so much time walking, it is no hardship to re-gather my strength, and generally explore the bay.

It is an area of such exceptional beauty I feel as though I've come home at last when, on my first evening I stroll down through the tall coast grey box to a little headland that overlooks the entrance to the Kiah Inlet. On my right is Brierly Point and, directly across the inlet, the Whale Beach, a narrow spit that separates the bay from the inlet. The sun becomes an orange ball as it touches Wog Wog, the Coolangubra and floods the coastal ranges beside Balawan with misty pastels. The mountain's distinctive shape clings to the water as mullet lazily take to the air and flop back down. Bream fins cut patterns in the shallows. Cormorants return to their roosts with heavy wingbeats. Their best efforts can't shake the reflection. A white-breasted sea eagle spirals overhead, on its way back to its nest in a tall tree not far uphill from the house. I am not the first to discover such beauty, for I am standing at the foot of a massive midden – stretching maybe 100 metres up the hill and into the trees – comprised of shellfish gathered from the inlet over thousands of years and consumed here. Overwhelmed, I ponder how many generations have done exactly what I am doing at this place, how it points to what has been common to human nature over the millennia.

The house at the whaling station is a simple old-style farmhouse with a broad verandah that looks westerly towards the inlet. Built by George Davidson of hardwood weatherboards in 1896 and named 'Loch Garra', it is now proclaimed as a Historic Place, and managed by the NPWS. The rough-hewn timber-slab kitchen block probably dates from an earlier time when there was no legal occupancy. It looks down over the Kiah Inlet, where, at the water's edge, is the site of the Davidson try-works.

Apart from the beauty of its forested foreshore setting, this site's main claim to fame is that it was a whaling operation. Its methods not unlike a shore based version of those described by Herman Melville in *Moby-Dick*. The try-works was a roughly improvised bush timber shelter with a corrugated iron roof in which the whale blubber was boiled down and reduced to fine oil, a product much sought-after at the time. Davidson's operations became a curiosity, much photographed and written about before World War I. He was championed by the photographer from Eden, CE (Charles) Wellings and his brother, storyteller HP (Harry) Wellings. An entertaining book by Tom Mead, *Killers of Eden*, mythologised the Davidson operations. In a fictionalised style, it claims to tell the true story 'of a bizarre compact between man and one of nature's most dangerous creatures'. First published in 1961, remarkably, it remains in print today, a bestseller at the museum in Eden. The story – a classic of the red-in-tooth-and-claw genre of nature writing – tells of George Davidson's relationship with Old Tom and a pack of killer whales, and how they helped round up passing whales for his crews to harpoon in exchange for first pickings from the carcass. Another side of the tale tells how he flouted the conventions of his time by paying the Aboriginal men the same wages as the whites.[2]

A little distance round the inlet I notice a small tent that stays day after day, a presence that mystifies me because camping is not allowed here. When I walk past, it is unoccupied. Piles of oyster shells lay all about. Billies and camping implements stand beside the fire as though the owner will be back any time.

It seems eerie when I find more old whalebones, festooned with mussels, almost buried in the sand while I swim in the channel of the inlet not far from where the try-works were situated.

Some time later on a visit to Eden, the closest town but located on the far side of the bay an hours' drive away, I call by to see BJ Cruse again. He's delighted I'm at Davo. 'Great place, Brother. I've pitched a tent there myself. Go and stay when things get too much for me in town. You know, sometimes everybody wants a piece of you. Sometimes you have to get away.'

Thereafter, every week or two he calls by for a chat. Most times he's bright and enthusiastic. There's always a new plan or idea. Often he harps on the need to retain cultural places, to have camps where Aboriginal people have always gone, where they won't be hassled for doing things the Aboriginal way, where they can show the kids the bush and help them have a broader experience of life. This helps keep them out of trouble. It's not good if they feel they're stuck in town. We often consider the old walking routes, which present an Aboriginal alternative to town, but he can't offer any suggestions about the precise location of the Bundian Pass. The mystery remains. He knows about it generally. Although he knows bush places of the region quite well, it was only his grandfather's generation that used to walk everywhere. Cars changed the old ways, the places people used to go, as well as so many other traditions. Not all of the changes have been good. He does reckon, though, that there was an easy way from Delegate to Twofold Bay, and we agree a route that follows the Bundian Pass should be known as the Bundian Way. We smile to also agree that if it followed the Wog Wog Pass, it should be the Wog Wog Way. 'Nowadays not many kids get to go camping the way we did when Dad worked in the forests. They're losing touch with all that stuff, like how to light fires and deal with snakes and spiders and all. It would be a great way to take kids on walks to learn about nature.' We wander up to the little headland to survey the countryside.

'This has become such a special place for me,' I say to him of the shell middens. 'I love being here. It makes me imagine the good times that took place on this very spot. Isn't it exciting?'

He looks at me a while with his quizzical look. 'It's strange to me,' he says, 'that you whitefellas pay more attention to our old garbage tips than you do to what's behind it.'

Another midden lay just down the hill, on the little waterside flat where George Davidson built his try-works. The bricks were fired from local clays, probably at Boydtown. The middens were plundered to make the mortar to cement the bricks together for the fireplace. All that remains are traces of the former uses: a few broken cast iron try pots and a replica of the spindle used to winch the blubber flensed from the whales in readiness to be boiled down to make the oil.

The house and surrounds, with their memorabilia of the whaling days, have become a popular tourist destination. Cast iron oil pots feature, some even used for bird baths. It's all lovely and olde worlde, but what I find beneath the touristy surface fascinates me more, the hints of a deeper, more complex story. My favourite place from that first day has been the knoll overlooking the inlet and its wide views westerly to Balawan and the mountain chain beyond. From here I check the tides and the fish and the coming weather while I consider the forests, deeply comforted by the sense that this was a place where the old Aboriginal people also came to contemplate the tides, the fish and the country further inland. It would have been a powerful dining room. The place brought me to think of its history as a living thing, that the Davidson story, though more visible, was only a small link in the grander chain. The evidence is all around in stone, some of it brought here from afar: flakes and stone artefacts, including fine-grained cherts and silcretes but also quartz. Bone fishhooks are common along this section of coast, as are the files used to fashion them. Deep in the midden under try-works, a dingo skeleton was discovered. A little above the house, overlooking the ocean, is a scarred tree. Although it is clearly very old, the woollybutt is 'believed to have been alive in the 1920s. It was long-butted (cut off) above the scar in 1938 ... The main scar is located on the north facing side of the main trunk. The scar is 1.5 metres long and almost 0.5m wide. There are numerous smaller cuts in the surface some of which are partially overgrown indicating their occurrence when the tree was alive.' From my experience, I would guess the age of the tree at over 400 years. The scars appear to have been made at various times, some possibly from before the coming of the European settlers. The largest, oval in shape, would most likely have been where a coolamon was removed. The trunk also has notches most probably cut as toeholds to climb the tree and look for whales across the bay. The tree is near a stand of other woollybutts, much favoured by koalas when they were more common before World War I. The 100-year-old Elsie Severs, daughter of George Davidson, told me of her first memories, 'I can remember when we went up to an Aborigine that was camped up on the hill above the house and he was roasting a koala. There was one over the fire, cooking. We were only small.

We knew it was a koala. Monkey bear they called them then.'³

A jumble of rocks in the water, I am told by BJ, was used to trap fish before it was rearranged for boat moorings. About the weedy beds of the rocks as well as in the inlet the bream, mullet, flathead and blackfish as well as mussels, oysters, mutton-fish (abalone) and pipis are not as plentiful as they used to be. It is a place where someone with as few skills as I have can usually manage to provide meals from day-to-day. It's a place where you sense the bounty of the old days. Occasionally I see dolphins using the inlet.

A few hundred metres round the inlet from the works is the site of Kiah House. Although it burned down in the 1930s the land is still owned by another branch of the Davidson family. This also has plenty of middens (some metres deep) and artefacts. In between, near the water's edge, stood two little one-roomed weatherboard huts that were used by the Aboriginal whalers during the season, and beside them an open boatshed and rude timber slipway.

At the conjunction of ocean and forest, relatively sheltered, with numerous inlets, the southern shores of the bay must have been remarkably rich places to live in the days before settlement. But also they were important places to visit as part of the seasonal rounds and I can see their stories coming together, taking a particular shape. Its plot is the Bundian Way.

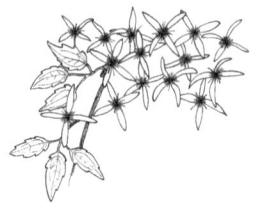

Brierly at Turamullerer

As I grapple with the spirits of the past one figure begins to stand out as a protagonist. And soon I come to see him as a neighbour. Brierly Point, part of the whaling station precinct, was named in 1842 so he could 'live down to future ages'. The artist Oswald Brierly built his home 'Merton' on the next headland to the east, on the other side of the small bay, Bilgalera (Fisheries Beach), about a kilometre and a half away. One morning after studying his 1847 watercolour of the scene I go and sit at the spot from which he composed the painting. Everything is still in place excepting his old home, demolished in the 1920s for the grander 'Edrom Lodge'. Beyond that where he shows some five vessels and a steamer rounding the distant point lies today's clutter of naval wharf and chipmill. A number of the coast grey box trees he portrayed are still standing. The rocky shelf, known as Toanho, on which he sketches a traditional Aboriginal family is still used to gather resources much as we shop at a supermarket today. Whale boats are gathering water from the creek behind the dunes. Two whales are surfacing, spouting offshore. Boyd's yacht, *Wanderer*, lies at anchor, more prominent than the numerous other vessels also harbouring in the lee of the southern shores. Beyond his house and the headland, smoke rises from the on-shore try-works he manages. A lively little terrier frolics or nips the heels of a sailor returning to the row-boat. Seagulls circle the water then as they do today. He only fails to record the pair of sooty oystercatchers that patrol my waterline. His shores are park-like, with a few tall trees that remain today crowded with younger trees and scrub. The scene is a vibrant seascape, undoubtedly accurately rendered, and yet it is domestic. The man has become a neighbour, and also a mentor and guide, such that I sense he is leading me deeper into the nature of this place and its Bundian Way. The visions he provides come as though through a window into the times and character of the old people who lived here, on the southern bay that I learn had been called Turamullerer. He always managed to find that other wrinkle to give his pictures an authenticity, signal their reality. Mostly he is drawing my attention to the imperishables, the things that continue through the ages, what we hold in common with the people who lived here so long ago. He is demonstrating what we should seek to keep. They include the cordial relations and need to recognise Aboriginal elements in the landscape as well as its deeper mysteries. Furthermore, it is Oswald Brierly who shows me how to find the eastern legs of the Bundian Way. The oystercatchers continue to work their relay, testing the sand. A whistling kite circles overhead.

Because of his importance to the Bundian Way in giving detail and inspiration, I search out his biographical details. Oswald Brierly was born in Chester on 19 May 1817, the son of Dr Thomas Brierly, but so much of his story is hidden it takes time for his fuller life to unfold. Perhaps Dr Thomas Booth Brierly, also spelt Brierley, of Tattenhall about 8 kilometres south-east of Chester was his father. In one summation he states that he is 'of an old English family bearing arms granted 1615', but it seems that date should be 1625. Perhaps his family became involved in Unitarianism. He has recurring Quaker associations.

That is the public man. It should not be too hard to find the man. Many of his works relating to his days in Australia are held in the Mitchell Library in Sydney, but the collection is not complete. The writings are usually on the verge of indecipherable and bits and pieces are scattered willy-nilly throughout the generally non-consecutive collection, all intermixed with sketches, drawings, notes to himself and general miscellanea produced as words failed him, which they frequently did. Many of his artworks are personal, lyrical, romantic. But he must have wrestled with demons from his earlier life because it is so seldom mentioned, barely hinted at. Only one note suggests the life but it is full of holes: words left out, names missing, raw emotion still bubbling. In Sydney, not long before their voyage southwards, he wrote of 'evening of walks with my dearly loved Mother. How my heart bleeds when I think of all her care and fond love to us.'

That is as much as I can find of an *idyllic* childhood, indeed any details of his childhood. He continues on a darker note

> there our departure for T – and gradually dashing fortunes – the Baneful influence of E over my mistaken Father. Our final setting down at all for a time where ——— took up the profession an artist to support his family – the large garden – rookery – orchards – fields – the solitary expanse of sea with a ship pushing[?] up or down channel dimly stealing along the Horizon ...[4]

The gaps he left between many of the words speak of the pain he must have still felt. And it is odd that in his father's loss of fortune and apparent shame and loss of his position in society, the doctor should have taken up the life of a professional artist to support his family, and then be followed in that life by his son. The family moved from Chester to the coast. Perhaps to

Ireland. His comment on the 'solitary expanse of sea' is telling, the meditation of a young man who, rather than in the company of other people, finds solace in the form of ships. For a period Brierly entered Henry Sass's art school in London, and after studying naval architecture at Plymouth he exhibited some drawings of ships at the Royal Academy in 1839. Perhaps these works attracted the attention of Ben Boyd of the Royal Yacht Squadron and led to his invitation to join the voyage to New South Wales. When on 22 August 1843 he received news of his father's death, he unemotionally records in his diary: 'Father dead.' Nine days later, in a similar tone, he observes 'Snow on Mount Imlay.'[5]

As I fossick through the writings from his days on Twofold Bay they slowly come to life and I begin to see the historic Bundian Way in my mind's eye. The world of the southern parts of the deep-water bay that he entered held little value for the other settlers of that time. The northern side where the township of Eden had started growing had all the advantages of a good, better-protected port. Beyond the town limits foot tracks ran hither and yon from one place to another but on the more difficult terrain, which lay in most directions, there were places you wouldn't choose to lead a horse. They could therefore hardly be described as roads as they weren't fit for transporting goods or produce which had to go by the sea roads. The soils, either rocky or sandy, were too poor for farming, the topography too irregular and steep for comfortable settler habitation, but tucked away in among those folds and assorted waterways of Turamullerer was an Aboriginal population of over 250, according to George Imlay's 1841 reports.

When Brierly arrived on 15 December 1842 aboard Ben Boyd's steamer, the *Sea Horse*, their ambition was 'to examine its capabilities as a Harbour and site for a town, and to ascertain the practicability of opening a road from it to the extensive cattle and wool growing districts of Maneroo ... making it easily accessible by sea to save the expensive land carriage of its produce to Sydney'. But he had already once visited Twofold Bay before he arrived to make it his home. Although I can find no journal entry recording the episode, it seems the *Wanderer* called in to the bay en route from England via Rio, the Cape (on 4 April 1842) and the Roaring Forties. I suspect Boyd's party was scouting for the best place to begin his empire. Brierly's sketch entitled *Primitive Australia – The Kiah Mount Imlay* is dated 1 May 1842. It portrays the inlet and mount romantically, with pelicans that look like brolgas and an Aboriginal woman in a canoe. The location's tranquillity made a big impression on him after the long voyage.[6]

Brierly, although trained as a painter, came with Boyd as a companion and to assist in management of the proposed settlement. After 7 months in Sydney his journal describes the joy he found after the *Sea Horse* anchored in the cove, and a party of natives wearing possum cloaks and armed with spears and boomerangs came to inspect them.

While the Boyd crew pitched their tents for the night, the natives made camp nearby and some in canoes brought a supply of fish to be traded for flour and meat. Later, he saw how 'The natives have collected from different parts of the Bay – their fires are blazing round us in every direction lighting up their dusky forms as they gather round them – some little children which have been playing on the Beach are scampering up the Beach frightened at our approach.' Their bearing and character and way of life impressed him greatly. Brierly scribbled his notes in a state of high excitement. 'The whole scene has a wild and grand effect, trees lit up by the fires which now and then Blaze up – lighting up for a moment the Forest round then die away again, the monotonous wash of the surf on the shore, the occasional scream of a flight of wild fowl passing high overhead – the unceasing chirr of insects.' But it was not enough to record his impressions, he had to go out among them and see what they were doing. 'I could not help stealing out at midnight to see the children of the Forest reposing (the fires had nearly died away) the dogs raised a suppressed growl as I approached. They are lying round the fire … closely wrapped in opossum rugs, some with blankets, with their feet to the embers. The Dogs crouching between them.'[7]

His first impressions and the magic of that first evening carried through in his later relations with them and were given weight by his drawings and writing. He had to draw the place where his party chose to settle, in woodlands and open grassy forest beside a peaceful freshwater lagoon called Beermuna. Its delights contrasted with the government township of Eden above Snug Cove on the northern side of the bay, where he was repulsed by the smell and general wretchedness. Whale bones were scattered all over the beach. 'The whole place looked as desolate and uninviting as any I had ever seen.'[8]

Brierly duly noted the progress of their new settlement, from the changing of the names of places and people to their attempts to enhance the landscape. Full of enthusiasm during the first days he made numerous sketches and wrote how 'the natives made themselves very useful – carrying Bark to erect a hut and water for the use of the people at the tents.' After breakfast they shot two black cockatoos.

On his fourth day during a trip on horseback around the bay to Imlay's camp at Snug Cove, the official port, he

> saw some natives carrying canoes on their heads at some distance down the Coast. Passed a native village – deserted. Native huts seen from the SW built to protect from NE breezes – 3 feet from ground in centre … Imlays Place Snug Cove – a store, Dr Imlay's house, buildings connected with the whale fishing. A wooden landing place, some bark huts. The natives make very good whalers and many of them are employed by Imlay who

> gives hops, provisions etc in return for their services.
> To some he has given Brass badges which are suspended
> round the neck by a chain – on these are engraved the
> name and capacity of the wearer ...[9]

Only 6 days after their arrival Brierly organised a journey with Ben Boyd to look for the best way to the Monaro. Of course the party had no idea how to go about it, so he enlisted a young Aboriginal man to lead them along one of the ancient pathways of the region, the precursor of the Bundian Way, a journey I'll look at in more detail later.

And Brierly was desperate for information. His friendship with 'a very remarkably intelligent fellow', called Budginbro (sometimes spelt Budgunburra but also known as Toby), had flowered soon after they met upon his arrival in the bay:

> he seemed quite aware of what we wanted when enquiring
> the native names of different things – White fellow call
> him 'Duck' Black fellow 'Ombarra' – and was not satisfied
> with our pronunciation until we accented the word
> properly. He then went on to describe the various weapons
> and in one instance where he could not make himself
> sufficiently understood – he took the pencil and drew the
> outline of the thing one he wished to describe – which
> was the Jincera or oval shield. He described too, with
> considerable accusation, the first appearance of ships in
> the harbour – how the Black fellows retreated to the hills
> round the Bay – how a few first ventured out – and finally
> how they began to carry 'hoo-roo' (Bark) for White fellow
> ... his Father – one of the oldest men in the Tribe – ... told
> in his own language (translated by his son) how the first
> White men came to the Bay, how the Blacks retreated to
> the Hills round the Bay ...[10]

In a later version of this journal Brierly added an extended description of that first contact between the land's first people and the newcomers, probably the shipwrecked sailors who walked past on about 31 March 1797, and how, 'after a time one or two bolder than the rest, ventured out but retreated again appalled by the horrid colour of the new comers, whom they took for spirits of their own people, as Toby said "jumped up again white"'.[11]

Budginbro was, from the beginning, Brierly's main informant on matters of land, fishing, culture and such. Their alliance brought about the treasure trove of shared history, a guide during my walking. Budginbro often became an intermediary, as described during their journey to the Monaro, when they came to the Snowy River, and once again Brierly showed his genuine interest in the Aboriginal people of the region.

> On the opposite side of the river among the trees on
> the mountain is a native camp – a number have crossed
> over to this side some are talking to Toby about us
> and then turning around and screaming the news to
> their companions on the opposite shore – they are
> communicating the information they have received from
> Toby concerning us to the rest of the tribe on the other
> side – he has been telling them (in their own language)
> all about our journey up and to increase his importance
> in their eyes he has put two shot belts on – one around
> his waist and the other over his shoulder – speaking of
> Mr B they say cabon white fellow that one – cabon being
> the general term among them to express anything great
> or important ... One – only one – sat apart from the
> rest – I was much struck with her appearance and manner
> so different from her clamorous companions – there was
> something so pensive in her downcast look – with the long
> shiny hair hanging in curls over her brilliant dark eyes.

His general attitude is probably best summed up in his note: 'I have ever found the heart of woman the same whether … the children of the forest or in the refined circles of our own dear country.'[12]

Brierly started making portraits of the people he most liked. His drawing of Toby's wife, Plomer or Korang.gin, shows the respect he held for her. She wears a government-issued blanket, as distributed annually by George Imlay at Snug Cove and, probably, Brierly's shirt.

Brierly described cultural values from the beginning and quickly grasped the weight they placed on trade and reciprocity: 'fresh fish for which we gave them flour and meat in exchange'. He regularly referred to their canoe culture, describing details, such as how 'When they landed they lifted their canoes, which were made of bark, out of the water with great care and carried them upon their heads to a shaded place near the beach, covering them over with green branches to prevent them drying up or cracking from exposure to the sun.'

Fish were a staple of the diet. He quickly understood the difficulties of mastering the canoes. When he tried using one sitting on his bottom, he tumbled into the water. And it didn't happen just once. In a drawing, eventually he showed the correct position, emphasising in a note: 'Mode of Sitting – kneeling and sitting on heels …'

The details in other drawings and paintings show the form of nets, lines, shell hooks and other implements used for fishing, including spears and the ingenious adaptation to allow a stable place for those spears to rest and the manner they were carried in the canoe. He also showed mullet, perhaps the favoured fish if not the one caught most regularly. 'Friday 29th September morning made drawing of canoe – returned on board wrote a letter, evening went to a Corroberie.' And he always shows genuine affection for the people involved.[13]

Things quickly began to change. In June 1843 he noted how Boyd had employed a surveyor to find a good road up to the Maneroo and they have already succeeded in finding the greater part of it without a single Ruction. When it is complete the Settlers of the back country will be able to ship their wool and cattle within a distance of fifteen miles instead of having as formerly to send it nearly three hundred to Sydney. Twofold Bay will also be the port where the Whalers may get their supplies instead of being obliged to go up to Port Jackson ... Every day now makes a visible change in Boyd Town – The first dray of wool came down to the Bay last Thursday – a practicable line of communication has been opened with Maneroo – a large new store is nearly completed. We have good water on this side – everything is in our favour – Mr Boyd has purchased a number of stations in the country behind this seeing very important advantages to himself – he has appointed me during my stay here, commandant over everything ... I am for once Governor of a Town and entire commandant afloat.[14]

After their whaling operations started on the southern side of the bay under Brierly's management, Budginbro was given the privilege of taking charge of the native whale boat. Most of those first whalers came from Twofold Bay or the surrounding districts including Pambula, Mowarry, Wonboyn, Kiah, Bega, Wangarabell, Boondiang and Cathcart. They were relatively young men, predominantly in their late teens and twenties. He wrote of how expertly they handled the boats and that 'their sight is better and they see the fish sooner than the white men'. But also raised their belief in souls of the dead going into the body of an orca.[15]

In 1843 the whaling season commenced at the beginning of August. Typically, in his journals, he marked the days when they caught a whale with a drawing of a whale's tail. When he painted features of the Aboriginal life he displayed painstaking attention to detail; as though he was reporting the lifestyle of the people of the bay. And he kept doing it. Most likely he had intended to publish his illustrated journals. But, perhaps, in the back of his mind he knew the writing wasn't adequate. Of some occasions, such as his journey to the Monaro, he wrote a second version, a little different in hope the better detail of the second might be more publishable than the first. It is surprising that a travel memoir entitled something like *An Artist's Six Years in New South Wales* wasn't published in his name. But his writings didn't conform to the genre which demanded the overstatement and dramatisation that might have brought him popular success. He stayed with what he knew, and the simple truths.

Brierly wrote on 4 September 1843 that he had 'commenced carrying out the plan of making a series of sketches of the natives'. Two days later he had 'made Drawing of Cherry – wife of Kalcut.'

In August 1844 he witnessed an event of some very great substance. It was a corroboree on the shores of the bay, where Aboriginal people from across the greater south-east region came to visit. Not by accident did they come at this time of year, for it was the height of the whale season, and a whale nearby was there to feed 60 or 70 travellers. But, of course, it was not just for a corroboree that they came so many hundreds of kilometres from the Monaro, even from Omeo. Knowing the routes they probably used, and the country through which they had to come, I can appreciate the difficulties of their trek. The distance from our perspective today looks so great and much of the country so rugged, I wonder if they saw their journey as something commonplace? What was so important that some walked for over a fortnight to get here? Was the 'new' corroboree a special occasion? Or was it because they knew there would be the whale feasts again? Could it have been a combination of many reasons? Ceremonies? Trading? To tell stories? Or was it all about kinship; getting together again with neighbours, friends and family? We will return to this remarkable event later, in other contexts, for surely it is the crux of the Bundian Way. A few days later when the old man, Tea Pot, died, the Monaroo people, who had set out for home, were called back for the funeral. A number of people from Bega, Towamba and Pambula, who weren't at the earlier ceremonies, also arrived for the funeral. More came from places north of Bega such as Murrah, Nerrigundah, Moruya, Belowra, Tuross, Tarraganda, Wandella, Brogo, Double Creek, Tathra, Dry River and Cobargo. Apart from whales on the shore, GA Robinson also 'saw a dead porpoise on the beach, Natives eat it'.[16]

Brierly described how, after the death, 'a fearful and terrible howling by the gins and dogs was commenced early in the following morning'. Obviously moved by the occasion, he described the funeral with dignity and drew the shrouded body.

Distancing himself from the activities at Boydtown, Brierly built the house he called 'Merton' a few kilometres away overlooking Bilgalera with views to Balawan. The artist could not have chosen a more dramatic position, one fitting for a man of his station. But also it was closer to the try-works and the onshore whaling station and had a better anchorage than near Torarago Point. Although the shores of the bay at that time were regularly described as park-like, and they appeared that way in his paintings, in one of his less buoyant moods one wintry morning, he set the mood, 'in the end the morning sun just appearing thro the dark forest of gum behind the house – but all cold and dreary – distant cry of curlew'.

Boyd's fortunes fluctuated with worsening economic times. During 1847 he reviewed his current position and circumstances. He had been noting bad feelings towards Ben Boyd's brother James and disagreements with the other superintendents, on account of which 'I am out of out of favour with BB'. He was now looking beyond the increasingly nasty intrigues of Boydtown society to the wider community. In view of their competition with the government town, Boyd would not have been happy when Brierly was made a magistrate in Eden and regularly attended sittings of the bench.

In 1848, as tensions increased Boyd faced imminent bankruptcy. Seeing Brierly's obvious talents during a visit, Captain Owen Stanley of the HMS *Rattlesnake* invited him to join their expedition as guest for a survey of the Barrier Reef, the Louisiade Archipelago and part of the New Guinea coast. Brierly was only too happy to leave the bay. He would not return.

That Brierly's pictures and writings show the countryside and its people so eloquently provides a foundation for the shared history. At the time of settlement, during the 1840s, few scholars were able to show what happened as clearly as Oswald Brierly. His evidence reveals typical stages in the dispossession of the Aboriginal people of the region. He reports sympathetically from the frontier but he was no missionary. Nowhere does he portray the Aboriginal people as worthless or savage or barbaric or as a doomed race. He employs them as equals and continues to work with them over the years. He deals with individuals, he portrays character.

The issue of European names was but one step in changing the old culture. Where at the beginning of Brierly's time on the bay its Aboriginal people wore animal skins against the cold, soon enough European clothing and blankets became common. In the early days there appeared to be fair trade. Reciprocity was demanded for use of the land by its people. But by 1848 and hard times, changes gathered pace.

What Brierly bore witness to were the better times. The efficiencies of off-shore whaling would inevitably decimate the whale numbers and make Budginbro's people less independent. Other marine resources were also being depleted rapidly round the bay.

Brierly at Turamullerer

After his voyage north on the *Rattlesnake*, Brierly returned to Britain where he eventually gained royal patronage. In 1867–68 he returned to Australia on board the *Galatea*, visiting Adelaide, Melbourne, Hobart and Sydney where an attempt was made to assassinate his friend, the Duke of Edinburgh, Queen Victoria's son. There is no record of him setting foot in Twofold Bay after his initial departure. He went on to be married twice, to Sarah Fry, a Quaker with connections to the Frys of chocolate fame, and later to Louise Marie Flore Huard from Belgium. He possibly left a child behind in Twofold Bay. The Brierly name has been handed down through generations of Aboriginal people in the region. He subsequently had two children by his first marriage, Emma and Keppel and two from his second – Louise and Alwyn. A comfortable renown settled during his later years. No longer the wild adventurer, his interests focussed on romantic but accurately detailed paintings of ships at sea, he was rewarded with the title of Marine-Painter to Queen Victoria in 1874. He exhibited at the Royal Academy, as well as at the Royal Watercolour Society. In 1885 he was knighted, and died 9 years later. But what is best remembered of the man and his days at Turamullerer is his mad enthusiasms, the relentless energy that kept him recording the sights of the place and its people in very fine, documentary detail.

Of course he had his depressions and darker times. It must have been difficult for a young man in his mid-20s to do without the companionship of others of his class. That seems to have bothered him little, he made do with his art. He was the young bohemian artist who could make his own rules. That watercolour of East Boyd 1847 is like his summation of all the best things of his time on the bay, his valediction. The painting is full of life and spirit and the joy of living. It represents commerce as well as nature. His house, with its neatly fenced yard and ensign fluttering above the humble dwelling on a pole, looks comfortable and appropriate, and far from being a castle. It amazes me that he can bring such an array of detail on such a broad canvas with such ease. His nearly manic need to get things right shows in the arrangements of rocks at the far end of the beach below his house. It is still the way they are, rock by rock. And the important trees, still there. Each of the vessels is so finely detailed that experts would be able to distinguish the whalers from the trading vessels and so forth. In coming chapters I explore the ways his determination to get things right have made such important contributions to the Bundian Way. But in this very busy scene one group stands out; they have dominion. It is the extended Aboriginal family on the rocks. They look as if they belong to the countryside as much as to the sea. They have their weapons and regalia. Two whales rise and spout directly over their heads. It is clearly their land. Their ease, and oversight of it underline the fact. And yet they might also be spirits. Ghosts of days past.

Balawan and first appearances

I have had to keep asking myself: what did the country along the Bundian Way look like before European settlement? How was it treated? Did that have any consequence for the existence of the Bundian Way and its survival? Answers are difficult, fraught with seasonal and topographical issues not to mention personal bias, but the questions help me move towards understanding what happened, and why. Routes that are impassable today might once have been clear and open.

On 31 March 1797, those first whites to walk the coast, the anguished and starving shipwreck survivors who quickly made friends with some of the local clans, reported of Twofold Bay, 'Walked about 18 miles round a very deep bay and many small rivers opening into it.' And on the next day, they 'Passed through a very pleasant country, whose delightful verdure, strewed over with a variety of flowers, rendered a walk of 20 miles this day extremely agreeable.'

The next close description came from an aristocratic Austrian. Baron Charles von Hügel was a captain of the Imperial Austrian Hussars and cut a dashing figure wherever he went in the colony. Tall, thin and sporting the sort of moustache to which a young Salvador Dali could only aspire, he was a distinguished naturalist with a clear eye. On a visit to the bay on 10 February 1834 he described its heath-free shorelines:

> The land rises from the rocky coast in gentle hills, with meadows in many places dotted with scattered trees, like an English park ... Behind the row of hills there rose several ranges of ever higher mountains, one of which, Mount Ballun (the native name) has a quite unusual pyramidal form ... Towards evening we saw several groups of Aborigines lighting a number of fires for the night which remained in view for a long time.[17]

When von Hügel returned in June, he found the hills along the lower reaches of the Towamba River had been burned by the Aboriginal people.

Oswald Brierly's images agree with von Hügel's description. The local people would have had more than a little to do in the meadow-like appearance of the land close to the water. Today, as with much of Australia's south-eastern coastline, the scrubs have run mad. The settlements dotted among the trees near the ocean mean the foreshores are unlikely to be burnt any more, other than through wildfire. A native plant, *Pittosporum undulatum*, has as a result moved out of its niche and is taking over, forming its own forests, making the old landscapes unrecognisable. Also called mock orange, it is a 'nice-looking' plant, so people generally don't want to remove it. And today, around the shores of the bay, the pittosporum scrubs proliferate.

The whaling station's long-time recognition as a significant historic site means many have described, drawn, painted and photographed its scenes, and these illustrations correspond to a remarkable degree. They also tell a story of the country. As the years pass, from one picture to another, you can witness how the scrubs rise up to clutter the park-like shoreline. In one book compiled by Rene Davidson of Eden, George's grandson, the 100-year-old photos of orcas jostle with the sadder whale carcasses rotting in the water beside the try-works. The faces of the whalers, many Aboriginal, show they were hard men, they had to be, for their battle with nature. In the oldest, the bay was a place of diverse forests and glades.

The longer I stay on the bay the more connected I feel. I have become deeply alive and completely alert to my surroundings. But it isn't just the coastal landscape that has grabbed me, it is that I'm still making connections all the way through to the high country. And my explorations continue every day.

Stand-alone mountains are unusual in Australia. Most peaks are part of a range that obscures their grandeur and individual character. Nobody would give two bob for Kosciuszko if it wasn't the highest peak. Balawan looks like a breast; from some places its nipple is more conspicuous. In the earliest years of exploration its name was also written by Europeans as Boolone, Bolloon, Ballun and various other permutations which variously hint at the true pronunciation. Ultimately, the settlers called it Imlay, after that tragic pioneer family, and its original name was erased from the official records.

The mountain was held in great regard by the old tribes. Throughout the Yuin Country are three major stand-alone peaks, which can be seen from each other in the right weather. These correspond to the three scars commonly made upon the young men at the time of their initiation. The whitefellas called them Imlay (Balawan), Mumbulla (Biamanga) and Dromedary (Gulaga), but to the south there is also Genoa. At least one, sometimes three, of the peaks can be seen from prominent parts of the coastal plains.

When von Hügel revisited in June 1833, always the avid botanist and collector, he set out to walk up the mountain via the Towamba River. There were plants new to science to be found. The way looked easy, but 'The banks rose from the river's edge as if to form a second, higher riverbed. This was very difficult to get to through the dense ferns and thorns, and the deep soil there had produced such luxuriant vegetation that it was almost impossible to push one's way through.' Above the river he was unable to find anything new due to recent fires.

His guide was the Aboriginal, Camimangua aka Constable, who regularly ran ahead making small fires, an action that would keep his firebrand alight. Not only would such a practice help keep the pathways free of scrub, but on this occasion it would also have helped pass the wintry time keeping warm while the naturalist slowly wandered attempting to identify plants in the unburnt spots.

> My blackfellow, dressed in Nature's garb, had taken a firebrand with him when we left in the chilly morning. He continually ran ahead a couple of hundred paces, squatted down and quickly made a fire of dry twigs, and then let me get 100 paces ahead before setting off again with his firebrand and doing the same thing.[18]

During his walk he did find some good plants, the now popular garden plant *Crowea linearis* (Hügel) was his favourite.

Balawan is a mountain best treated with respect, so much is clear from any view of it. The first time I climb it, I approach from its southern ridges. All I am looking forward to are some interesting views. But as I climb higher and higher it becomes obvious it is a very special place, and unusual, strange. It would have been a floral wonderland for von Hügel had he made it up the deceptively steep ridges, for he might have been the first to record a tree that is now regarded as critically endangered.

Balawan and first appearances

The Mount Imlay mallee only grows over a small area near the summit. Then there are the *Boronias* and grasstrees that form a magic garden along the summit. Difficult country lies in all directions, extremely difficult country. Roads and houses are so very few, that in spite of all I know about this landscape, I am shocked to my core. Even though I know ways to get through, I feel I am fenced in by its extreme ruggedness.

Fire obviously plays its part on the vegetation of the mountain. It would have rushed up the various faces regularly. The signs are there on the boles of the ancient grasstrees as well as the eucalypts. This evidence of fire has been like a motif in all my walks even though its influence varies from one landscape to another. It has helped me find the story of the Bundian Way and that's turned out to be a complex story, all the more so now I come to consider the coastal areas. The paradox of fire, as I keep suggesting, is that the hotter it burns, the more the country scrubs up afterwards and will burn even hotter next time; the cooler, the more the land is cleaned up and becomes open. In the coastal ranges a cool fire might trickle along hither and yon until it goes out with the coming of nightfall. In one sense a hot fire that gets into the crowns is a disturbance, and has much the same effect as any other disturbance, like bulldozing, grazing or ceasing to graze the land. It can make the land more fire-prone. Researchers confirm the relationship between fire intensity and scrub formation, and that reduced use of low-intensity fires has caused declines in forest health, increases in pest and disease populations, invasion by shrubby understoreys and more extensive high-intensity fires.[19]

Even though the eucalypt is a rapidly evolving genus, there are still niches to which it has not adapted. Many parts of the high country – and sometimes even the lower country – are too cold for eucalypts. When surveyor Stewart Ryrie reported from Delegate in 1840 that there were very few trees, 'which the Blacks ascribe to a heavy fall of snow some years ago', I wonder what was meant. Perhaps they were talking about events of a long, long time ago. Many thousands of years.

If we can imagine the topography and its wildlife as constantly in motion, its vegetation coming and going over the hundreds of years in fast forward, the Coolangubra would, say at 15 000 BP, have appeared very much like the high country today with snowgrasses and fields of alpine wildflowers. As the climate changes, in fast motion the eucalypts arrive, small at first but growing taller, colonising the alpine herbfields and rocky outcrops, while the sea rises to cover kilometre after kilometre of the rich coastal plains displacing their people, who become refugees and have to find a place in other clans' country. Each group has to adapt to the encroachment. Some of the difficulties are reflected in AW Howitt's retelling of the Aboriginal creation story from Gulaga, of the totemic ancestors and the strife that comes, for 'At this time when the earth was only inhabited by animals the land extended far out where there is now sea.' Stories still passed on tell of the drowning of the country and conflicts between totemic ancestors as the lands changed and the waters rose.[20]

The moral might be that we could all be displaced at any time, we should be understanding of others in that predicament. Aboriginal culture as I understand it has always been welcoming of the displaced, the orphaned, the homeless. There has always been a way to accommodate those needing refuge. Children especially are accepted; regularly raised by relatives other than parents and others. Elders step into the counselling role of parent. The culture is inclusive, resilient. Constant adaptations have been necessary. The climate has always been a restless force.

Looking at the high country, ecologist George Seddon, said that 'Aborigines rarely burnt this country'. In fact, the alpine tops and the wet ash forests of the shady slopes are seldom capable of being burnt. They don't dry out sufficiently. Studies of charcoal at Club Lake suggest fire frequencies at about 100-year intervals. And a knowledgeable Aboriginal man, Rod Mason, has said that burning thereabouts was only to clear travel routes as necessary, 'for spiritual reasons they rarely went to the highest tops'.

During Oswald Brierly's journeys in 1842, he wrote of fire-blackened landscapes in the mountains and grassy scenes along the Towamba River. This kind of evidence confirms how widely fire was used, albeit selectively.

At the height of the most recent Ice Age about 14 000 years ago, for example, when much of today's high country was under ice, the Monaro and coastal ranges had a similar climate and vegetation to parts above the present tree line. The alpine, sub-alpine or cold steppe was so cold as to limit the vegetation types. Most of the land between Kosciuszko and the coastal plains would have been treeless, apart from the best-protected refuges.

Meanwhile, scientific research at different ends of the Monaro, at Lake George and Bega Swamp, show a considerable increase in charcoal some 140 000 years ago. Could this have been when the first Aboriginal people arrived with their concerted fires? Or is it due to climate change? Through the analysis of pollen grains in cores taken at each site, it appears that grasses and daisies and some casuarina predominated. Eucalypts didn't start their spread through parts of today's Monaro and south-east forests until more recently in the past 10 000 years. The research suggests that rather than wresting grassland from eucalypt forests, the grasslands of the Monaro have been there for an exceptionally long time.[21]

Those golden landscapes were managed by the Aboriginal people in many ways, not only with fire. Their skilful fires helped not only to keep the basalt grasslands treeless, but also encouraged the bountiful wildlife and yamfields. In granite country, burning patches of grassy woodland produced the patterns suitable for the fire-stick hunting techniques historian Bill Gammage has described. Tree-growth rings confirm that high-intensity fires only came with any regularity after European settlement. The old Aboriginal people followed ways that minimised the consequences of fire. The extent of their 'farming' or intensive land management across the continent pre-1788 has at last been confirmed by a non-Aboriginal historian. What we thought was natural was man-made.[22]

Local observations can reveal complexities that underlie the greater landscape. My puzzlement over that early account of Australian fire written by natural historian William Howitt concerns his statement that only 15 years after European settlement in the region, the countryside was still subject to Aboriginal burning practices, and other fires were being lit all the time. And yet none of these were enough to prevent the terrible conflagration of 1851.

Other accounts describe how the sky turned dark and burning leaves rained down upon the decks of boats in Bass Strait as well as northern Tasmania. Intense flames were seen near Mallacoota that same day and the fires extended into the southern Monaro. Some scars are still apparent, I believe, in the form of scrublands.

Along the old pathway, especially on the Monaro, many descriptions of local conditions tell us how the countryside came to appear as it does. But those tall forests are now only occasionally park-like. The small-scale, trickling cool burns are no more. Much of the land, particularly that closer to the coastal settlements, has not been burnt for a very long time.

Weeds like pittosporum are rampant and could potentially explode when the big fires eventually do come, as surely they will. Perhaps that open form is unachievable again, certainly in the short term.

    These are matters I discuss with BJ Cruse during his regular visits. We still talk about the Bundian Pass. Neither of us is able to let go. Maybe it's all a myth, one of those local things that now only exists in memory, its specific location long lost and never to be found again. Maybe it is one of those cultural matters that were deleted during the mission days when everything old was labelled bad. This torments me as much as if it were completely imaginary and yet still I believe it's there, like a will-o'-the-wisp, we only have to pin it down.

Another side

The associations between the Aboriginal people and whaling have been recognised as special since the earliest days and many have documented its scenes in journals, drawings, paintings, photographs as well as in oral history. These correspond to a remarkable degree. It's especially interesting to drill down to find the snippets that talk about what everyone knew, the common day-to-day knowledge that was so unremarkable nobody bothered to systematically write it down.

It's there in the stories passed down from generation to generation of the Aboriginal families who are related to the old hunters manning the boats for George Davidson during the whaling season. For example, Burnum Burnum, a grandson of the whaler Bert Penrith, wrote that although the ancestral relationship with the orcas was traditional, it was later exploited by the whaling industry engaging Aboriginal crews. The orcas drove migrating whales close to the whale boats so that they could be easily harpooned. As a reward the orcas were allowed to eat the lips, tongue and fluke when the whale sank.

Similarly, the greatly respected storyteller and Elder, Percy Mumbler, told Roland Robinson that

> The dark people would never go lookin' for whales. The killers would let them know if there were whales about. Ole Uncle would speak to them killers in language. They must have been bugeens, clever blackfellers. They'd go as far as Narooma lookin' for whales. Two would stop with the whale and one would go back to Twofold Bay and leap out of the water. 'Pook-urr!' He'd slap his tail and let the whalers know.[23]

In the 1950s he added that his old Uncle Brierly was a champ whaler. He'd use the harpoon-spear and 'had a knack of killin' the whale, he'd put the harpoon right into him an' kill the whale stone dead'.[24]

Many accounts tell of how the killers were seen as Aboriginal ancestors come back in a different form. Each orca had distinct markings and fin shape and a name that honoured the ancestor, who maintained communication through the spirit of the orca. In 1844, Oswald Brierly wrote that the Aboriginal cries of welcome to a big orca were so loud the whalers thought it must be a whale and prepared their boat for the chase. The Kooris believed, it was said, that any harm inflicted on an orca would bring repercussions to those responsible. Biamanga, whose smile revealed a missing front tooth – a mark of his traditional initiation – spoke in the early 1900s 'of the spirit of a long departed brother ... "He go into a killer [whale] ... I saw him once at Eden, and his eyes looked up at me out of the killer's head."' The best known orcas included Albert, Brierly, Charlie, Jimmy, the Kinscher, Humpy, Hooky, Stranger, Jackson, Old Ben, Cooper, Young Ben, Typee (probably referring to Toby) and of course the longest lived and best known, the mischievous Tom.[25]

Although the Aboriginal whalers amply proved their value in the whaling industry, it was only a relatively brief time – barely 100 years – before the increasingly efficient killing methods brought the big whales to the verge of extinction. It doesn't take much imagination to see the days before the whale boats arrived in the bay, when the migration passed northerly and then returned at a more leisurely pace in springtime. Hundreds of whales might be seen in a single day. Occasionally, the old or infirm might succumb to weather conditions and be washed up on the beaches. But the killer whale pack also came back every year and based itself in Leatherjacket Bay, from which it could easily herd the slower moving whales into the bay.

In 1904 ethnologist RH Mathews recorded an account of an Aboriginal whale hunt. The account by a 'Thoorga' man appears to fit with other accounts of the traditional whale practices in Twofold Bay and provides a link to what followed when European whalers took over and made an industry of whaling in the bay.

> When the natives observe a whale, 'murirra', near the coast, pursued by 'killers', Mananna, one of the old men goes and lights fires at some little distance apart along the shore, to attract the attention of the 'killers'. He then walks along from one fire to another, pretending to be lame and helpless, leaning upon a stick in each hand. This is supposed to excite the compassion of the 'killers' and induce them to chase the whale towards that part of the shore in order to give the poor old man some food. He occasionally calls out in a loud voice, ga-ai! ga-ai! Dyundya waggarangga yerimaran-hurdyen, meaning 'Heigh-ho! That fish upon the shore throw ye to me!' If the whale becomes helpless from the attack of the 'killers' and is washed up on the shore by the waves, some other men, who have been hidden behind scrub or rocks, make their appearance and

run down and attack the animal with their weapons. A messenger is also dispatched to all their friends and fellow-tribesmen in the neighbourhood, inviting them to come and participate in the feast. The natives cut through the blubber and eat the animal's flesh.[26]

I have been told accounts of whales swimming close off-shore in the bay feeding on what appeared to be schools of small fish, or perhaps krill. One nearly beached itself directly across the inlet from the station while chasing a shoal from the deep channel of the Whale Beach. That would have been the best part of the bay for the killer pack to keep an old whale penned up while they exhausted it. It is where the Aboriginal men could so easily have assisted the process with their spears. Between themselves and the orca pack, they developed a process that worked to mutual advantage. While the orcas could herd the much bigger whales it was more difficult for them to disable or kill even a weakened one. This is where the Kooris and their spears came in, for they could deliver the first disabling blows to the whale with their heaviest whale spears. The Whale Beach is one of few places from which shore-bound men could attack a whale with their spears. Once dead, the orcas could have their preferred part, the tongue and lips, while the Kooris prepared for their feasts. The Kooris have often noted how the slapping of a paddle against the water mimics the tail-slapping of the killer whales, the signal to alert the Davidson whalers that a whale was in the bay.

That rip-roaring Tom Mead novel of 1961 – written from information primarily supplied by George Davidson with a lot of imagination to glue it together – has kept the legends alive with its 'documentary' approach. Numerous references to the Aboriginal whalers seem to capture their life in the industry as well as their camps and some of the characters involved. Mead's writing catches the colour of the chase, the activities of the orcas and the mood of racial relationships from the Davidson era. But by the time Davidson moved to the whaling station in 1896, the old Aboriginal families had been 'obliged' to leave Twofold Bay for Wallaga Lake with the exception of Charlie Adgery, who held out as long as he could. So long as whales kept coming in sufficient numbers, the other whalers continued to return year in year out as part of their long-standing seasonal migrations, now undertaken for work as much as for the social get-togethers.[27]

Over the years it was often recorded that although there were few jobs for the Aboriginal people, from the days of first settlement seasonal work was always available for them in Twofold Bay whaling. In 1853, AW Manning reported, 'At Eden however they have for some time past been used by the different whaling parties and practice has made some of them most expert – one person having five boats had four of them manned entirely by natives during the greater part of the whaling season just closed. The most expert Headsman in the whole fishery was a native.'[28]

When Baron von Hügel visited again in 1834, he noted how Doctor Imlay and his brother had an establishment of 10–12 men, to catch whales and seals. However, local Aborigines probably became part of the industry when Captain Thomas Raine started his whaling operations in 1828. George Imlay's primitive bark hut, with young Aboriginal women in attendance, rather took von Hügel aback.

The Imlays ran their operation from two shore based stations, one at Snug Cove, Eden and the other at East Boyd on the southern side of the bay. In 1843 they produced 200 tuns (barrels) of oil which could have been taken from up to 40 whales, or roughly one whale a day during the peak season.

Dr George Imlay took on the role of honorary guardian of Aborigines and made an annual census of the Aborigines of the region. The blanket returns say he was in charge of distribution from 1835 until his death by suicide in 1846. In his 1839 return to the colonial secretary he stated that they had two Aboriginal whaling crews (of six men per crew) responsible for the harvest of eight whales during the season. Furthermore, he added that Aboriginal whalers lived in huts, slept on beds, used cooking utensils, made bread from flour and were paid the same wages as the other whalers. But once the season was over they returned to their old bush ways. The Imlays apparently had good relations with the Aboriginal people, although in one report of the time George describes the 'savage and merciless predatory warfare which is constantly going on between the stockmen and the unreclaimed tribes which hover on the outskirts of the pastoral tracts'.[29]

All had to abide by the land's capacity to provide for those who lived there year round. The increased population on southern shores of the bay due to whaling soon stripped it of its natural food resources. And yet the area was renowned for its ceremonial gatherings. Aboriginal people came long distances for what the settlers called corroborees, as related by GA Robinson. There were of course other places to which the people travelled for seasonal food sources such as swan eggs, burrawang seeds, bogong moths and yams, places where the people could congregate for a while. But on the southern shores of the bay it is clear what drew so many for weeks at a time.

On Wednesday 14 August 1844, Oswald Brierly had a guest on board the *Wanderer*. George Augustus Robinson, the chief protector of Aborigines in the Port Phillip district, which at the time was still part of New South Wales and included Maneroo, wrote in his notebook

> On board 'Wanderer' RYS ... Boats (whale) roving about, black crews and white ditto. Two whale boats manned by crews of Aboriginal Natives, 17 whale boats white Crew. One whale boat (Imlay) Aboriginal Native crew ...[30]

Then, later, he adds news that is central to the Bundian Way. Information that has led me along all those bush tracks on the quest for the pathway that brought the old people here by way of the Bundian country. He wrote in his rough excited scribble about activities on the southern bay shore, with some telling details of an Aboriginal gathering:

> This evening went on shore in South Twofold Bay and witnessed a very interesting corroberry by the Maneroo Natives, they were on a visit to their coast friends to introduce it, was composed and arranged by Al.mil.gong, an Omeo Black from Tongio-mungie. There were about 60 or 70 Blacks present including the Twofold Bay. Number of whales were on shore. Dance commenced late on the finest acclivity of hill, singular effect, men had a broad streak of white round small of arm and legs, women were covered with white spots and white down of birds, cheeks and round forehead, their bodies also reddened. Three sheets of bark had been prepared – painted the centre one represents women the two outer – men. Three women danced with boughs beside and behind the back … each side alternately changed side. It lasted about an hour and half. The last was by men entirely. The dancing behind the … and beside it and the … as before and lastly two men danced face to face being opposite each other resting and residing in a stooping pose and occasionally changing sides. The Twofold Bay, like the whites, were spectators. The words were 'mun.der.rer.nar' then 'nay.ar.de.ning.e.o' and had two L. To courtship these men sing a rather pleasing air. Retired to the 'Wanderer' about 10, all went off peacable.[31]

I find great beauty in this. Where I had a notion that the old gatherings followed a rigidly circumscribed well-known ritual, this event helps me see their excitement at coming for a newly composed song and dance performance. I can feel in my guts the excitement and expectations rising among those gathered. I can understand why people walked such long distances, endured hardships just to be here for the event because I have done the same. I readily imagine Al.mil.gong's thrill and how he thought nothing of his walk of about 400 kilometres to present his show because I too have travelled long distances to present song and dance dramas, and thought nothing of it. Similarly I have travelled great distances to witness singers and theatre. Such events are part of my lifeblood as much as my ongoing appreciation of the local birds' dawn chorale each morning. Would I have walked a distance as far as that renowned performer from Tongi-Mungie? You wouldn't have been able to keep me away from it. A man with local wisdom once told me that the Aboriginal people of the region were not renowned for their rock art or their painting. But they were held in the highest regard for their abilities in song and dance, for storytelling, for music, for their own form of high opera, for their comic abilities and the keeping of their history and ancestral tales. Large gatherings had many purposes and went by various names. Here, at this point in time, what they called corroborees were the speciality of the closely associated family groups from all across the south-east of Australia. Tonight, about half were Maneroo, whom we are assured walked from places like Maharatta, Bibbenluke, Cathcart (which he gives many names including Tal.li.goor), Delegate, Tingaringy, Rock Flat near Cooma and Nimmitabel. Others were from more local places like Nyangutter (Nangutta), Nullica, Bemboka. But also, that very far-away place nestled in the high ranges due south of the Snowies and Targangal, Omeo.[32]

At about the same time as Robinson was writing his account, Brierly also scribbled notes of the occasion:

> Evening a Corroberee of Maneroo Blacks different from any that before seen – it was divided into three part or scenes between each of which the dancers retired and freshened up the paint on their bodies – coming on again with a different dance – they had also three very broad sheets of Bark propped up – behind which the performers would move and then screen themselves – this was their scenery – they danced with boughs in their hands.[33]

In his excitement he drew a quick sketch and added that

> ... a sort of scenery used pieces of bark marked with the white chalk behind which the gins retired – it was also in three acts or 3 difft descript of dances. Each time the whole party retired behind and repainted themselves – howling of dogs – distant fires blazing up amongst the trees. Dusky forms by dim fires touching and retouching themselves ...[34]

Beryl Cruse, BJ's mother, and his father, Ossie, in different ways assure me the gathering would have been signalled by the pale flowers of certain shrubs, including the sallee wattle. Their flowering coincided with the time of year when they knew they should get together, when the whales were passing and there was the means of feeding large numbers of people. Given the number of whales passing on their annual migration, it was relatively common for dead whales to be washed up at random, and, Robinson assures us, travellers were always keeping an eye out for them. These presented an opportunity for the people to feast and make merry. As soon as one was sighted, word went out on foot through the networks to alert all and sundry to the event. But such events were unpredictable. What was more predictable was that, with the assistance of ancestral beings in the form of killer whales, the people of Twofold Bay could provide a bountiful food resource with reasonable regularity. The other clans could safely visit from far afield to participate in the ensuing celebrations. Like the burrawang feasts further up the coast and the bogong feasts of the high country, ample food in season provided opportunities for renewing and finding kinship obligations, reciprocity, trade, ceremony and a wide range of social activities for a considerable number of visitors. Most importantly, there is a deep artistry threaded through all such events.[35]

Ways through Towamba

A pair of black swans glide very slowly on the mirror surface of Bilgalera Lagoon. Not long after dawn the reflection of the coloured stone on the hillsides appears more sombre than it did in the evening. A willy wagtail performs frantic acrobatics between the shoreline and a low sand island as I wash my face in the salty water. The dawn chorus is only just beginning to fade into the general sounds of the day. This is not the first time I've camped at Bilgalera. What regularly surprises me about the place is the grass cover. It is a couch grass as closely cropped as a golf course fairway, compliments of the mobs of kangaroos that move onto the flats as the evening light begins to fade. One hundred and fifty years ago when Oswald Brierly painted the scene there was a small freshwater lagoon at the western edge of the flats but it has since silted up. It could be rejuvenated by digging out the mostly wind-blown sand. As I'm packing up ready to begin my walk, I'm chided by hundreds of New Holland honeyeaters. The old Fisheries Flat is scrubbing up with coast beard-heath, painted white with its edible berries, and coast wattle but even in living memory it was clear of any shrubs and trees. Very old photographs confirm this. Wind-blown sands have covered the shell middens but scrape anywhere and you come down to the level of shells and stone brought here long ago. The southern shores of the bay were important places for people to gather. The more I look round the bay, the more it becomes clear that the corroboree described by Brierly and GA Robinson took place at Bilgalera, against its finest acclivity of hill, the bare hillside that would best amplify their words and music. Not that there weren't other ceremonial places around the bay. As I walk past the site, it's a simple flat, grassed and sandy underneath. Sometimes I think I can detect hints of a circle where dancers went about their motions so many years ago. It's a special place, abutted by stony hillside but with an aspect that looks towards the ocean. Fresh water and rainforest on one side and the flats beside tall forest leading down to the lagoon on the other. The Toanho rock platform is only 100 metres away. My heart feels what a rich locality this has been, and still is. It's now owned by the Eden Local Aboriginal Land Council after having been used as a free primitive camp site for very many years. BJ Cruse regularly expresses the need to keep this as an important Aboriginal cultural place, to continue the gatherings here and maintain its rich legacy of story. For weeks now I've been reflecting on the direct connections from here to so many other places I've been. How did those old people actually get from one place to another? More specifically, the coastal districts have seen so much more development than the high country and it's going to be a lot harder to follow the old routes as precisely here. As I ponder the old time travels I imagine the Bundian Way coming to life, its route twisting through the mountains like a snake, flexing to be rid of its old skin.

 I hoist my backpack onto my shoulders and begin the walk towards Towamba. A little past the corroboree site at the foot of the rainforest gully two white-headed pigeons sit in a muttonwood tree. This is one of the relic plants from the days of the super-continent Gondwana, which bears its flowers and deep purple fruit along its trunk and branches rather than at the terminal ends. Veering easterly, an easy track winds up the slope and heads along the top of the broken cliffline towards the Kiah Inlet only 10 minutes' walk away. Both parts of the bay open up from this vantage, an intense blueness pervades to the coloured cliffs and multiple sandy bays and inlets. Forests top all the hills. It feels as though I'm coming from my back yard to the front as I approach the Kiah Inlet and its complex shoreline and amazing array of habitats. A walkway leads past the old whaling station buildings to the shoreline beside the try-works. Oyster covered rocks guard either end of the beach. Just before the Kiah House holding I cut uphill beside the fenceline to where the route runs westerly along the back of the private land. The track here was once shaped to take horse-drawn vehicles and it's not hard to follow down to the wetlands. Once, the creek had a bridge over it, but now you have to detour up the creek to keep dry feet. Small fins cut through the waters. A school of mullet lazes near the headwaters where I find a fallen tree; a makeshift bridge. On the other side it is about a kilometre to the river crossing. Along the way you look over a vast estuarine wetland occupied by armies of rapidly scuttling soldier crabs. The mangroves look low and stunted. Above the tidal extremes stand tall paperbark thickets, eucalypts further up the slope, elegant roosts for flocks of cormorants. At the river it's boots and pants off for a wade through waist-deep water. This is the traditional crossing at the shallowest point, where the sand fans between tides. When lots of rain buckets down this crossing might require a swim to get across.

Then it's into Boydtown land, still pastoral. Following the ancient route, the public road reserve leads gradually uphill past curious cattle and very tall coast grey box before a steeper descent into Boydtown proper. Today new houses in a subdivision cling to the hillside. Trees have been cleared from beside the old Beermuna Lagoon and slime clogs the waterway. The historic Seahorse Inn has been revamped to provide high quality food and accommodation. It looks nothing like the building Ben Boyd almost finished but still, it looks old. Its location is only a little closer to the ocean than where Brierly made his camp in 1842.

Their first ambition upon arrival in the bay was to open a road to the Monaro. Within a few days of his arrival, Brierly had persuaded Budginbro to lead them there. The route he was to show them was an important Aboriginal pathway, which had of course been followed by the Imlays' workers and other landholders on their way to and from the rich grassland flats for a good 10 years. In a sense I'm joining him on my walk, or following him. Brierly wrote in his journal of how 'upon leaving the Bay we struck at once into the forest keeping a general north-westerly direction and began to ascend the mountain ranges that overlook the Bay'. My route, after crossing the Princes Highway, follows in his footsteps, along what is now called the Short Cut Road beside the sandy Nullica flats and eventually onto the crest of a gently rising ridgeline to join the Towamba Road in Nullica State Forest.

Brierly complained that 'the country for miles had been swept by bush fires, and for some hours after starting we rode through a most dreary looking forest of blackened gum trees, without a blade of grass or sign of vegetation'. The fire-blackened landscape he witnessed in the range is another indication of the extent of burning that took place. The country was burned as regularly as there was fuel to burn, which is to say the burning was cool enough that the fire sensitive silvertop ash, some huge and very old, could survive. His notes complement those of von Hügel and tell of a time when grazing and logging had not developed on any intensive basis. The route follows the crest of the ridge which permits a reasonably direct way through otherwise very complex, difficult, steeply dissected country. Men cut sleepers and mine props here between the wars. Sawmills took the best of the A-grade hardwoods. Then the forests were cleared of trees in coupes that are today regrowing. In a few years passers-by will probably not realise the extent of logging that has taken place here. It might be stating the obvious, but in the days of the Imlays, grazing took place only where there was enough native grass. The cattle were fenced in by the steeper slopes where they found little grass. Due to the predation of dingoes, sheep were restricted by their ever-present shepherds to daytime grazing only. Brierly talks of Budginbro 'setting fire to a single tree for the purpose of starting an opossum', a not uncommon practice. Some records state Aboriginal people lit fires against eucalypts to create hollows, which made suitable homes for the possums. It's one of the ways they tended their flocks. Create a predictable estate. Once hollowed, possums will take up residence and, when needed, it is easy to make another fire to smoke them out.

The oldest route, directly over the tops of the range at elevations rising to 350 metres in a westerly direction, would not have been difficult. Today, the Towamba Road generally follows a similar route except that roadmaking technology has allowed side-cutting into the steep hillsides to give vehicles a better grade.

It's a pleasant enough walk along the road and here and there I follow the older route that goes up a hundred metres or two over the top of a few mountain crests. The road itself is incredibly dusty. Near the top a car goes past me trailing a thick pall of dust that blocks all vision. I jump off the surface in case another is trailing it. But on the steeper sections and side-cuts, I realise, a walker can't get off the road as there are cliffs on both sides. The road is barely wide enough for two cars to pass. Notwithstanding all the Towamba Road's historical values, it is no longer a safe way to walk. Not at all.

Budginbro led Brierly's party along the well-trodden route down a ridge to the river near the present village of Towamba, about 15 kilometres inland as the crow flies. After their 3-hour ride, Brierly's party stopped by the river where 'open flats along its banks showed beautiful patches of green among the surrounding gloom and desolation; here we lighted a fire, made some tea, and cooked some bronzewing pigeons we had shot'. He drew the place, illustrating how bullrushes (cumbungi, a staple Aboriginal food) grew in the river. Then they continued their journey until evening, when they halted in 'a beautiful park-like spot at the base of a great mountain'.[36]

Typically, in eastern Australia, the richest alluvial flats are about a similar distance inland. At Towamba station came a fork in the road. One branch continued north-westerly generally following the river to Burragate, Rocky Hall and the head of the river while the other passed the Imlay stations located at Towamba and Pericoe, then continued up Pericoe Creek towards Nangutta and the Bundian Pass. They chose not to cross the river here and visit.

The first time I visited Towamba in the early 1970s it had all the hallmarks of a traditional Australian village with a store and wine bar. Today, there are no shops, but it has a vibrancy that is enchanting and houses with wide verandahs mostly built of locally milled timber. Disappointed about the dangers of the road, I propose exploring an alternative route from Towamba passing south of Balawan, also rich in Aboriginal history. The Pericoe Road, a wonder of very old road management skills, survives in its ancient form on a different, far less dusty, geological base. After much testing of ways to go, the historic Pericoe route has great potential.

In his *Mt Jingo, Stop for the Night*, drawn on that first night in the Towamba Valley, Brierly shows open grasslands with scattered trees. Their tent was made from slabs of bark, probably from the local stringybarks, but some nearby trees appear to be old man banksias. The grasses are quite luxuriant, perhaps kangaroo or wallaby grass. Tall forests are apparent on steeper slopes. Later, in the somewhat enhanced, second draft of his journal of the trip, Brierly drew *An Exploring Breakfast*, which shows grassy flats beside the river and very occasional trees, and he describes the forest: 'Mimosa, gum, banksia, Stringy bark. Delightful bush in Kiar.' Indeed, the scene shows his swag rolled beside his saddle, his fowling piece (gun) leaning against a tree with furrowed bark that could be stringybark or banksia. A stem of bracken or fern grows near the tree. Later, at the junction of Mataganah Creek, another important old pathway leading via Wyndham from the coast north of Twofold Bay joins the Towamba route.

His drawing of the head of the Kiah points to the sheer rugged wildness of the walking route and its unsuitability for bullock teams and drays. A few days later he drew the *Snowy Mountains from the Plains of Maneroo* which illustrates their extreme dryness at certain times. Willy-willies of dust spiral across the grasslands. This is the route so many would follow in later years, especially the diggers on their way to the strikes at the Kiandra goldfields.[37]

Later in 1845 assistant surveyor Francis MacCabe completed a map of part of a road between Monaroo and Twofold Bay. Essentially its route followed the classic old pathway that Budginbro had shown Brierly. At the eastward point, at a 50-acre property called 'Yuglamah', on the upper Nullica, his route splits, one branch going to the southern bay and Boydtown, the other to Eden. He describes the mountain country as 'High ranges very heavily timbered good grass in the valleys.' Along the Towamba Valley, which he calls Bibendeloe, a name that has since disappeared, he notes: 'Good grass, in some places thickly timbered with honeysuckle, wattle and gums.' His route continues to the head of the river where he finds 'A very broken country of granite formation good grass along river.' But on the Monaroo tableland headed to Hibburd's Inn at Talequong (Cathcart) he finds 'Undulating open forest land good grass interspersed with swampy flats without timber.' All his descriptions hold true except there are fewer grassy flats along the river and a lot more scrub.[38]

On his way past during his most detailed survey, MacCabe was invited to luncheon at Tuamba cattle station, now run by the Walkers who had taken over after the Imlays' financial distress. His field note book for 17 January 1847 (he first surveyed the line of road in 1843) which records his progress through the valley, chain length by chain length, shows the layout of the station. Then 4 miles further upriver he records stringybark and a little further on, '1st Women's camp'. And then four pages later, on 4 May, shortly before the 5-mile point comes the 'Second Women's Camp' before a pinch and then, obscurely, 'Hooky nets'. The only stations in the catchment of the Kiah/Towamba were at Pericoe, Wog Wog, Puragete (Parrokeet, Burragate) and then further upstream, Boyd's new buildings block at the Mataganah Creek junction, where the route from Pambula joined with the river.[39]

Once on the Monaro, the main route was via the present-day places: Cathcart, Bibbenluke, Dalgety, and Berridale, thence on past Kiandra and Yarrangobilly generally following the same route as the Snowy Mountains Highway, and on to Tumut and the western slopes and plains. Kiandra was the main gap through the mountains north of the high country, while the Omeo Gap lay to the south. Destinations for the Aboriginal people included their ceremonial places near Jindabyne or on the Snowy Plains. Another, for diggers, was the goldfield at Kiandra. The common theme to all these stories is that the way through the mountains was by routes pioneered by the Aboriginal people.

The very deeply dissected mountain country of the upper Towamba River valley is not necessarily easy-going, but it's much easier than taking to the hills. In fact, the river follows a geological fault that cuts through in a reasonably direct line to the Monaro without the intervention of layer upon layer of the mountainous country all around it. The last few kilometres are in a gorge where sunlight rarely visits. In the vicinity there were major routes for the old Aboriginal people, that much is well documented. But details are still being uncovered. In 1988 a young resident, Jason Meek, was wandering one of the creeklines not far from the head of the river when he saw an unusual stone in the creekbed. He took it to National Parks and Wildlife Service and the Eden Local Aboriginal Land Council, whose interest was raised. One of Australia's foremost archaeologists, Isabel McBryde, looked at the stone and declared it to be one of the most beautiful artefacts she had ever seen: 'The hatchet head is an outstanding example of the skill and craftsmanship of Aboriginal stone knappers.' It is a dark green-black, with a fine grain, a distinct gloss and green glow from one surface. She came to believe it hailed from Mount William, north-west of Melbourne; an ancient Aboriginal quarry. Such artefacts were traded over very long distances, usually following the trade routes running the length and breadth of the country. Over many years she has traced the record of management of the quarry through the traditional years to when a record was given to AW Howitt in the 1880s by William Barak, last 'ngurungaeta' (Elder) of the Woiwurring people, a traditional custodian of the quarrying productions. Her research found the distribution of Mount William hatchet heads extended to the north and west, to beyond the Riverina to the Willandra Lakes and along the Darling and the lower Murray rivers. Traditionally, the Kulin greenstone producers did not have close ties with the south-eastern coastal groups and few of the hatchets have ever turned up here, but some attention to the subject has brought more to light, as well as greenstone hatchet heads of a different quality quarried near Tumut, which lies not far across the Kiandra Gap from the Monaro. McBryde speculates its discovery is, an exciting addition to our knowledge of Mount William and Aboriginal exchange. It is the first witness to an exchange item of very high quality which must have travelled through many exchanges to the south east of NSW ... For me it opens up a new chapter in my research on the Mount William Quarry ... especially in relation to links between the mountain groups and the coastal peoples.[40]

What really sparked my curiosity was that it had travelled over 400 kilometres as the crow flies through the high country to arrive at its resting place on the Towamba River. Not the sort of object you could easily lose; so did its owner die and it was buried with him, and later sluiced into the creek where it was found? That grand and tantalising question – along with all the others – will have to wait until more evidence can be considered. Even though virtually all flat places in the catchment are rich in artefacts, some are particularly so, usually for obvious reasons, but one curiosity near Rocky Hall is the presence of stone walls, apparently made by the old Aboriginal people. Similar to others I have seen at Jindabyne, Nadgee and Pambula, I can only guess they had ceremonial import, for they are usually near places I understand to have been ceremonial. Such things have led me to thinking the special places across this country are many, not few; the lands so rich with meaning it's hard to know where to begin.

And so the ancient route up the river was a major thoroughfare. But you could not conveniently walk it today. After Burragate it once crisscrossed the river from one flat to the next, where the roadworks cut into the hills to stay on the one side. Fenced freehold land blocks the old way along the river and at the crest of the tablelands.

The regular hard times of drought, when the river and creeks ran dry, pestilence, flood and fire took a greater toll due to the settlers' farming practices. The Imlays were neither first nor last to go broke and lose their holdings.

The days of Aboriginal people living along the river ended with the coming of barbed-wire fences which seized the best parts. Economic hard times for the settlers meant the increasingly dependent blackfellas would also suffer. When the resources had been swallowed by a growing population, the Kooris were cleared from their favoured places, which had become white-fella real estate, and it was now every man for himself.

One of those most difficult journeys was forced upon Charlie Adgery, a whaler who lived with his clan on the clifftops overlooking the bay at Eden. He absolutely refused to live anywhere else but on his own place, until the family was *unwillingly* relocated and they went to Cocora, on the bay west of the Eden township in about 1890. He was the last of the old people to reside on their traditional lands beside the bay. In 1904, at the age of about 70 he and his family were forcibly taken to Wallaga Lake by order of the Aborigines Protection Board. He died there within 12 months. But, until the whale numbers were too depleted for whaling to continue, Aboriginal whalers returned year in year out as part of the long-standing seasonal migrations, now undertaken for the work as much as for the social get-togethers.[41]

Not until the end of the 1960s were Aboriginal people allowed to return and make their homes on the shores of Calle Calle and Turamullerer, also known as the Twofold Bay.

Master of all he surveys?

Countryside has a profound effect on the lives of its inhabitants – who can be as changed by the land as it is changed by them – none more so than the surveyors who were obliged to systematically follow the byways of Aboriginal Country, regardless of its ruggedness. They were often alone, with Aboriginal guides or sometimes with a recalcitrant crew, a very long way from the reach of the law. In many districts the old Aboriginal law still prevailed. These men changed the older system and often left records of the old ways for posterity. And so I find myself wondering: if the first surveyors were painting out the land's Aboriginal ethos, then what was the land doing to them?

Although many of the most valuable old maps and records of the early days were lost in the 1882 Botanic Garden Palace fire, the mapping was published in the form of parish and country maps, which were the first detailed representation of particular localities. Much copied and traced, the early editions are still held in the New South Wales archives. The 'parish' concept, adopted from Great Britain, is a peculiar over-writing of the land's Aboriginality, all the more so because there are still no churches in most of the 'parishes'. But their inconsistent detail, at a time when the old Aboriginal people were still in residence, can help tell how the old people used the countryside. An accumulation of detail has built up over time, layer upon layer of it, laid over the original surveyors' information. The surveyors and their maps are one key to the story of the land.

The wild country with its present Aboriginal spirits could begin to play terrible tricks on a man's mind, especially one primed with the experience and knowledge of Britain's green fields. Any mood of doubt and suspicion would have been reinforced by the terrible death of surveyor GC Stapylton, who had served with TS Townsend on the Monaro, and his assistant at the hands of Aboriginal men while surveying near Brisbane on 31 May 1840.

So much time spent constantly in the wild bush made life difficult. For example, Irish-born MacCabe was reasonably forthcoming in notes during his survey along the Towamba Valley. He mentions curiosities in his contact with Aboriginal people and in the landscape, however his subsequent expedition along the Genoa River (where the New South Wales–Victorian border would go), very much more difficult country, seemed to stun him into silence. His field books present only the survey measurements, without comment or footnote or other amplification.

Surveyor Thomas S Townsend, was about 175 centimetres tall, with red beard and hair, and, although excitable when roused, his letters show a quiet, sensitive man who was methodical and determined in his pursuits. Time was running against him when, after his work in the high country and following the route through Gippsland and the Snowy, in 1843 he was ordered to survey 'the principal features of the Colony'. It presented too many problems, especially along the Great Dividing Range with its seasonal extremes and the sea coast from Moruya to Cape Howe, which was so rugged and inaccurately defined that the orders were impossible to carry out in the time allowed. The gulf between expectation and reality was like an abyss. He was expected to traverse country so terrible and threatening that anyone would be daunted. Some of the slopes and scrubs are still so heart-stoppingly fearsome there's always the possibility you'll go in with crew and equipment and won't get back out.

These surveyors had to become consummate bushmen and find accommodation with the Aboriginal people whose lands they entered to obtain the ways and names for places. But their work in capturing the landscape in the terms required for the taking of possession by British officialdom did not come without personal cost.

Before the land was surveyed no official boundaries existed. The first survey of the coast, undertaken by Townsend, was nearing completion in 1843. He met Ben Boyd and Oswald Brierly and must have liked something about Eden because at the first lands auction that year, the government gazette noted that he purchased one of the blocks. Boyd purchased three. The sales were a result of laws that extended the limits of authorised settlement.

The surveyors did not have an easy life round the edges of the Monaro. It's one thing to visit an area and follow your feet along the best course, but when your job demands you pass along terrible slopes through scrub where even snakes wouldn't venture, there is a cost. Add to that the deprivations and solitude and we begin to understand why Townsend's mind began to give way.

In a letter to Sydney finalising arrangements to survey the township and facilities in Twofold Bay, Townsend points to the shortage of manpower as the reason he had to take men from MacCabe's survey party, which he met on the way to Eden near the Towamba River by the Jingo Mountain. At that time the isolation of the south-eastern region was such that the only means of correspondence was by courtesy of George Imlay, who used his trading networks to secure a form of mail.[42]

And when Townsend reported back in December from Camp Wiacon, he said in a classic understatement that the land about the bay is 'excessively scrubby, consequently my progress has not been as rapid as I hoped'.

Maybe an aggregation of misfortunes helped bring Townsend down. On 16 July 1846 in the middle of the harsh winter on the Monaro one of his survey team died. Not just any member, but Murray Mitchell, the son of his boss and mentor, the surveyor-general, Sir Thomas Mitchell, who would subsequently write of how 'He died at the age of eighteen, from want of medical aid, when surveying, in winter, in the Australian Alps ... He had served the public, gratis, upwards of 2 years, as a draughtsman and surveyor.' In September 1847 Townsend applied for 2 years' leave of absence to go to Europe to benefit his health, but he was talked out of it. In 1850 he was held up by bushrangers, stripped and robbed. Somehow in spite of so much time deep in the wilds, Townsend managed to find a social life. He was married in Queanbeyan in 1853. By 1855 Mitchell had to tell a commission of enquiry about the misfortunes of his surveyors, 'some have died miserably, amongst them, two of my sons; madness had deprived the services of others ...' Perhaps he had Townsend in mind. Finding what happened to this 'sensitive' man when his years in the bush ended in about 1853 is difficult. That he married, had a son and soon separated from his wife is established, and it is probable an unsoundness of mind would haunt him for the rest of his life. In 1854 he went back to England. At a hearing to grant probate of his will in 1872, the judge reflected there was no evidence as to his mode of living or the circumstances of his death. Some said he lived happily, others that he committed suicide.[43]

It is true, after all, that the bush can get to you. Being in wild country you have one eye on the weather, the other on the topography. All the while you're looking for human presence. Your senses work overtime seeking it out, often unconsciously, involuntarily. Voices. Figures. Friend or foe? Sometimes places feel like they're inhabited by spirits. Stories you've been told replay in your mind. Those dark, Gothic campfire tales aren't just imagination. In some wild places I feel great and so at home I don't want to leave, in others – not too many – I feel uncomfortable, and these I avoid. I get out, go round, or generally do my best to keep to where I feel more at home. I wouldn't like to be a surveyor whose job was to work in those difficult places, like it or not, especially with Aboriginal people in the vicinity who had, if they chose, many, many ways to put the fear in you. It's not just other people, but also snakes, ticks, fires and floods … Survival in rawest nature, where nobody else is there to advise or lend a hand, demands inner resources. There is a word for it that perhaps came from the Scots: *raugh*, as in Wallagaraugh, which referred to country in its natural state, rough and not yet processed or worked. To come through the experience is one thing, but transitioning back to society can be even more demanding; I know only too well. The difference lies in the way you use your wits, and when you realise the gulf, doubts begin to creep in …

As they attempted to master the wild land a strange thing happened to so many: it mastered them. So many failed. In fact, as the early settlers wrestled to change their land into something they could regard as hospitable, it also changed them. All of them.

Scotsmen, rats and lice

The arrival of the Scots surprised no one. Like the rats and lice, it was said you can travel to the ends of the earth and find them everywhere. Perhaps the experience of managing small acreages in the Scottish lowlands, often in rugged country, equipped the Scottish immigrants to cope so well in the wilds of Australia's south-east. One of them became the land commissioner for the Maneroo Squatting District from 1837 to 1852. He was what could be described as a hard man. Hailing from Ayrshire in the south-west of Scotland, John Lambie had become ruthlessly efficient at his clerical duties by the time when, at 46 years of age in July 1839, he took up residence at Coomer Creek. This served as a base for him to oversee a veritable kingdom of some 240 000 square kilometres – big enough to rival many European states – that was quickly being populated by the hungry men who would dispossess its Aboriginal people. Acting as the official administrator of the land for the British Crown, he was law and order, the taxman, the allocator of property and recognised its ownership by possession. A Scots background in common brought comfort to some landholders, nonetheless he was not a man to be crossed. This society looked more towards a new feudalism for want of better ideas, and still the going was fragile. Learning as they went, even the strongest could fail from uncontrollable circumstances.

His travels on horseback – in the early days accompanied by Aboriginal guides – had a purpose: to describe for the first time the countryside and its new inhabitants who so often had secrets they wanted to keep. In order to fill in names on officialdom's map he explored his empire several times and in his very own cryptic but consistent reporting – punctiliously written down in the columns of his official itineraries almost as though they were his journals – gives the first overall views of what the country was like at the time of settlement. His code for describing the countryside was not sophisticated. 'Open Forest' meant grassland such as found on the Maneroo Treeless Plains or the Bega Valley grasslands. The older meaning of forest, from the *Oxford English Dictionary*, is of 'the outside wood (ie not fenced in)', which appears to have been his principal meaning, but also he used it in the sense of 'an extensive tract of land covered with trees and undergrowth, sometimes intermingled with pasture'.

Few areas of fertile ground could be found south of the Towamba grasslands. One lay on the lower reaches of the Wallagaraugh at Timbillica. He could afford to ignore the country to the south as too rough, and he travelled beside the Genoa to Wangarabell and Nangutta following the well-established Aboriginal pathways the settlers had adopted, thence to 'Bondia' and onto the tablelands to 'Maratta'. Until 1851 when Victoria was split from the colony of New South Wales Lambie had jurisdiction across the entire south-eastern corner of Australia (including Gippsland) and was obliged to search out the stations of the region. Although without ownership of his squattage, the squatter had 'legal status as a tenant of the Crown from one year to the next, provided he was a man of good character and paid every year a fee of ten pounds for his license to depasture stock'. And to finance the police and judicial powers of the commissioner, a tax was levied on all stock at a rate of one penny for each sheep, threepence for each head of horned cattle and sixpence for each horse. This meant it was in the interests of the hungrier squatters to hide the full extent of their herds.[44]

An 1841 map showed the grazing district of Maneroo with 133 stations, 1031 acres in cultivation, 1554 people, 2133 horses, 78 473 cattle and 230 130 sheep. The numbers had multiplied by 1847, when Lambie described his own holdings at Cooma as having five residents in four huts and 80 horses, he had naturalised. The Maneroo had made him recognise it was home. He was there to civilise it, and, like the rats and lice, he'd come to stay. He died at Cooma in 1862.

In the early 1800s unusual factors drove Lowland Scots from their homes. Schools in the parishes produced a literate populace. Five universities served a land of less than a million people to create an educated class for whom, in their underdeveloped economy, there were too few appropriate jobs. Migration was the answer, when the 19th century revealed land and opportunity in New South Wales they came as traders, governors, surgeons, adventurers, officers, officials, craftsmen, administrators and such, and, most crucially, many of them had experience of rural life where the land was difficult, even harsh. They brought characteristics of hard work and thrift, and every one of them knew how to write and calculate. And so they spread across the colony, especially in the south-east and took responsibility for its administration.[45]

Their influence on the countryside, still evident today as I continue my walking, has been critical to understanding what lies about me. The Scots are an integral part of the Bundian story. They came into the Aboriginal landscape bringing Scottish attributes. Everywhere I go, from the forests to the cleared land, I find evidence of the Scots. The route, I have come to suspect, not only connects Aboriginal places but also far-flung and scattered little Scottish provinces. In between bouts of research I talk to people and walk to get a better understanding of what the records suggest. Every day I feel I'm coming closer to joining the dots. The smaller walks coupled with the history seem to be shedding light on the location of the Bundian Pass.

About Twofold Bay and along the streams of the Towamba, Wog Wog, Wallagaraugh, Genoa and Nungatta, some parts are not dissimilar to how they were when the settlers arrived and people began keeping records. As I walk their old lands I get to understand how and why they did things that were otherwise inexplicable. Whales played one part.

Peter Imlay

Captain Thomas Raine's onshore whaling station in Snug Cove, Twofold Bay, was working overtime when the *Elizabeth*, en route from Launceston, entered Twofold Bay in September 1832. A 40-year-old Scot from Aberdeen, Peter Imlay, was standing amidships when he noticed the spouting of a whale close inshore, then another near the southerly shore. On board was a cargo of wheat, kangaroo skins and wattlebark he hoped to sell once he reached Sydney. He was a big man in many senses: close to 2 metres tall, well-built and strong, but he had the mindset of an enthusiast. The glow in his eyes was roused by the opportunities for new trading ventures.[46]

Then, with profits of his trading, he enthused to his brothers, the older by 2 years, George, and younger Alexander, both surgeons recently come to Sydney. He suggested they start a family business. They would use their influence with the governor to obtain a grant of land near Eden and develop a trade in the natural resources of the region. They would have their own port. Twofold Bay was, after all, a lot closer to Sydney Cove than Tasmania. Although some squatters had already moved into the northern parts of the region, the brothers had first pick of the rich farmlands of the south. Dr George would take responsibility for the whaling and agricultural pursuits including cattle and sheep.

The lands they claimed were the grasslands of the granite country. They had convict labour, and encouraged Lowland and Border Scots to join their enterprises. There were no fences. Huts made of bark sufficed as accommodation for shepherd and overseer alike.

When the Imlay family first occupied the coastal plains, they focussed on the richest of the grasslands where trees, mostly forest redgum and rough-barked apple, were few and widely separated. The tracts seemed tailor-made for the first herds of cattle, building blocks for emerging agrarian dynasties. The river flats and floodplains with their freshwater lagoons were the richest, most resilient places of all. The Imlays had the run of the countryside from the ranges to the ocean. The boundaries were natural, steep and distant. There was no conception in those early days of how grazing and the build-up of stock numbers would change the rich 'open forests' forever.

Their holdings included Kameruka (18 600 acres), Bega (20 000), Tarraganda (6500), Murrah (1000), Cobargo (6400), Double Creek (10 000), Corridgeree (10 000), as well as Tantawanglo, where they had their horse paddock at the foot of one old Aboriginal pathway to the Monaro, and Nungatta, as well as leaseholds at Pambula, Candelo, Bittangabee, Bournda and, of special interest, Towamba and Pericoe. In other words, they chose well, taking up the best of the region, including the gateways to the Monaro.[47]

Scotsmen, rats and lice

Life was primitive. Baron von Hügel might have scorned George's rude bark hut at Eden and yet the Imlays were as close to being gentlemen as anyone else in the region. Be that as it may, there were few niceties of life. By 1838, with reputations firmly established, they were shipping their stock to South Australia, and Dr George Imlay settled at Tarraganda, where he eventually built a fine home across the river from where the Bega township would be established. The 'Bigga' property was said to be 'superior to any in the colony'. Cattle and whaling produced their best profits. But financial turbulence was just as unforgiving as the climate, and the general decline in stock values and difficulties of trade in 1843–44 put the Imlays on the long list of businesses in financial difficulties. In order to keep going they had to sell one part after another of their holdings. They had ample grass in the best years, but finding winter grazing after the annual native grasses died back was a problem. Worse, being in rain shadow, the grasslands dry out terribly in drought. Grazed and trampled, the grasses could simply disappear.

In October 1839 John Lambie described the Imlay's massive Biggah station, which took in virtually all of the grasslands in the catchment of the Bega River, as having 45 residents, 23 slab huts, 50 acres of wheat, 9800 cattle, 230 horses, 5800 sheep while producing 13 hundredweight (660 kilograms) of butter and cheese located in open forest. Their Pambula flats had only 10 residents, five slab huts and 150 acres under winter barley, six head and eight horses in thick forest. At Twofold Bay and Kiah there were 31 people in two slab huts and a weatherboard cottage with six head of cattle and two horses in thick forest.

Hard times savaged those with the biggest stations, and although the Imlay brothers held 3885 square kilometres of land, their fortune quickly dissipated so that by 1844 they only controlled four runs (still totalling 15 135 hectares) in the Bega district. The Walker brothers, William and James, of William Walker and Co, merchants based in Pambula, then Kameruka, had originally been agents for the Imlays and had to foreclose on the bills and acquired most of the Imlay land and the whaling interests in Twofold Bay. When they entered into possession at Towamba it had 19 people in seven bark huts with three stockyards, 14 acres under wheat and 4000 sheep, and was producing three hundredweight (152 kilograms) of butter in 'thick forest and scrub'.

Their business operations effectively ceased in 1847 after George, supposedly suffering from 'incurable illness', went up onto the mountain overlooking his home and committed suicide. Alexander died a few months later. It took until 1853 before Peter Imlay could sell the last of the holdings, the Bega and Double Creek stations, and the remaining sheep and cattle in order to move to Wanganui in New Zealand. The migration of labour from farmlands to the gold rushes in the 1850s finally signalled the days when their style of low cost, labour intensive farming could no longer be sustained.

The countryside beat the Imlays, its changes, its demands. To burn or not to burn? The cycles of too much and too little. They battled but could not hold on to it. It was too complicated, and burdensome. Too much land. They tried to farm the land as they found it. And failed. They didn't change the landscape but they started the process of settlement. If only they could have upped sticks and moved on as the seasons demanded.

Nonetheless, lessons were learnt from their experiences, not the least by the countrymen who came in their wake.

Captain Stevenson

When I walk the Genoa River below the Bondi station I experience 3 or 4 days of unutterably wild yet beautiful gorge country that suddenly, shockingly, gives way to broad green expanses of floodplain with well-spaced trees of extraordinary height and girth. This is the Wangarabell land stamped with the influence of the redoubtable Henry John Stevenson, from Fifeshire, Scotland. He came to Twofold Bay as an experienced whaler before the end of the season in 1836 to become the Imlays' captain of whaling operations out of Snug Cove. On 21 July 1844, GA Robinson reported on how the captain had 'taught natives to whale'. In his off seasons Captain Stevenson set out to find land to try his hand at farming. Some of his Aboriginal whalers were from country south of the Imlays' stations, from the Genoa River catchment at Wangarabell, Nangutta and Boondiang. These men would repay his lessons.

In 1839 Stevenson took out a depasturing license over the rich river flats and open forest country at Wangarabell while he continued his whaling operations for the Imlays. In 1840 he spent the season at windswept Gabo Island where there is a risky harbour. By this time the competition for whales was vigorous between the land based whalers and the sailing vessels that could range further to sea.

Early in 1842 Captain Stevenson travelled further up the Genoa River to visit the Boondiang station, a run which had been taken up in 1839 by Thomas Liscombe. There he met an emancipated convict named Joseph Lingard who had just been freed at the end of his 7-year sentence mostly spent as an assigned labourer for the Campbells on the Monaro. Lingard had hatched a plan to spend the early days of his freedom collecting bird and animal specimens which might be valuable when he could return to England. In 1842 Lingard wrote how he accompanied Stevenson to the coast near Cape Howe and on the first night came to Nangutta after following the creek down to the station:

> One [Alexander] Weatherhead kept this station as overseer it was a cattle station. We staid (sic) all night the mistress ... said we had better stay another day ... as the way we

had to go was a very rough one. I saw trees there, I should
think one hundred and twenty yards high and twenty-five
feet through the ball; the natives call the trees stringy-bark
or messmate.[48]

It would have surprised no one at the time that Lingard and
Stevenson's peregrinations were made easier by following a
long-established road. This was the old Aboriginal pathway
that ran from the Monaro, through Nungatta, on to Wangarabell and along the Genoa River to Genoa. Its route would
have followed the flatlands, avoiding the extreme wildness of
the gorge country, with a longer, steeper detour that passed by
the hospitality of old Boondiang, soon to be better known as
Bondi station.

Through their mostly Lowlands and Borders affinities a close
community of Scots developed in the district. The McDonalds
had moved nearby at Merramingo when the Weatherheads
went a little north to Nangutta. They ran family farms, where
everyone did their bit. A helping hand was always available and
cooperation was invaluable in dealing with mustering stock,
fires, pests and such. They assisted each other through difficulty and when there was something to celebrate, they sang and
danced together. They shared an ethic of self-sufficiency, and
their family farming methods also involved helping each other
out whenever necessary. This made all the difference when, for
example, the Imlays' empire failed due to labour problems and
financial stresses. Ben Boyd's desperate dependency upon labour
also told, and in the end the small family enterprises triumphed.
The irony was that when Boyd's failed empire was being wound
up, Stevenson purchased the Bondi station on the headwaters
of the Genoa, giving his family a monopoly of the best parts
of the upper river catchment. The families intermarried. It was

a lifestyle that agreed with him. Stevenson died peacefully at Bondi on 28 March 1874, aged 95. His grave is on a hilltop overlooking the Genoa River flats and the great bowl of mountains from Gulgin and Coolangubra past Nangutta to Coopracambra. To this day the outlook is still unutterably wild. They say he was buried standing up, facing easterly, to look over his lands towards the ocean. It would also be fair to say those were the lands of the Bundian-mittong.[49]

Ben Boyd

Ben Boyd was a relative fly by night, a blow-in, as they say, a man whose borrowed monies and mad, hungry dreams gave him so much clout locally and nationally that he became a veritable archetype of the corporate villains Australians have come to love and hate. But the impact he made on the region has been considerable and lasting, for reasons not all negative. That he soared so high only to crash and burn has reinforced a mythical status for him, perhaps as the corporate Ned Kelly. Historian Manning Clark made him a character with a god-like appearance 'and an appetite for glory to match the garments of display with which he bedecked his body'. And the type has been visited by other important Australian writers, such as Francis Webb, who suggests in an epic poem that one thought could become 'a drum for Ben Boyd'.[50]

After their journey to the Monaro, Boyd's party returned to the bay on 4 January 1843 to find his men had been making their mark. A fine bark hut had already been completed.

They had decided to imagine themselves the founders of a second Rome and they would 'point to various spots which are to bear our names and thru them live down to future ages'. This euphoria at establishing an empire based in such a beautiful place led them to decide to change its name from Beermuna to

Boyd or, optimistically, Boyd Town. But it would never achieve the lofty ambitions of Ben Boyd's wildest dreams. In the excitement of founding a new empire, their first step, after changing names of places, was undertaken: 'a blanket nailed to a pole is the first ensign passed in the Town'.

The empire of Boyd's dreams was grand. He would make his own fleet of modern steamers to connect his capital, Boydtown, with the rest of the world. New South Wales was the blank slate upon which he would draw his grand designs. Twofold Bay would be his port from which his roads would snake out into countryside that he would own and work for produce in such abundance that trade in both directions would spring up, along with villages, towns and cities. His capital was raised in London, where interest rates were low, to be used in New South Wales where the rates were high. So what could get in the way of his adventurous developments around Twofold Bay and purchase of land all the way across the Monaro and beyond? As benign overlord he would bring prosperity to the wilderness.

Before long flaws appeared in his plan. Every feudal economy needed a peasant class, but he could find no people to act as his serfs. While the Imlays already had assigned convicts who worked out their time for a reward of clothing, food and a roof, in 1840, just as Boyd was starting his operations, it was decided the convicts were no longer to be transported to New South Wales. It meant he would find no cheap, readily available workers and it irked.

Boyd never considered life in a bark hut like the Imlays. He brought his own luxury yacht, the *Wanderer*, to serve as hotel-style accommodation while his visions were being realised.

The Seahorse Inn was conceived in a spirit of grandeur, but the dream, like the building, would soon crumble.

Scotsmen, rats and lice

He was born on 21 August 1801 at Penninghame, Wigtown, in south-west Scotland, the second surviving son of a merchant in the Glaswegian West-India trade. His arrival in Port Jackson on board the *Wanderer* on 18 July 1842 came with fanfare and celebrity, for it was believed he had all the influence of patronage and privilege necessary to have his way with the colony.

A few months later, his expedition to inspect Twofold Bay on board his steamer the *Sea Horse* made a big splash as he cut the grand figure. The only question was whether the theatrical dash would sustain his privileges and the patronage upon which his schemes depended. His ferociously combative nature could not accept the hold the Imlay brothers had on the village where Eden is situated today, even though it had the better anchorage. Like a clan chieftain back home he wanted things done his way, which was to focus on the southern side of the bay and make his own place there as his base for tapping the far-away riches of the Monaro.

To gratify the demands of his ego the necessary infrastructure was being made by skilled artisans; his Seahorse Inn was being built in an incongruously grand style – as much Elizabethan as it was Norman – out of bricks made on the estate, local stone and sandstone brought from Sydney. The slate roof was brought from India, the doors and mantels from England. By 1845 he advertised in the *Sydney Herald* that the Seahorse Inn was now open to travellers 'at English prices'. His road to the Monaro employed a high level of skill to negotiate the problems of topography. Many of the ancient pathways which had survived for countless years could not survive traffic by hard wheeled vehicles, such as drays. The wheels cut furrows into the loose granite soils so that the next time heavy rain fell, the run-off followed the wheel ruts and liquefied the hillside causing massive erosion. Sections of Boyd's road still exist in unmodified form, for example along the Cow Bail Track where skilled masons were used to clear the route up a long ridge overlooking the source of the river. Mighty granite outcrops were neatly cut through to make passage suitable for the bullock teams. Along its route artefacts remain of the Boyd days in chimneys used for fires at stop-over points made from well-crafted granite building blocks. On the flatter places you can see the signs of its earlier users in the form of flakes of stone and other Aboriginal artefacts.[51]

He continued to accumulate squatting runs: Mafra, Gennong and Matong for sheep and at Bibbenluke, Myalla Downs, Wog Wog, Cambalong and Boco Rock he concentrated on cattle. As economic conditions became worse, he found higher prices for his produce in Tasmania than Sydney. Soon, rather than export livestock, like the Imlays, he found he could get some return on his capital by boiling down the oversupply for tallow, which made for easier shipment. He exported 700 tons (635 029 kg) in 1847.[52]

Boyd treated his employees badly, pushing always for greater efficiency, saying there was no mystery to shepherding and making his shepherds superintend larger flocks than the Imlays. The colonial system had originated in the early days, without fencing, so the sheep would graze by day and at night be enclosed in folds or 'hurdles', while the shepherd slept in a hut nearby. The shepherd had to protect them from dingoes and disease like scab. If he lost sheep they were paid for out of his scant wages. During the late 1830s the size of the flocks to be superintended increased from 350 to 1000 or more, and as pastoralism moved to the back country, the shepherds increasingly had to allow them to run on larger, more hazardous areas each day.

In the mid-1840s Boyd introduced his new, more labour-efficient system of 'camping'. Instead of being folded at night, the sheep were now left unconfined and the shepherd had to lead a nomadic life sleeping with his larger flock.

No evidence suggests Boyd had any ill feelings towards the Aboriginal people who refused to serve as his peasant workers.

In fact, his early dealings at Twofold Bay appear to have convinced him to regard them as unsuitable for employment, to ignore them, as distinct from the way resident managers of many runs struck mutually advantageous relations with their local people. Oswald Brierly, however, as his manager of whaling operations did trust them and gave them employment on equal terms. But for his wider operations Boyd wanted a more stringent master and servant relationship than was possible with the land's original owners. His new shepherding arrangements undoubtedly increased tensions with the Aboriginal people who were pushed further into the less-hospitable backblocks. Competition for resources became fiercer. At a time when the free rural workers would prefer their own run to the miserable wage Boyd would offer, Boyd looked further afield to solve the problem of populating his empire. He quested widely for an answer, first looking to Asia but, on finding coolies unsuitable for labour in the bush, in 1847 he brought some 65 Melanesians from Tanna, Lifou and other islands to Twofold Bay to serve as shepherds and labourers. This was as disastrous as any of the other schemes he dreamed up. It had no practical application to the countryside where it had to be implemented. The Monaro winter is tough enough for those accustomed to such cold. Inadequately dressed people from the tropics simply could not acclimatise. The publicity was bad. Most of them had to be sent back to the islands by the end of the year. One by one his ventures failed and were sold up. And with all the irony of natural justice his 'black-birding', as it was called, would be the end of him. He went ashore on one of the islands and was never seen again. Perhaps his most lasting influence was that he raised expectations of the land. His empire had come and gone in less than a decade.

On 2 December 1854, Mort & Co advertised the auction of the leases of many of Boyd's runs, including Bondi and Wog Wog.[53]

His vision became a wreck. As a child, one of my strongest memories was visiting the very much down-at-heel Boydtown. As I wandered through the tumbled-down, broken mess of a church he had built on the hilltop overlooking his town I couldn't but help marvel at its ruination. And to this day I remember my childish wonderment at how aspirations so grand could have resulted in such a sad, empty, smashed-up place.

Alexander Weatherhead

Why I have to keep visiting Nangutta/Nungatta is a mystery to me. It's one of those places that got under my skin, not so much for its paddocks, but for those strange, mysterious mountains that surround it, and the wild, wild river that hems it in to the south along the New South Wales–Victoria border. Although I've always figured it must hold clues to the location of the Bundian Pass, it remains the last of the region's old runs still in anything like its original form. During my explorations I find an eagle's eye view of the place from the ramparts of the sandstone cliffs of Nangutta Mountain, it is as though past and present intermingle. Today, as ever, it is a bowl of grassland surrounded by mountain peaks and tall forests. In the middle of nowhere is the phrase I hear most often to describe its location. The vision laid before me incorporates the landscape's history as though its people had only arrived in the last five minutes. The routes people walked stand out, obvious and clear. The whole outlook invigorates me, exhilarates me as I walk southwards along the crest towards the nearby border line. I cross the rainforest of the upper Neenah Creek and soon, as thornbills chide me with their insistent *tsk, tsk, tsk*, I find I'm I fighting my way through razorgrass scrub. This is horrible stuff that slashes at my clothes and skin. Its infestations can be managed with light burning. There is no way round, so I plough right through as it rips at my clothing and skin. By the time I arrive at the junction of Nangutta Creek and the Genoa River all the front of my jeans have been torn from my legs and they flap behind like ribbons. Fearful of how my skin will be savaged on my way back next morning I put them on back to front like cowboy chaps, but the southern crest of the horseshoe-shaped mountain is not so infested. Along this walk I first make contact with the long-footed potoroo. Other parts of Nangutta are not so interesting.

This part of the story tells me about ways people walked through this landscape as well as the many ways they did not regularly walk. But Nangutta does have another story. In 1840 when a thick-set but energetic 31-year-old named Alexander Weatherhead arrived in Eden there was only one white woman in the district and 'the land ... was in a state of nature and inhabited only by Aborigines'. He started for his new employment as manager of Nangutta station as soon as practicable, but he needed help to find his bearings and so after he found 'a blackfellow to go with me, we walked to Towamba that day' following the old Aboriginal pathway from Twofold Bay, the same one that would be used by Brierly and Budginbro.[54]

Towamba and Pericoe are those kind of grassy places that are all the more idyllic after the hard journey you have to make through the hard, slaty mountains to get there. Early in the second morning he passed the Imlays' station at Pericoe and then came into the tall forests to follow upper Pericoe Creek through its gash in the Black Range. The saddle at the head of the creek is where he at last came out of the Imlay lands and crossed through open forest into the Nangutta catchment. It is at once typical of the old stations and also atypical because it has remained relatively intact, and is therefore worth close examination for it has many lessons to teach us.[55]

Nungatta had been purchased as an investment by William Morris, an absentee landholder, who employed Weatherhead as manager. His approach to the land is explained in his story of the early days of white settlement, written as the reflective memories of an old man, and published as *Leaves from My Life*. He was born just south of the Tweed in England in 1809 but 'endowed with the instinct of a Scotchman'. Emigrating with 'a sound constitution and good wife' in 1834, his affinities with the Lowland and Borders Scots brought him advantages and enough favours to make a success of his farming life where so many others would fail. His Scottish wife, who hailed from just north of the Tweed, had a similar dogged capacity for farmwork. They made a good pair. She could keep the place going while he was away, which was much of the time. This was in 1840, when the Imlays had already picked the eyes out of the land between Balawan and Mumbulla, including Towamba. Nangutta, at the time, was described by surveyor MacCabe as being 'thick forest stringybark' in the north, as it still is today, but along Nangutta Creek towards Yambulla it was 'honeysuckle and gum open forest'. Once his wife and three children were settled at Nangutta, with the nearest neighbour 12 miles off, they got down to mustering cattle and running a small dairy to sell the butter for transport to Sydney by boat from Eden. When John Lambie paid a visit just over 12 months afterwards, he found the Weatherheads had improved the place with a dairy, acres of wheat and an extra 300 head of cattle. Their heifer station was a long way downriver at Genoa. There were no fences.[56]

But even quantity and quality of land holdings was not proof against drought or wider economic circumstances, and with Nangutta cash-strapped and in drought, Morris and his partners foundered and sold the station. The Weatherheads had to leave, but stayed in the district and attempted to farm on their own account. He moved downriver to a property called Wallagara, near the junction of the Genoa River, 'a poor place', and then Timbillica, a richer place for farming on the Wallagaraugh River. Suggestions are that blackfellas showed him the place, but he would have passed by on his way to and fro from Twofold Bay with produce and provisions. Around Timbillica there were the richer alluvial flats, where the otherwise narrow fast-running stream could spread over a larger area in flood time and deposit the topsoil carried for long distances from upstream. Here, the river meandered. There were spring-fed lagoons and swampy clearings with patches of grassland and open forest over a few hundred acres. Even so, it was nowhere near as extensive or as rich as country on the Genoa at Wangarabell. He split slabs and gathered bark to make a house. His practice was to run cattle rough, which is to say they ran free wherever they could find grass. But also the family kept a dairy and grew crops. As he acknowledged, his greatest asset was his wife – unnamed throughout his memoirs – who worked tirelessly and under conditions of extreme isolation. She milked the cows, separated the milk, fed the pigs and made the butter and all the while kept their rude accommodation and the family going while he was off exploring and taking their products to market, such as when he and neighbours John Rixon, Thomas Doyle and James Allan cleared a road of some 25 miles between Timbillica and the Kiah River near its entry to Twofold Bay. One evening, while bringing in the cows for milking, she was lost in the wild hill country and didn't find her way back home until lunch time the next day. Not all the family's tribulations are stated in his book. GA Robinson heard that he 'shot his own child, fine girl, by accident (eldest) when tying his sister frock. Mother almost distracted, not recovered since'.[57]

All the time he was getting to understand the country north of the Genoa and how it could be best used on a year in, year out basis. This is a district where, as my many walks demonstrate, at the best of times the rain can turn the meadows into bogs while the native grasses supply luxuriant summer feed, and at the worst, when the creeks dry up, the grasses and ferns shrivel and all hint of green disappears from ground level.

The coast

When his neighbour Doyle left for Wog Wog in 1846 to take over from the Boyd estate, he moved to Merrimingo and applied for a license of all the land he was occupying. It was a better spread of land than Timbillica alone, and with the run of all the country along the Wallagaraugh to the Genoa River, some 15 kilometres away as the crow flies, it presented the prospects of at last moving beyond subsistence towards producing real income. In general it was not great land but the smaller flats scattered among the scrubs in the steeper forest country were like an insurance policy against the worst conditions. Many gullies had green pick for the cattle and the ridgetops and higher parts where the silvertop ash grew formed boundaries against the cattle straying too far, indeed there was little to entice them to stray there. He now had land on the Genoa flood plains good enough for cultivation of wheat, maize and oats. Their house was on a rise by the side of a waterhole a few hundred metres from the river but when the 1851 floods came they lost just about everything and he had to return to Timbillica where he still had enough wheat stored to see his herds through the worst of winter. Two years later came another flood. This would have spoiled their best pastures for a few more years. The Victorian Crown Land Licenses record he had applied for a license to cover an unspecified area with 10 horses and 28 cattle at Merrimingo. It was here that GA Robinson visited in the course of his travels south of Twofold Bay. Weatherhead had just returned from Boydtown, bringing a sack of wheat, and within 4 miles of home he saw the bag had been punctured and half the wheat had run out onto the ground. In his typically dogged way, he returned next morning with Robinson in tow to help pick up the grains. Never one to forgive easily, 50 years later Weatherhead wrote, 'and so he did, he would walk along leading his horse and when he would come to where it was thick he would stop and let his horse eat it. Some people are very thoughtless.'

Scotsmen, rats and lice

Weatherhead's outrage and frustration is understandable. Fancy losing his hard-won wheat like that, to an otherworldly idiot of an Englishman who was being paid by the government and could well have afforded to buy his own! On the other hand, miserable, scrawny Robinson did not often find the chance for a good feed. As often as not he had to subsist on bush tucker. His time aboard *Wanderer* in Twofold Bay had been rather a paradise; not so for his even scrawnier horse in the sandy flats round Boydtown, before the party had to trip through the thorny coastal heaths round Cape Howe to Timbillica.

Robinson was more generous to Weatherhead. He recites how it was rainy and Captain Stevenson and the Liscombes from Boondiang also stayed the night. 'Good fire, good food, good bed. Horses were out to graze in good feed opposite; did till morning.' They all seemed to have got on well enough, with much talk about Aboriginal whalers, and after the wheat episode the next morning Robinson went downriver and across the lakes to Stevenson's property at Mallacoota where he was in his element talking with Aboriginal people gathered there, mostly from the Bemm and Cann rivers. His usual frenetic gathering of information appeared to come from a deep inner compulsion, he found greater peace when he was actually with the Aboriginal people. He met the old man: 'Cooperer Billy, Mallokoterer mitter near Mr Weatherhead's, Tummeric, wife to above, a Ben mitter, 40 miles west of Mallakoter'. Three weeks later, bedraggled and half-starved after a difficult time in the scrubby mountain country west of Mallacoota, he arrived back in the rainy late afternoon just as the Weatherheads returned from Timbillica. His mind too restless for anything bar chasing down yet more information about the Aboriginal people, the Weatherheads must have been delighted.[58]

In about 1843 Campbell & Co took over Nangutta, made little enough money from their investment, and in about 1847 Peter Imlay purchased it to try his hand, but, as Weatherhead said, 'never made much of a go of it. Cattle being at a low price, they were neglected and went wild'. He had to ask Weatherhead to catch store cattle to fatten for boiling down at a price of 15 shillings per head, delivered at Bega.[59]

In 1850 Imlay sold to a consortium that stripped the property, selling off the stock for what they could get. But after 1851, when the gold rushes began, cattle prices doubled. A year later the price had doubled again. Weatherhead was also now getting good money for his wheat in Sydney and oats and corn in Eden. Other big landholders couldn't get labour, especially as the rushes proliferated and came closer to home. In 1854 Weatherhead purchased the Nangutta property for £800 plus £35 for the horse and cattle brand. He sold Timbillica to James Allan for £150.

When the family arrived back at Nangutta as owners, he says 'There was a large bush paddock, everything else was a wreck, not even a bit of garden, and not a hut, I won't say a house, fit to live in.' He doesn't say how happy his wife and family were to arrive on their new property in about 1859. Furthermore, the cattle on the station had gone feral during Imlay's time as he had nobody who knew the countryside. Mustering was difficult with so much of the stock running wild in the hills, a problem the previous owners who'd hoped for quick profits had faced. Much of the country was rugged, especially along the steeper ridges. The stock left behind was scattered in the grassier parts of the forests, often near the heads of meandering creeks. Weatherhead observed, laconically enough, 'We got a good few cattle, but it was rough work.' He rounded up a few of the horses but found it was easiest to shoot the rest, thus avoiding the problem of brumbies in later years. At the same time they managed to get a decent house up.

And so it was that Weatherhead's small-scale, multi-use farming gave him the edge where the big operators like Boyd and Imlay had failed. Rather than put all his chances in accumulating bigger and bigger herds, he and his wife focussed on the small things of a farming life. Following the regional tradition, they used all the land they could, catchment wide. But their main focus lay on the home paddocks where they ran a small dairy herd to make butter. They grew their crops and ran pigs, always working with their neighbours in a spirit of sharing and cooperation. Between them they controlled a tract of land over 3000 square kilometres. As the friendships grew, their families intermarried.[60]

Things were never properly secure for the squatters. Few could afford to, and many didn't want the expense of converting their squattages to freehold as Weatherhead did, progressively block by block. There was much agitation among the increasing population of settlers who wanted access to land in the vast estates assembled by the squatters. Not all big landholders were as hungry as the Weatherheads, but he had the doggedness to make his way through the difficult times, to push on regardless, to be self-sustaining, even to get on in the world.

He now began to call the place Nungatta, apparently because he preferred not to be associated with a gutter, 'gatta sounded more respectable but denied its Aboriginal name and roots.

In 1885, in the official view, according to Weatherhead's Return of Crown Lands lodged at the Court of Petty Sessions at Eden, Nangutta consisted of only 6187 acres with 50 sheep and 24 horses. The run's actual area as he usually described it would have been in excess of 40 000 acres (or 180 square kilometres).

Life would not have been easy. The roads became impassable after extended rain. He said one bog hole was so bad it had been filled with a dead bullock, 'it appeared to fill the hole nicely'. Whole sections of track became swamplands or were eroded into deep ruts. He described how, 'Before we got to Rocky Hall Mrs Weatherhead got pitched out, it was a heavy wagonette we had, she went between the wheels, one of the hind wheels went over her back and her face got bruised. She got up quick told me I had killed her, then laid down again. Was she Irish? No, she belonged to the neighbourhood of Canny, Newcastle ... it was a good while before she could get over it.'[61]

A stereoscopic photograph by C Walter of the station looking south-westerly across Nungatta Creek towards the southern end of Nungatta Mountain, circa 1869, shows a collection of rude buildings on the steeply sloping rise above the creek. Split post and rail fences divide the scene into paddocks. The home paddock has a four rail fence around perhaps a hectare of crops, including corn. Many trees have been ringbarked in the mid-distance. And yet the cycles came with an unerring regularity. He says their losses through drought were never heavier than in 1865–66 when they lost 300 head. 'Then to mend the matter, when rain came and we had plenty of grass we got the pleura [pleuro-pneumonia], and that stuck to us a long time. I kept account of the deaths until I had four hundred, I then gave it up.'[62]

This happened just before the heights of the gold rush to Kiandra and then closer, on the Monaro at Craigie when supplies and transport were fetching premium prices. Chinese appear to have been frequent visitors, mostly from the Chinatown at Craigie. His family was in the ideal situation in 1891 when the rushes began a few kilometres away at Yambulla beyond the Waalimma Mountain to the east. At their height a town was planned and surveyed, but failed. There never had been or would again be such a large population in the district.

Weatherhead employed the local Aboriginal people whenever they could be of assistance to him. He wrote of how they helped him find his way through the unfamiliar country, how they minded his children and stripped bark for him to roof his new slab house in the desperate times after floods on the Genoa, but he does not mention how much of a problem they were. The station could, at times, have been a frightening place. It was about as remote as you can get from towns and civilisation.

Scotsmen, rats and lice

The glowering cliffs of Nungatta Mountain had his home full in their stare. The peaks of Nalbaugh, Wog Wog, Wallagara, Waalimma, Merragunegin and Yambulla stand like boundary markers. But this home rested directly on a very important pathway, the main Aboriginal route from the Mallacoota coast to the Monaro. The ponds and damp grassy clearings at Nangutta would have been important stages in the local people's calendar. There were wild food plants and game aplenty here before the whitefellas came, enough to sustain the group on a year-round basis. Perhaps the old clans brought in the whitefellas and their stock to provide even better resources. They would have been proud, and happily showed it off as a good place to settle.

There were resident Kooris. And like all those other travellers, other clans would have continued to pass through on their way up to the mountains or down to the salt water. But once the station was established, transient groups of Aboriginal people would not have been so welcome, especially when they were in competition for resources that were more limited at certain points in the climatic cycle. The coming of barbed-wire fences not only interrupted free passage, it corralled stock in paddocks where, especially in drought, they would trample and destroy the yamfields as well as herbage the kangaroos and emus relied upon. The old Aboriginal people had a deep hunger for fats. Their normal diet, apart from whales and moths, included few foods that had much fat content. The arrival of the Europeans with their cattle and sheep was a veritable bonanza. Would it have been little wonder that when the Weatherheads left the milk out overnight to separate, the Aboriginals could not resist skimming off the best part? Or that, as historian Mark McKenna recounts, Weatherhead retaliated by poisoning one vat with strychnine? In various forms I have heard another story that has been passed on by families of the region: Weatherhead massacred a local Aboriginal clan that roused his anger. They fled to seek refuge above the homestead in the Neenah Gorge, but he found them there. All were shot. A Monaro man whose mother lived on Nungatta during the early 1900s told me she saw human bones lying in the paddocks. This brutal approach was also seen in the practice carried out until the mid-1900s whereby, when the dingoes became too much of a nuisance, an old horse would be led out into the bush and shot. Its body would then be laced with strychnine. Harold Farrell told me the scene would soon be surrounded by the bodies of the dogs as well as eagles, quolls, magpies and such. The settlers believed they had to be ruthless, especially towards what they saw as 'vermin'.[63]

HP (Harry) Wellings was a shipping agent, accountant and writer, whose greatest passion was for the history of the Eden region. He wrote numerous articles for local newspapers and historical publications. Without his contributions – often verging on the conversational – the history of the region, including the lives of those like the Imlays, Ben Boyd, the Davidsons and the Aboriginal whalers, would be a far less colourful subject. His writings check out against other historical sources, and he had a close working relationship with many of the players in our story. In the *Bombala Times*, 1 July 1932, Wellings told the story related to him by an old stockman, identified only as 'Bill', about 'Tailing stock on Monaro fifty years ago'. One of its characters, Old Tongihi (Tangiai), was presumed to be the 'last of his tribe, all the others were shot down near the Cann Valley years ago.' The man Bill knew as Tongihi was only about 8 years old when the old stockman's family found him near their home on the edge of the mountain. At that time the blacks were often employed on the cattle stations in tailing stock to see that they didn't wander off into the thick scrub and get lost. Bill told Wellings Tongihi's tribe lived on the edge of the valley where they oversaw lots of cattle. Another tribe that lived more towards the sea were often causing trouble. Bill described how

> one of the settler's sons living down the mountain came on three-half eaten carcasses and their brand was on them. So they ups and swears they'd get the blacks for it ... These young fellows collected some more of the cattle owners about that part and they swore they'd hunt the blacks out of the mountains. Well, they hunted around a bit and ... after a while they heard a devil of a shindy going on away up the mountain.
>
> They ... finds that a sort of battle was going on between the blacks. One of the chaps who was always a bit hot headed, ups with his rifle and lets go at the crowd and drops a young black fellow dead. Away the lot goes in all directions, and the cattle people made after what looked like the main body of blacks making down the mountain ... no questions was asked but the bullets and slugs were poured into the blacks as they ran. They told us afterwards that they must have killed thirty or forty that day ...

When the cattlemen came to inspect the dead, they found a woman who was critically injured, but she managed to tell them 'her tribe had been watching the coast blacks from the Bemm River and had caught them spearing a bullock. Her people attacked and it was during the fight that the white people had come up.' Before she died she told them her young son, Tongihi, had escaped. The cattlemen left the dead Aboriginal people where they fell, 'because they could not bury them'. Young Tongihi went to the station and was cared for there.[64]

The massacres were seldom clean. Memory is long. The perpetrators could not engage the whole district in complicity. Reminders and evidence survive. Unease lingers.

The coast

I should note the Cann River valley's catchment runs southwards from a gap below Bondi station and the country of the Bundian people. The Cann, like the Bemm, is part Bidawal, with Krauatungulung and Kurnai/Gunnai Country along the coast to the south, while the Genoa, including Bondi and Nangutta, seems to have been occupied by Thaua speaking Yuin, the Bundian-mittong. I would expect some overlapping of country and inter-relationships. The editor of the *Bombala Times* saw fit to add as footnote to the Wellings article:

> Tongihi was a great hunter, and would climb after a native bear, cut him down, and be on the ground as soon as the bear, ready for the kill. He would go after wombats, and would be no time returning with a couple of carcasses slung over his shoulder, with the hair shaved off them with the tomahawk fit for the pot. He could locate a wombat in its burrow by placing his ear to the ground, and would go right to the spot where the wombat was sleeping and spear it with a special spear, while a white man would be making ready for an hour's work digging out the burrow. Mr Cootes heard that Tongihi's father was shot by one of the white settlers down Nungatta way, and this may have been the occasion of the shooting mentioned by Mr Wellings.
> Editor[65]

Many years later in a matter of fact voice 'Billy Bamboo', an old, blind man who was then living at the Wallaga Lake Aboriginal Reserve, in 1956 told Roland Robinson: 'Well, my tribe got shot up. A white man found/a baby near the camp and took it back/to the station on his horse. That baby grew up/to be my father.' The violence and tragedy that has been a recurrent theme in the landscape of the Aboriginal heart is probably nowhere better expressed as old Billy in a matter-of-fact way continued his tale. He described a tribal fight, black against black — which happened more and more often after their dispossession as competition for resources heightened — an old man and his wife running away along a path, and how they hid their baby in a hollow log. A white man was riding by. 'He took the child and reared it and gave it / his name. And that baby was my mother.'[66]

Such stories are only too common throughout the region and beyond. Most Aboriginal families have one or more.

In February 2002 at the Nungatta homestead I fell into conversation with a young Aboriginal woman who told me her great-grandmother had lived on Nangutta. I introduced her to Pat Osborne, whose family has owned Nungatta since 1946. In conversation he surmised that one of the flats had been divided from the station, apparently for one of the Weatherhead boys who was at the time in a relationship with a young Aboriginal woman. Aboriginal stockmen had also been employed to work on the station.

Alexander Weatherhead died at Nungatta in 1901. One of his sons continued on but gave up ownership during World War I. Emotional attachments aside, it would not be hard country to walk away from for economic reasons. The vacant crown lands surrounding the property with their wet meadows and tall forests, once part of the run, were over the years variously reserved for state forests and then eventually, after long-running forest wars, made part of the South East Forests National Park, proclaimed by Premier Bob Carr on 28 January 1997.

Nungatta South was once part of the greater Nangutta run but never part of the freehold. It was selected from the run or purchased in about 1906. Alan Brown, whose father purchased the land in 1923, described how his mother, when her babies were due, had 13 gates to open on her way on horseback to the nearest neighbours at Nungatta station. The route she followed was once part of that old Aboriginal pathway between the Monaro and the flats of the Genoa and Mallacoota, and then one of those first 'roads'. The ridgeline dividing the Nangutta catchment also hosts the old Rockton Road, now little more than a memory, that comes from Pericoe and follows clear ridges all the way to Nungatta Creek. This is the easiest way to go, and the dividing point where that track to Nungatta South, Wangarabell, Genoa and Mallacoota leaves it is clear.[67]

I understand the strong feelings of attachment many people feel for Nangutta/Nungatta. Some parts attract me, others disconcert. It's such a strange, particular place – a great tract hemmed in by mountains – that it gets under your skin.

The dark side of the Weatherheads' occupation of the station was evidenced in their actions 'defending' their property. Their reprisals, however inexcusable, came at a time of drought and economic difficulty when many squatters no longer suffered the obligation to share 'their' land with its Aboriginal people and had no compunction about taking the law into their own hands. When a selector wrote to the *Bega Gazette* observing that Aborigines put the land to better use than the squatters who kept it as a private domain, an anonymous but angry squatter replied typically, 'Why should squatters let lots of people on their lands? ... Squatters are not philanthropists, they are each one for himself.' It was the springing of the trap, the point at which the Indigenous people were finally and officially dispossessed, which did not only happen at Nangutta or across Australia, but in many lands throughout the British Empire. Despite all the nice words and calming entreaties, the Indigenous possession was eroded slowly enough for the final act of its taking to be misrepresented as compassionate.[68]

In the shadow of waratahs

The mountain range that overshadows Nungatta to the north is where I believe the jigsaw of the Bundian Pass will come together. So in the springtime I spend weeks there, walking and looking closely. In between expeditions I talk with locals, especially those who know their country in the older ways – before modern maps, bitumen roads, 4WDs, Google Earth and helicopters – where the creeks and hills carry their own logic. I keep looking in even the most unlikely places. I hold sure the pass will reveal itself when I'm ready. Anyway, it's always exciting to get back into the Coolangubra. I'm taken in by a mixture of its big peppermint, brownbarrel and ribbon gums and entangled in old mysteries I still feel I can resolve. If I go deep enough. As if answers are there, just beyond my reach.

The first place I visit in my renewed quest is tucked below Pheasants Peak (unfortunately named in the old parlance for its large lyrebird population) or Yarramgun (WB Clarke's name for it), not far from the yamfields. Huge trees appear to float in the air above Waratah Creek's wending course through overhanging ferns. Waratah trees lined up like uniformed guards are covered with crimson braid. In the early morning mist, before shafts of sunlight break through, the flowers seem switched on. They create a carnival for the birds who respond with waratah antics: silvereyes en masse – popping in and out of the blossoms in their frenetic feeding – successfully outflanking the scolding of thornbills, the soft bell notes of crimson rosellas always nearby, eastern spinebills like southern humming birds hovering over one flower awhile, then darting to the next while various honeyeaters – the guerrilla platoons of New Holland and more cautious white-naped – compete with the bigger wattlebirds, so much clumsier and raucous and conspicuous.

The Gippsland or tree waratah is reasonably common in the damper gullies of the south-eastern montane forests. Its form is anything from a shrub to a tree 20 metres high with dark green leaves that in some places can form a sub-canopy underneath taller forest, a Gondwana plant that has adapted to the rise of the eucalypts. I have experienced these waratahs in many contexts. Sometimes they intertwine their branches with other species to form an impenetrable barrier. On one occasion, desperate to pass, I ran and threw myself at it only to be bounced, cursing, back again. Its wall was too high to clamber over, perhaps 6 metres tall. The place was so damp it would only burn on the very rarest occasions, say once every 50 or 100 years in the hottest weather during drought, and could therefore remain impassable for the duration of my lifetime.

At other times it is easy enough to pass them without noticing. And yet eventually comes their moment when, with a will-o'-the-wisp character, they stand out like bright red traffic lights. From here earlier I walked the other mountain passes: Wog Wog, Myanbah, Burrimboco, Wambamgarragun and others further north to no avail. I'm confounded, and decide to look southwards again. Sometimes I climb mountains to clear my mind. Today I'm headed up Yarramgun, at the head of the creek; the most impressive peak of the region. With sharp slopes at the crest, it looks as if it has been constructed from massive granite boulders, all tumbled together, countless tors and crannies abound. White and silvertop ash sprout impossibly tall from the crevices. Caves are formed in the gaps between its building blocks.

One aspect of the Coolangubra Range is its similarity to the present high country peaks, today's bogong places. The flats that lie below might well be where the moth ceremonies once took place, where many pathways led.

Vistas from the tops of the mighty rocks give me a special appreciation of how the country fits together. Insights come and go. Near dawn on the next day I see Delegate Hill, Tingaringy and all those peaks back to the high country. It's all so simple. The way is obvious.

When I head off to the line of peaks that reach southwards, I always see something new: signs of mines, prospecting. But especially I'm entranced to be in such remarkably beautiful and varied forests. Behind White Rock, on top of Nalbaugh, is a forest like no other I know: tall, mysterious, double-canopied: tree waratahs below, almighty brownbarrels an impossible distance above. It's a mist forest, at 1100 metres, very often in the clouds. The values of these forests were recognised in a proposal by ecologists Alec Costin and Geoff Mosley promoting World Heritage recognition for the south-east forests because they are:

> the most diverse of the Australian areas (and hence the world's) dominated by sclerophyll forest vegetation. The moist Eucalypt forests of the region are amongst the more diverse temperate mesic forests in the world and have a rich marsupial fauna. These and the dry grassy eucalypt woodlands and forests have a high species diversity compared to open forests around the world. The Far South East has one of the richest bird faunas of any Australian region.[69]

Their report explains the evolution of the region's vegetation that 'originated in East Gondwana, first appearing in the fossil record about 80 million years ago'. It goes on to describe how at the height of the last glaciation (25 000–15 000 BP) the eucalypts were confined to a few refuges and during the warmer periods that followed they spread to occupy the whole countryside excepting the small areas now occupied by heathland, closed forest and grasslands. Some 183 eucalyptus species reach their geographical limit in the Eden region, 137 at their southern limit and 38 at their northern. The big thing is the *eucalypt* genus.[70]

Climbing Wog Wog another afternoon, two-thirds of the way up with magnificent views across Nungatta, I find beautifully formed silcrete artefacts in a small clearing where the tree waratahs form a grove, lit by their flowers and surrounded by masses of heavily white-flowered daisy-bush. Further along the ledge to my right lies a core from which the artefacts might have been manufactured, as though the owner was sitting here not 10 minutes ago. This in itself is not so unusual, but as I look out from this northern wall of Nungatta towards the New South Wales–Victoria border and the wilderness areas of the Genoa and Coopracambra, the find sets my mind racing. I see new contexts. If I unfocus my eyes slightly, the landscape before me would be just as the old Aboriginal tribes might have seen it. Even in a place as remote and rugged as this, being part of the way on a direct line between Bombala and Mallacoota, I am following older footprints. The immediate surrounds must be as beautiful as any place on earth. Pale trunks of extremely tall, well-spaced shining gum contrast the more darkly toned understorey of daisy-bush and tree waratah. If I happen to kick a big rock, it would likely as not hurtle 600 metres down the slope all the way to the Sheepstation Swamp, one of those halfway kind of places, not quite tablelands and not quite coastal. From the sharp crest of Wog Wog Mountain the difficulties of the ranges easterly towards Balawan are obvious. It is an easy crossing through banks of crimson spider-flower grevilleas to Nalbaugh again, where I find mighty amphitheatres walled in granite, so many dreamlike places. Unusual plants. But it is the artefact from the mountainside that most haunts me. What brought the old people to these steep slopes? Somehow deep in my bones, I already know, and yet I am desperate to find out more.

And then, with the intensity of fruitless searches weighing on my mind, I drive from my camp into Bombala to speak with Harold Farrell, bushman and dingo trapper now in his 90s, the father of a long-time friend. Harold had lived much of his life in the mountain forests between Coolangubra and Balawan. He wears an old Tweed jacket and bushman's hat. Bent over, speaking so quietly he might have been talking to himself, his eyes blaze excitedly as he tells me about little animals he calls pademelons that once kept the teatree at bay. 'Before the foxes came there were thousands of them,' he says. 'When you approached a big tussock they'd go hurtling off in all directions much too fast to ever catch.' We talk about how you go from here to there in the forests, and when I tell him I can't locate the Bundian Pass he laughs, saying, 'Ah, but you must know ...' He pauses, as if to say he thinks I'm joking. 'It crossed Sheepstation just below the Swamp, where the bullockies from Nangutta put in a stone corduroy to make the crossing safer. It came from the tablelands near Nalbaugh Falls, then along the White Rock before crossing a gap in the hills. Past Umbach's old place. From the swamp they went up the ridge beside the Surveyors Gully ...'

I had been thinking of it as a mythical place; so long lost it had disappeared. So I am gobsmacked he can be so precise, so clear in his recollection. That means it passed beside WB Clarke's Nelbung and the Windindingerree Cataract, now known as Nalbaugh Falls. It's a matter of names. But here he is telling me about it as if it is a perfectly current thing.

The coast

The clouds of disbelief are still with me when the next day I visit another old local, Keith Brownlie, who owned land below Wog Wog. His response is to take me there immediately. He knows the district well. We soon find the creek and walk to the lower end of the swampy grasslands. The stone crossing is there, exactly as Harold described it. This is the foot of the long-missing Bundian Pass.

'It can't really be as simple as this?' I say to Keith.

He smiles back shyly. 'Never know, do you?'

Turamullerer: Coming to Bilgalera

BJ Cruse is sitting on his verandah at home looking out to sea, full of wisdom.

'Well I've got some news for you. You're not going to believe this ...' I say.

'I reckon you've found that pass,' he says, nodding sagely as if he'd known all along.

'How did you guess?'

He laughs. 'It's written all over you. S'pose we've got ourselves some walking to do?'

The pass has been the missing part in our puzzle and, while we have something to celebrate, there's a whole lot more to do. We had talked previously about that rarest of Australian animals, the long-footed potoroo, and the search for it at that very Sheepstation Swamp where the national parks scientist found a remarkable Aboriginal place. When its vast collection of artefacts was bulldozed by Forestry interests in 1987, headlines in the *Sydney Morning Herald* on 10 February screamed: 'Aboriginal site destroyed as Govt scratches its head.' The environment writer mourned the 'destruction of the most important Aboriginal artefact site on the far South Coast of NSW' and how 'while National Parks and Wildlife Service staff were attempting to evaluate the site, Forestry Commission bulldozers overturned it ...' This is when BJ became an activist, he tells me on our way to visit the place. After that, he did his best to ensure such a thing would never happen again; and a system of site inspections and monitoring was introduced in the forests.

Even with the swamp now protected as part of the South East Forests National Park, the fact remains that the surviving fauna of these forests is secretive and well-secreted. It takes a lot of energy to investigate the habitat of the long-footed potoroo, a small and very cute, hopping marsupial which might be the rarest mammal in the world. Parks scientist Dan Lunney recognised its presence and the few hairs that turn up in hair-sampling tubes and the odd tooth in dog or fox scats suggest they have managed to survive. My sightings remain unverified.

A team from the land council joins us on our visit to the pass. We follow a track then dodge through regrowth to get to the creek crossing. First thing, BJ goes up the rise to a flat. 'This is it alright,' he calls to us. 'This is the spot the Forestry bulldozers levelled.' He faces us, happy, with twinges of resignation. 'This is it, no problems about that, they bulldozed it when they were finishing the quarry for the Imlay Road, just up the hill there.' We have rediscovered the place we'd thought was lost. And then we begin finding artefacts. They're rising to the surface again. The old site is taking back its place. It wasn't destroyed, it was changed.

The importance of the location at the time was that it proved the old Aboriginal people lived in the forests. In 1987 these forests were being passionately contested by conservation and logging interests, and this find put a new element into the equation. The assumption before then was that Aboriginal people had only occupied the easier, clear places such as those indicated by the coastal middens. And this is a pretty place, just within sight of the creek but looking northwards to the grassy meadow from underneath stringybark, messmate and blue and ribbony gums, a good place to spend the night in anyone's language: grassy, clear enough, permanent running water. It's that same old story. The settlers learned their lessons from the Aboriginal people, followed in their footsteps. That corduroy of stones – like a paved roadway – was carefully placed there by the drivers of bullock teams going to Nangutta so they could ford the swampy creek with their heavily-laden wagons. The place lies at the foot of the Bundian Pass.

Then just across the creek at the base of the ridge that leads to the pass, we find a scarred tree from which a coolamon or shield might have been cut. Other signs and artefacts are evident. Further up the ridge scars on the trees at just about the right height tell us a horseman might have wielded his tomahawk to blaze the trail for those who would follow, as Alexander Weatherhead said he'd done. Furthermore, when we pass through the gap and onto the White Rock River we find more stones laid in a similar corduroy to form a track up the sandy riverbank.

About the swamp the patterning of woodland and grassland hint at periodic burning. Yams grow there, and patches of orchids suggest yamstick cultivation.

The Bundian Pass was the easiest way to go from the Monaro eastwards, and it led to the legendary Aboriginal place that was bulldozed during the forestry operations. Things click into place.

The Sheepstation Swamp, with its tinkling creek running out the bottom end, has always demanded a thorough exploration. I'll come back, I know, many times. It is as though the doorway has opened for me. So much makes sense now. The details all connect, add up to something very special, transcend, and we have our Bundian Way. It becomes a way to view the landscape with fresh eyes. Charges it with new meanings. The location, like so many other 'sheepstations' of the region, was probably named by the early shepherds who found it a discrete place to run their sheep, especially when drought settled across the Monaro. It would be warmer than the tablelands. Situated at the foot of the Bundian Pass, its swampier parts alternate with grassland and open wet meadow. Grassy ridges of stringybark, not as rich or tall as the forests higher up the slopes, reach down to the swamp in long fingers; and so it runs hither and yon for more than a few square kilometres in a basin at an elevation of about 500 metres, over-shadowed by the massif looming directly to the north, where its headwaters reach into the gap at about the 1000-metre mark between Nalbaugh and the Wog Wog crest. All in all it has a much-varied and lovely mosaic of swamplands that merge with the rainforest in the higher parts. And so it is that at last, when we finally have the chance to walk together through this wild country of the Bundian Pass, all manner of things I would otherwise have missed come to light. I'm saying, 'Look at this BJ!' while he's pointing me in the other direction towards some other remarkable detail. He spies a chert core, for example, from which small tools have been flaked.

Among all the ruggedness of the coastal ranges not many easy routes exist. This is one: sometimes looking like an animal pad along the crest of the ridge or in other parts as a regular indentation from the long-time traffic of feet.

Why had the place eluded my search for so long? Maps show the route of a crown road reserve, a disused road. But it is discontinuous. Once the dots are joined, the route is exactly where it should be: along the White Rock River, then across a low point in the ridgeline to the swamp. On the route below the falls, a lyrebird swings along in front of us with a jaunty

Turamullerer: Coming to Bilgalera

sway. There are forestry trails further up the hill, but the lyrebird leads us along old tracks beside the river. When the bird disappears his song rings out. The most wonderful of all the songbirds, his voice seems to encompass all birds singing in praise of the place. So many birds rolled into one, the smartest of all birds, the trickiest, the most powerful. He leads us for many kilometres. Or perhaps many birds collaborate to guide us along this way among extremely tall eucalypts. And then across the river and through the gap. Artefacts appear regularly. Beautiful artefacts of many colours, but predominantly a jade blue-green. Both the White Rock and the Sheepstation have the corduroyed crossings. This is it. That excitement is here, we're back on track. This is the Bundian Way.

It's a comfortable walk from the south-eastern corner of the tableland near the yamfields, easily undertaken in a day. Plenty of excellent camping places present themselves along the White Rock, but that old spot overlooking the swamp would have been hard to beat. That other route via old Bondi station was longer and more challenging, taking in two sides of the triangle, and yet it was the social route for the settlers, like going out of your way to stop at a comfortable inn overnight.

And then as we strike out for the coast, along the very old track from the swamp leading above Surveyors Gully to the ridgetop, we find the vestiges of the old Rockton Road. This leads through the grassy stringybark forests of the Nungatta run, then across a gap to Pericoe Creek.

We talk about the issues of finding heritage recognition. And BJ's passion sees how the old Aboriginal brought the present landscapes into being. He understands, deep in his guts, the uniqueness of these forests. Nowhere else, as we find along the Bundian Way, does one plant genus dominate the landscape from the highest part of the continent to the sea. And with a unique diversity. BJ would like to see this country made World Heritage, knowing full well the recognition would be symbolic. It would recognise the Aboriginal people's role in shaping Australia.

'We have to bring kids, blackfella and whitefella, up here to see how things are in this bush,' he says with deep feeling. 'If this Bundian Way can teach them about culture and Country, why not? That's what it's all about, get them a taste of real nature. It would bring respect. Yeah, that's what we need,' he says, his eyes alight. 'We can't afford to lose touch.'

Through the Nungatta catchment the ridgetop road is not exactly exciting, mostly following the disused Rockton Road and firetrails. But its relative bareness seems to be a result of the ancient management. The pathways were kept burnt. Clear. Clean. When I dive off the route to look in this gully or that, I find the most gorgeous glades. Exciting, vivacious places among tall trees; delightful camping sites. The route from the White Rock on lies within the South East Forests National Park but once out of the Nungatta catchment it enters Yambulla State Forest.

The way then crisscrosses ferny Pericoe Creek following the old Pericoe Road past tree ferns and towering mountain grey gums. The wet forest scenes become drier as we walk downstream, still dominated by the pale trunks of extremely tall eucalypts. Plenty of excellent camping places present themselves. At one old crossing place with a new concrete bridge, we find nearby the remains of an older timber bridge and beside it a ford from the early days. And stepping stones as well, most likely marking the oldest crossing of all. Artefacts are common along the way, many with that appearance of jade. The road still essentially follows the original course taken by Weatherhead at the time of earliest settlement. It leads all the way to the grasslands by the river and Towamba, a very pretty little town, old fashioned and charming. The weatherboard houses and wide verandahs welcome you, and its oval and community facilities provide an inviting 4-star campsite.

Turamullerer: Coming to Bilgalera

To avoid the dangers of the narrow, dusty Towamba Road, the walking route from Towamba leads southwards and around Balawan. The track out of town leads up a sharp ridge to the Black Range and then into the sheltered catchment of Imlay Creek. As I come on to the crest of a small section of pine forest I feel some trepidation the area might have been heavily logged. But it's a treat to walk through, following minor forest trails through the forest, damp on the southerly slopes and incredibly rich with birdlife. Eastern spinebills hover and quarrel over grevillea and bottlebrush flowers. Already I can feel the influence of the coast. There are plenty of well-watered campsites. Lyrebirds strut out of my path indignantly. An ideal campsite lies just over Imlay Creek, and another at the foot of the mountain is the perfect jumping-off place for a walk to the summit, surely what must be one of the great experiences of the Bundian Way. As I climb higher it seems to assail me or derange me or at least disarrange my senses as I pass into the layer of misty cloud that so often shrouds the crest. First, come aromas of the eucalypts and then the colours, such fields of colour. The Mount Imlay boronia, a plant endemic to the mountain, flowers so prolifically the entire understorey is washed in tones ranging from mauve to white, but mostly pink. Yellows and orange-browns frequently intrude. Near the top, the boronia becomes the principle understorey creating the effect of a sea of pink punctuated by the starbursts of grasstrees and their spear-like flower stalks. The fireworks displays of colour glow brightly against the slightly bent but stark black trunks of silvertop ash, and then the scribbled-upon upright trunks of the tall white ash.

In a while, when the mists lift suddenly, one aspect might well have frightened the life out of von Hügel, had his quest reached the summit. It is as though one stumble could send you tumbling down the slopes to the bay that seems to lie directly below. But from this point and all about the crest, the secrets of the landscape are revealed. You have command of Towamba as well as the bay, you see how it all connects. It is a fundamental point of the Bundian Way, a place where understanding of the scope of things becomes possible. Small wonder it was held in such awe by the old people.

Tracks follow obvious ridges all the way through the tall forests to the ocean. Mustering Ground and Shelleys Road are seldom used forest trails that lead through silvertop ash forests towards Bilgalera and the sapphire waters of the bay. I experience a genuine thrill when I finally walk out of the steep, stony forests and onto the sandy flats which mark the eastern limit of the Bundian Way. Twofold Bay gleams as brightly as ever it must have been, and each layer of story that lays behind the Bundian Way adds to the walk, brings greater depth. I make camp in a perfect spot by the lagoon and yet I itch for something more. The walk can't just end like that. I set off up the nearby hill to find those places overlooking the bay and its beaches where everything seems as wild as it was back when Oswald Brierly and Budginbro trod the shores.

On the hill above the entrance to the Kiah Inlet at the head of the midden that points all the way back along the Bundian Way to the high country, stands the old carved tree which I now see in a different light. Whereas the Kurrajong beside the Snowy was probably marked by one set of hands in more recent times to show a message about the people and countryside, this dead tree is infinitely more complex. In death it retains the scars of many generations. More recent marks made by steel axes indicate the coming of the whitefellas. The step holes point to getting a better vantage to see fish or whales or find a better vision of the seas, or even to look back into the country along the old way. but perhaps it could also have given access to koalas and possums near the treetop. A rude roof has been erected to protect its remains from the elements. It's not at all beautiful, but I see how it stands as a symbol of the shared history. That it has not been chopped up for firewood or allowed to rot away is a triumph.

This vulnerable stump overlooking the ocean and flats of Twofold Bay has its own magic and tales. It stands for all the stories brought here over the millennia, to be played out in song and dance, or told around the campfire, or even scribbled hurriedly into a notebook. The story is of survival against the odds, of tribulation and triumph, reconciliation and renewal.

Afterword

Many years ago as I was setting out on my back country walk behind Moruya, by accident I happened to have coffee with a group of academics. They asked me why I was going bush for so long, and one of the reasons I gave was that I thought we might learn from the ways of the old Aboriginal people. Someone took exception to this, roundly criticising my attitude towards the enlightenment and what the British had brought to this continent. He finished by lowering his voice scornfully to exclaim, 'I'm afraid you don't know which tribe you belong to.'

Maybe my trouble is that I still don't know. But in truth I believe I belong to the greater tribe of those who call themselves Australians. Some are black and some white; many like me have Aboriginal ancestors. We all benefit when we learn more about the land we inhabit. So much of our knowledge today, white and black, is hopelessly compartmentalised, inaccessible, so increasingly specific and lost in jargon it has become fragmented and in danger that like Humpty Dumpty it cannot be put back together.

Afterword

On the shores of Twofold Bay, we are talking about the issues. But I'm restless, and so is BJ. We keep coming back to the Bundian Way. For some reason, the name has stuck. It's the way that uses the Bundian Pass. We don't know it well enough. What about those stone arrangements? The yamfields? The scarred trees? The springs? How does it all fit together? On and on ... We have to know it better.

'We gotta do something about that, Brother,' BJ says to me in all earnestness. 'We gonna go out and survey it. Only we won't do it the way we did before. We'll go along carefully, walking all the way. We'll keep a record of everything we find. That way, I reckon, nobody'll be left wondering. We'll have it pegged.'

I give a groan but the idea appeals to me. And there is too much I still don't know about the Bundian Way. We begin to make our plans. The walking is not over yet.

It seems to us the route should be more widely acknowledged; protected from being bulldozed during fire emergencies, for example, or turned into roads. 'That's the sad truth,' he tells me. 'Today some people would recognise the Bundian Way by covering it with bitumen, whereas the old Kooris could recognise it in song. We've gotta protect it from people who don't understand.'

Along its route no day's walk is quite like the next. Some are so varied it's as if you have stepped onto a different planet. Having now followed it many times, my excitement levels rise just thinking about it. There's so much to it, so much to see and do. So much way beyond the ordinary.

The time will come for me to do something else with my life, but for now it's strange that after I close my eyes to sleep those landscapes return and I search them in my dreams. The way, I suspect, also exists as a dream. Nonetheless a counter impulse tells me that I can't allow it to become a mere dream.

Although details of the oldest song-stories that identified the route have partly been lost under the impact of European settlement, it strikes me that even today the richest way to map the route is through story. Not with a physical map, but a mental one, one you can carry in mind, one that makes a pathway your imagination can follow. We each tell our stories of it, the way pulls the strands together. As it was in the beginning, before history arrived with the Europeans.

Ossie has a lot of ideas. He sees an important role for the Bundian Way. It is, he says, 'All about connection.' And I realise that I most feel connected to that country through the Aboriginal vision, past and present interwoven, with my civilisation simply part of the whole. That's how I have now come to understand my country. It's the way that rings truest.

As we search for innovative ways to deal with the Bundian Way, BJ likes my idea of shared history as a way of publicly recognising the route. Blackfella and whitefella cultures continuing separately but connected. Independent, interdependent. Insights shared. 'In the old days there were new things and ideas come along. We have to let them happen today as well. We can't live in the past. We renew as we go along.'

The Bundian Way should be an inclusive concept, maintained for the benefit not only of those who have a family affinity with the clans that lived along the route, but also for those with kinship, tribal, community and other links from further afield, not to mention anyone else who is interested, especially schoolchildren. It could be a tool for better understanding of the Aboriginal people and their ways with the land. A reconnection with nature. We come to regard it not as a collection of connecting sites, but as a single long-distance place.

And it's a matter of respect. The fact is that we do have a lot to teach each other. During the mission days a very great deal of cultural knowledge was lost, nevertheless, even though a lot was passed down regardless, much can still be recovered from the discussion of historical sources. At the same time, few Aboriginal people nowadays get the chance to go bush the way their parents and grandparents did. It's the same for many other Australians, there are just not enough hours in the day to make the break. You get stuck in town at work, or sitting behind a computer, or doing your homework. We decide an important aim is to see a process in the region by which the Aboriginal people can rediscover closer actual ties with their Country and its nature. Find new ways to deal with the world as it is around us.

Noel Pearson laments how his people of Cape York are losing their culture and languages, along with their distinctiveness:

> The development and possible disappearance of a culture is the product of an enormous number of minute incremental changes in a large number of behaviours and beliefs of the individual members of that culture. I believe we should think of the Aboriginal Australian peoples as a population of individuals, who each have a particular relationship to culture and particular living circumstances ... Aboriginal Australians need to be brutally honest about the threatening demise of Aboriginal culture. We need to face the evidence and be less rhetorical. The cultural survival of Aboriginal Australian peoples does not hinge on declaratory assertions that 'We have always been ...', that 'We will always be ...'[1]

He adds that in a globalised world, the old way of passing down knowledge by word of mouth doesn't work any longer. Disadvantage has deprived people of the means to keep abreast of technological communications. And I agree, it seems to me that Hollywood is displacing the Dreaming.

But Pearson should be thankful for what culture his people in the far north, remote from the big cities, actually do have left; that it was not swamped, crushed, converted, hidden, forbidden, criticised, twisted, misrepresented, overwhelmed and in so many other ways generally denied in the rush to Australia's 'civilisation'. If his people's losses continue, it could eventually put them into a similar position to those of the south-eastern corner of Australia where the culture is not what it was. But even so, a distinct, strong Aboriginal culture survives here. It might not be the culture of old. But it's a culture nonetheless. Or better, it is a number of cultures which are not necessarily in accord. As ever.

We all need to understand our country and its organic nature better.

In too many ways, without 'Country', the Elders appear to be losing their authority over the young. Too many of the older people suffer from obesity, diabetes, kidney failure, heart problems and other ills of the modern lifestyle. Every member of the community is touched by the problems of the few that result from alcoholism, drug addiction, dysfunctionality ... When I try to see Ossie – one of many who don't drink or smoke – he's only too often on his way to another funeral. He laments how there are funerals every few days for Kooris, too often dying before their allotted time of causes attributable somehow to alcohol. It's not just sad, it's tragic.

The Bundian Way today is not only a route to be walked. It is a story composed of many strands that weave together to form a necklace laid over the landscape. New South Wales allows the recognition of Aboriginal Places, kinds of mini-national parks, which are a way of recognising and legally protecting Aboriginal cultural heritage. Under the New South Wales *National Parks and Wildlife Act*, any land may be declared an Aboriginal Place if the area 'is or was of special significance to Aboriginal culture'. And we currently have in progress numerous nominations along the Bundian Way with an aim that these will be like pearls threaded in the necklace, places with the highest values that can be used for education and conservation but especially as places where a story brings Indigenous

Afterword

cultures into focus. Our understanding of the country has many dimensions.[2]

Stories are the most vital way to map the magic of the Bundian Way. Fundamental is the story of Al.mil.gong's new corroboree in 1844. Another is WB Clarke's record of the Bundian Pass. They give the sense of it better than strip maps. How much more interesting to follow the stories?

Accounts from the cusp of settlement, when the traditional lifestyle began to change, enable us to see the stages of colonisation and that final trap of complete dispossession. And by the same token, as the shared history stories unfold over time, we see the resilience of the Aboriginal culture. Other stories reveal themselves in the ways that traditional management has influenced the landscape we see today. The stories also animate landscape in the walker's mind, they show its circumstances through time, and form the impress that can guide its management. They are the key that links past and future. They promise much for the Aboriginal people of the region, especially in the desperate need for cultural healing and learning in Country. As they come together in the Bundian Way, they will also bring recognition, jobs in tourism and natural resource management and new insights for culture-based storytelling. Perhaps most importantly, this can result in better understanding and reconciliation with the broader community.

In following the Bundian Way step by step the stories gradually reveal themselves. Its ever-changing landscapes are illustrated by the stories. They allow other stories to be told. They fix the route in the mind. Your way becomes an odyssey. And so you readily rediscover nature, and respect for it, not by following lines on a map but by becoming part of a greater engagement. You weave your own stories into the necklace. But no matter what part of the route we follow, when I walk it with Aboriginal friends, we invariably find yet another special quality to our way, some new magic. Walking the distances involved becomes less of a chore than a light-hearted movement of the spirit. Indeed, feeds the sensation that the old route somehow sings to us. If by chance we come off-track, I am not sure what sense it is that tells us. Perhaps the heart, perhaps all of the senses in concert. A short backtrack, the lightness returns. We are on track. The songs are in the air and the country makes sense. That is the Bundian Way.

Postscript: Keeping on track

April 2015

To conclude, some details. The Bundian Way goes through the old Bundian lands. It is a shared history pathway between Targangal and Bilgalera that, after surveys with a Koori crew, was entered on the New South Wales Heritage List on 18 January 2013. Both the physical feature and its conceptualisation have demanded exhaustive explorations: they've taken more than 10 years and the overall project is ongoing.

During its early days, the project was all about walking, to search out its route, find its background and make connections. But nowadays there is more to it than simply managing a walking trail. Already it is providing training and employment for Aboriginal people and has become a tourism destination. The young visit for its educational values. People describe its qualities as reawakening, inspirational, healing, a reconciliation. A dedicated Bundian Way Aboriginal Art Gallery has now been operating in Delegate since 2012. Scientific research continues ...

While it is one thing to find the route, it is entirely something else to formalise it as a modern walking track with minimal facilities open to the general public. A steering committee of the region's agencies was formed in 2010 to establish the walking route. Renowned architect Glenn Murcutt is designing the structures. Aboriginal community workers and inmates from correctional centres contribute their labour and find cultural connections in Country. Government funding has helped the Eden Local Aboriginal Land Council construct a high-quality walking trail around Twofold Bay. But many tasks remain, including development of primitive campsites on the open country of the Monaro, completion of a wilderness lodge, updating our website <www.bundianway.com.au> and developing social networking and a volunteer base.

The Bundian Way has come to be an innovative tourism, cultural and shared history project that promises international attention and economic benefits for the wider region. The land council and its partners have worked tirelessly, often on an honorary basis, towards creating 380 kilometres of public infrastructure. Unfortunately, while developments are in progress, the full route cannot be officially opened to the general public. Government support has not been ongoing, and comes on a program by program basis. Volunteers can only achieve so much. And so, more slowly than anyone wants, the momentum builds.

Following Aboriginal footsteps has been such a rich experience for me I feel I now see the land with fresh eyes, as though it opened a doorway on how to truly know Australia. It pointed to connections, highlighted elements that made me sense the power there at the same time as I realised the cultural view is manifold, a phantom that varies, sometimes in major respects, wherever you look. The blessing was to have excellent guides to help me find deeper respect for the many pathways to understanding. It's been tough at times. Would I happily do it all again tomorrow? Well, new ways have opened.

Notes

Epigraph

1. Clark, D (ed), *Baron Charles Von Hügel: New Holland Journal November 1833–October 1834*, Miegunyah Press, Melbourne, 1994, p 420.

Introduction

1. *Historical Records of Australia*, 1924, series 1, Vol 22, Library Committee of the Commonwealth Parliament, Sydney, 1924, pp 649–50.

Part 1: The higher country

1. AW Howitt, *Native Tribes of South-East Australia*, Aboriginal Studies Press, Canberra, 1996, p 35.
2. J Blay, *Trek through the Back Country*, Methuen, Sydney, 1987.
3. Geehi Bushwalking Club, *Snowy Mountains Walks*, 8th ed, Geehi Bushwalking Club, Cooma, p 48.
4. Discussions in AB Costin and DJ Wimbush, 'Trends in vegetation at Kosciuszko', *Australian Journal Botany*, 27(6), 1979; NA Wakefield, 'Bushfire frequency and vegetational change in south east Australian forests', *Victorian Naturalist*, 87(6), 1970; JCG Banks, A history of forest fire in the Australian Alps. In RB Good (ed), Proceedings of first Fenner Conference, Australian Academy of Science, 1989; Dane Wimbush, Bermagui, 2007, personal communication (pers comm).
5. *Recollections of GH Dawson*, 1834–90, with additions from his son, HJ of Rockton, Bombala, A1805, Mitchell Library (ML) MS, Sydney.
6. M Young, *The Aboriginal People of the Monaro*, 2nd ed, Department of Environment and Conservation, New South Wales, Sydney, 2005, pp 245–46. Annual reports of the New South Wales Aborigines Protection Board in *Annual Reports*, in New South Wales, *Votes and Proceedings of the Legislative Assembly*.
7. Young, *The Aboriginal People of the Monaro*, pp 105–09; J Lingard, *A Narrative of the Journey from New South Wales, including a Seven Year Residence in that Country*, Taylor and C, Chapel-en-le Frith, 1846.
8. AW Howitt Papers, Letters to his family 14 January 1866–28 December 1867, MS 9356 Box 1046/2a(3), State Library of Victoria, Melbourne; also Young, *The Aboriginal People of the Monaro*, p 227 (after Phil Boot).
9. Discussion in V Kruta and Australia Felix Literary Club, *Dr John Lhotsky: The*

turbulent Australian writer, naturalist and explorer, Australia Felix Literary Club, Melbourne, 1977; AEJ Andrews, *Earliest Monaro and Burragorang*, Tabletop Press, Canberra, 1998. There has been much debate over who climbed which mountain first.
10. Young, *The Aboriginal People of the Monaro*, pp 226–27, as reported by WB Clarke.
11. Howitt Papers.
12. WB Clarke, Papers and notebooks, 1860, ML, Sydney, p 222.
13. Geehi Bushwalking Club, *Snowy Mountains Walks*, p 97.
14. The Clarke Papers in the ML are the invaluable point of reference, and include his meteorological data.
15. ID Clark (ed), *The Journals of George Augustus Robinson, Chief Protector, Port Phillip Aboriginal Protectorate*, Vol 4, 11 August 1844, Heritage Matters, Clarendon, 2000.
16. Rod Mason, Aboriginal Heritage Officer, NPWS, Jindabyne, 2008, pers comm.
17. See H Selkirk, 'The origins of Canberra', *Journal Royal Australian Historical Society*, 9(2), 1923, p 61.
18. An addendum to his letter of 7 June 1828 to Elliot, Archives Office of New South Wales (AONSW).
19. Mitchell to Survey Staff, 5 September 1829, 4/6908, AONSW.
20. D Clark (trans and ed), *Baron Charles von Hügel: New Holland Journal November 1833–October 1834*, Miegunyah Press, Melbourne, 1994, p 421.
21. Mitchell to Townsend, 6 August 1841, AONSW 4/5429 Reel 2827 and Townsend to Mitchell, 5 October 1842, AONSW and discussion in AEJ Andrews, 'Surveyor Thomas Scott Townsend – his work in Australia 1831 to 1854', *Journal Royal Australian Historical Society*, Vol 79, 1993, pp 156–64.
22. Young, *The Aboriginal People of the Monaro*, pp 93–94 and Felix Mitchell's *Back to Cooma Celebrations*, Back to Cooma Committee, Cooma, 1926. Also WB Clarke, *Researches in the Southern Goldfields of New South Wales*, Reading and Wellbank, Sydney, 1860, p 117 on visiting Kosciuszko and Omeo with Brooks; also generally, Clark, *The Journals of George Augustus Robinson*.
23. Moyangul Parish Map, 2nd ed, 1898, New South Wales Department of Lands, Sydney.
24. Generally, see D Watson, *Caledonia Australis: Scottish highlanders on the Frontier of Australia*, Collins, Sydney, 1984 and Howitt, *Tribes of South-East Australia*; or more on reprisals see M McKenna, *Looking for Blackfellas' Point: An Australian history of place*, UNSW Press, Sydney, 2002.
25. Shirley Foster, Wallaga Lake, 2005, pers comm.
26. Clark, *The Journals of George Augustus Robinson*, p 94.
27. *Magnet*, 25 January 1979.
28. *Bega Times*, 14 February 1979.
29. *Bega Times*, 28 March 1979.
30. McKenna, *Looking for Blackfellas' Point*, pp 175–90.
31. *Bega Times*, 4 April 1979.
32. *Bega Times*, 25 April 1979.
33. B Egloff, N Peterson and S Wesson, Biamanga and Gulaga: Aboriginal Cultural

Association with Biamanga and Gulaga National Parks, Research Report, Office of the Registrar, *Aboriginal Land Rights Act 1983* (NSW), 2005; B Egloff, *Mumbulla Mountain: An anthropological and archaeological investigation*, NPWS, Sydney, 1979.
34. Egloff et al, Biamanga and Gulaga, pp 56–57.
35. Young, *The Aboriginal People of the Monaro*, p 228.
36. Wimbush, Bermagui, 2007, pers comm; D Keith, *Ocean Shores to Desert Dunes: The native vegetation of New South Wales and the Australian Capital Territory*, NPWS, Sydney, 2004.
37. B Ingram, 'Excursion to Willis', *Bombala & District Historical Society*, 26 October 2002, pp 2–3.
38. Ingram, 'Excursion to Willis', pp 2–3; Clive Cottrell, Merambego, 2002, pers comm.
39. Young, *The Aboriginal People of the Monaro*, pp 251, 420 although there are numerous instances.
40. Ingram, 'Excursion to Willis', p 3.
41. Pat Ryan and Barrie Reed, Delegate, 2003, pers comm.
42. AB (Banjo) Paterson, 'The Man from Snowy River', *Bulletin*, Sydney, 26 April 1890, p 13.
43. AW Howitt, 'The eucalypts of Victoria', Transactions of the Royal Society of Victoria, 2, 1890, p 107.
44. J Wright, *Collected Poems*, Angus & Robertson, 1971, p 121.
45. W Howitt, 'Black Thursday – The great bush fire of Victoria', *Cassell's Illustrated Family Paper*, 1(6), 4 February 1854, pp 46–47. See also subsequent issues, 1(8) and 1(9), 18 and 25 February 1854, pp 59, 67.
46. Howitt, 'Black Thursday', 1(6), p 46.
47. Howitt, 'Black Thursday', 1(9), p 67.
48. Howitt, 'Black Thursday', 1(6), p 46.
49. W Howitt, *Land, Labor and Gold; or, Two years in Victoria*, Ticknor and Fields, Boston, 1855, pp 73–74.
50. Howitt, 'Black Thursday', 1(6), also, 1(8), 1(9), 18 and 25 February 1854, pp 46–47, 59, 67.
51. Egloff et al, Biamanga and Gulaga, also Egloff, *Mumbulla Mountain*.
52. AW Howitt, 'Notes on songs and song makers of some Australian tribes', *Journal of the Anthropological Institute*, 16, 1887, Melbourne, pp 327–35. Many details are discussed in DJ Mulvaney, 'The anthropologist as tribal elder', *Mankind*, 7, 1970, pp 205–17.
53. IF Pulsford, Disturbance history, Thesis, Australian National University, Canberra, 1991; IF Pulsford, JCG Banks and L Hodges, Land use history of the white cypress pine forests in the Snowy Valley, Kosciusko National Park, Centre for Resource and Environmental Studies, 1993. In J Dargavel and S Feary (eds), *Australia's Ever Changing Forests II*, Proceedings of the Second National Conference on Australian Forest History, Ch 7.

Part 2: The Monaro

1. Pastor Doug Nicholls (Sir Douglas), from a sermon he gave at his church in Gore Street, Northcote, Victoria in ABC, 'Bloodlines: The Nicholls Family', *Message Stick*, 19 September 2010, <www.abc.net.au/tv/messagestick/stories/s3014566.htm> (accessed March 2015).
2. RH Mathews, 'Ethnological notes on the Aboriginal tribes of New South Wales and Victoria', *Journal and Proceedings of the Royal Society of New South Wales*, 38, 1904, pp 350–51.
3. R Mason, 'Dyillagamberra – the local rainmaker', NSW Department of Environment and Climate Change, *Resort Roundup*, Issue 25, Winter 2007, <www.environment.nsw.gov.au/parkmanagement/ResortRoundup25.bak.htm> (accessed March 2015).
4. Travels with the *Town and Country*'s special correspondent who visited the South Monaro in 1872 in *Bombala & District Historical Society*, 20(4), February 2008, p 12.
5. Much of this is reflected in a series of articles by SA Elliott in the *Bombala Times*, 1946, also in WK Hancock, *Discovering Monaro: A study of man's impact on his environment*, Cambridge University Press, Cambridge, 1972 and in the works of AB Costin, especially *A Study of the Ecosystems of the Monaro Region of New South Wales*, CSIRO Publishing, Melbourne, 1954 with special reference to soil erosion.
6. *Historical Records of Australia*, Vol 26, Series 1, pp 224–25.
7. Charles Darwin to Howitt, in MH Walker, *Come Wind, Come Weather; A biography of Alfred Howitt*, Melbourne University Press, Carlton, 1971, p 221.
8. L Fison and AW Howitt, Kamilaroi and Kurnai: Group-marriage and relationship, and marriage by elopement: drawn chiefly from the usage of the Australian Aborigines: also the *Kurnai tribe, their customs in peace and war*, G Robertson, Melbourne, 1880, <https://archive.org/details/kamilaroikurnaig00fiso> (accessed March 2015).
9. These documents are reproduced in full in Young, *The Aboriginal People of the Monaro*, pp 338–55.
10. Young, *The Aboriginal People of the Monaro*, pp 338–55.
11. Young, *The Aboriginal People of the Monaro*, pp 338–55.
12. Young, *The Aboriginal People of the Monaro*, pp 90–91; MJ Currie, Journey southward of Lake George. In B Field (ed), *Geographical Memoirs of New South Wales*, John Murray, London, 1825.
13. W Clark, Journal, Reprinted from the *Asiatic Calcutta*, 27 December 1797, 10 January 1798, *Historical Records of New South Wales 1797–98, 1893–1901*. See also discussion in M Nash, *Cargo for the Colony; The wreck of the merchant ship, Sydney Cove (1797)*, Braxus Press, Sydney, 1996, pp 13–14, 41–42. AEJ Andrews discusses early settlement on the Monaro in *Earliest Monaro and Burragorang*, Tabletop Press, Canberra, 1998, pp 94–102.
14. J Kerr and H Falkus, *From Sydney Cove to Duntroon: A family album of early life in Australia*, Hutchinson, Sydney, 1982, pp 12–15.
15. *Bombala & District Historical Society*, 20(4), February 2008, p 12.
16. The theme of the Highlanders and the Aboriginal people is thoroughly

explored in Watson, *Caledonia Australis*, 1984.
17. Hancock, *Discovering Monaro*, pp 66–71.
18. G Dunderdale, *The Book of the Bush*, Ward, Lock & Co, c 1870, p 266, <http://gutenberg.net.au/ebooks/e00014.html> (accessed March 2015).
19. Young, *The Aboriginal People of the Monaro*, p 224 and in Clark (ed), *The Journals of George Augustus Robinson*, Vol 4, 9 September 1844.
20. Clark (ed), *The Journals of George Augustus Robinson*, Vol 4, 25 August 1844, p 158.
21. Ryrie journals, Dixon Library, Sydney, pp 8–18 cited in Young, *The Aboriginal People of the Monaro*, pp 203–04.
22. J Lambie, Itineraries Moneroo District, X85, 1839–47, AONSW, Maneroo, 14 January 1842. In Young, *The Aboriginal People of the Monaro*, pp 152–53.
23. *Historical Records of Australia*, Vol 26, Series 1, pp 224–25.
24. Henry Haygarth's 1848 *Recollections on Bush Life in Australia* quoted in Young, *The Aboriginal People of the Monaro*, p 114.
25. On koalas, Te Whare, *A Bush Cinema: Made in Australia*, Carters, Sydney, 1922, p 9. On bustards, Bishop Broughton journal, 11 February 1845. In Kerr and Falkus, *From Sydney Cove to Duntroon*; Lingard's report on waterfowl and animals from Young, *The Aboriginal People of the Monaro*, pp 131–32.
26. C Harpur, 'The Kangaroo Hunt', holograph MS 14, ML, Sydney, pp 125/108. The original poem is reproduced by the National Library, Trove, 28 July 1860 <http://trove.nla.gov.au/ndp/del/article/72484741> (accessed March 2015).
27. Harpur, 'The Kangaroo Hunt', pp 125/108, 142–43/125–26.
28. Young, *The Aboriginal People of the Monaro*, pp 247–48; Monaro census information attached to reports of the Aboriginal Protection Board (APB).
29. AW Manning, who replaced Lambie, reported from the Crown Lands Office Maneroo, Pambula on 6 January 1855: Young, *The Aboriginal People of the Monaro*, pp 171–72.
30. A McFarland, *Illawarra and Monaro*, W Maddock, Sydney, 1872, p 113 quoted in Young, *The Aboriginal People of the Monaro*, p 229.
31. AGL Shaw on economic history in *Australian Encyclopaedia*, Vol 3, pp 334–38 generally as to the times. Work on Delegate station: Peter Jeffreys, Delegate, 2010, pers comm.
32. For more on Robinson's role and duties, see Clark (ed), *The Journals of George Augustus Robinson*, Vol 1, pp vii–xiv.
33. Egloff et al, Biamanga and Gulaga, pp 31–37 and Young, *The Aboriginal People of the Monaro*, pp 84–86.
34. *Bairnsdale Advertiser* and *Omeo and Tambo Chronicle*, 14 May 1910. In Young, *The Aboriginal People of the Monaro*, p 392 per John O'Rourke JP in 1910.
35. All extracts and details in this chapter are selected from the New South Wales APB Reports published in Young, *The Aboriginal People of the Monaro*, pp 281–92; copies are held at State Records Authority of NSW and at the Australian Institute of Aboriginal and Torres Strait Islander Studies (AIATSIS) in Canberra. The National Library of Australia is digitising the collection <http://nla.gov.au/nla.aus-vn1447508> (accessed March 2015).
36. Young, *The Aboriginal People of the Monaro*, p 281.

37. Young, *The Aboriginal People of the Monaro*, pp 281–82.
38. Young, *The Aboriginal People of the Monaro*, p 286.
39. Young, *The Aboriginal People of the Monaro*, pp 289, 297.
40. Young, *The Aboriginal People of the Monaro*, p 290.
41. Young, *The Aboriginal People of the Monaro*, p 292.
42. Young, *The Aboriginal People of the Monaro*, p 292.
43. Young, *The Aboriginal People of the Monaro*, pp 281–99. Original documents are at AONSW: Letters received 7/3644; Minutes, AIATSIS Reel MF 229; Letters sent, AONSW 4/7128; Expenditures, AONSW 7/3643, Reel 1851.
44. Dunderdale, *The Book of the Bush*, pp 268–69.
45. Michael Smithson quoted in Young, *The Aboriginal People of the Monaro*, p 44. Other historians like Bob Reece, also quoted, have considered the problem in detail.
46. Egloff et al, Biamanga and Gulaga, pp 44–49. The report cites *Royal Commission On the Aborigines*, John Ferres, Government Printer, Melbourne, 1877 and Clive's letter to Howitt, 5 December 1881.
47. Oral history for Bundian Way project, 2008. For more on families of Delegate see Young, *The Aboriginal People of the Monaro*, pp 281–305, 409–23.
48. Egloff at al, Biamanga and Gulaga, p 45 in a tape recorded by Janet Mathews, a relative of RH Mathews, and held in the AIATSIS archives.
49. Egloff at al, Biamanga and Gulaga, pp 45–46 and further information from oral histories by Sue Norman, 1986, AIATSIS archives.
50. Oral history Bundian Way project, 2008. For more on the families of Delegate see Egloff at al, Biamanga and Gulaga, pp 44–49 and Young, *The Aboriginal People of the Monaro*, pp 409–23.
51. Stewart Ryrie; Journal of a tour in the southern mountains, ML, Sydney, 1840, transcribed by Bredbo Landcare Group, 1995, pp 46–49.
52. *Bombala & District Historical Society*, 20(4), February 2008, p 12.
53. Stewart Ryrie, pp 50–52.
54. Clarke, *Researches in the Southern Goldfields of New South Wales*, p 202.
55. 'A trip to Genoa and Lake Malagoota', *Bega Gazette*, 30 April 1884, cited in *Bega District Historical Society Newsletter*, 14(6), May 2002, pp 6–7.
56. Stewart Ryrie, pp 46–47.
57. D Lunney and T Leary, 'The impact on native mammals of land-use changes and exotic species in the Bega district, New South Wales, since settlement', *Australian Journal of Ecology*, 13, 1988, pp 73–74.
58. I am indebted to Dave Hope, brother of poet AD Hope and first ranger in Nadgee Nature Reserve, who gave me the kernel of the story. More details are recounted in M Devine, *A Dissertation on the History of Wonboyn Lake, including the Nadgee and Narrabarba to 1960*, Unpublished, 2005, pp 19, 22, 30, 33, 45. Other particulars were sourced from Parish Map for Hayden, 1st ed, 26 August 1889 and Parish Map for Narrabarba, 2nd ed, 1910.
59. Most of this information comes from the early edition parish and county maps.
60. Gordon Platts, Bombala and Menlo Park, 10 and 11 August 2009, pers comm.
61. RD Fitzgerald, *Australian Orchids*, Government Printer, Sydney, Vol 1, Pt 1

1875, Pt 3 1877, Pt 4 1878, Pt 7 1882.
62. *Bombala & District Historical Society*, 8(9), August 2006, p 8.
63. Eden Local Aboriginal Land Council has a Yamfields Research Project and a Women's Business Project called AWAY, see also A Blackburn, J Blay and A Dorrough, AWAY on the Bundian Way. In N Williams, A Marshall, J Morgan (eds), *Land of Sweeping Plains: Managing and restoring the native grasslands of south-eastern Australia*, CSIRO Publishing, Sydney, 2014, pp 14–15.
64. Clarke, *Researches in the Southern Goldfields of New South Wales*, pp 174–83.
65. Clarke, *Researches in the Southern Goldfields of New South Wales*, pp 177–84.
66. Clarke, *Researches in the Southern Goldfields of New South Wales*, pp 197–98.
67. Clark (ed), *The Journals of George Augustus Robinson*, Vol 4, 13 July 1844, p 118.
68. Ryrie journal, 11 June–30 July 1840, 7 July 1840, reproduced in Stewart Ryrie, pp 23–24. The Ryrie map is at AONSW M.3b.1170, Sheet 19 and M.3c.1170, Sheets 16 and 17. See also the early parish maps which provide details of the various landholdings.
69. Keith Brownlie, Harold Farrell and Neil Platts, Bombala, 2003, pers comm; Bondi Parish Map, 1905, Land and Water Conservation, NSW, 102670.
70. Harold Farrell and Neil Platts, Bombala, 2003, pers comm.
71. Clark (ed), *The Journals of George Augustus Robinson*, Vol 4, 12 August 1844, p 143.
72. Clark (ed), *The Journals of George Augustus Robinson*, Vol 4, 13 July 1844, p 118.
73. Clark (ed), *The Journals of George Augustus Robinson*, Vol 4, 11 August 1844, p 145.
74. Clark (ed), *The Journals of George Augustus Robinson*, Vol 4, 14 August 1844, pp 147–49.
75. Clark (ed), *The Journals of George Augustus Robinson*, Vol 4, 30 August 1844, p 166.
76. Clark (ed), *The Journals of George Augustus Robinson*, Vol 4, 26 August 1844, pp 161–62.
77. Clarke, *Researches in the Southern Goldfields of New South Wales*, p 202.
78. Howitt, *Native Tribes of South-East Australia*, pp 80–81.
79. Young, *The Aboriginal People of the Monaro*, p 351 citing Howitt's drafts for *Native Tribes of South-East Australia*.
80. AP Elkin, 'RH Mathews: His contribution to Aboriginal Studies: Part II', *Oceania*, 46(2), 1975, p 132.
81. RH Mathews, 'Language of the Birdhawal tribe, in Gippsland, Victoria', *Proceedings of the American Philosophical Society*, 46(187), October–December 1907, p 346.
82. See generally Howitt, *Native Tribes of South-East Australia*, pp 616–42, but especially the early pages and pp 640–41 re sharing the ceremonies across tribes.
83. The South Australian Museum quotes Norman Tindale's original work of 1940 and the 1974 revisions, regarding the Bidawal on its website at <http://archives.samuseum.sa.gov.au/tindaletribes/bidawal.htm> (accessed March 2015). AIATSIS publish the widely distributed Aboriginal Australia wall map with a 'Disclaimer: This map indicates only the general location of larger groupings of people, which may include smaller groups such as clans, dialects

or individual languages in a group. The boundaries are not intended to be exact ...' See <http://aiatsis.gov.au/explore/culture/topic/aboriginal-australia-map> (accessed March 2015).

Part 3: The coast

1. OW Brierly, 'Wanderer' journal of voyage from Plymouth to New South Wales 1841–43, Journal ML A528.
2. T Mead, *Killers of Eden*, Angus & Robertson, Sydney, 1961 (cover).
3. *Davidson Whaling Station Historic Site Management Plan*, NPWS, p 257; Elsie Severs, Eden, 11 March 2003, pers comm.
4. OW Brierly, Papers relating to Twofold Bay, 1842–47, Abstracts, P 151741, Sydney, 4 September 1842, ML A, CY 1067.
5. W Hirst, *Upon a Painted Ocean: Sir Oswald Brierly*, ML A, Catalogue, 2004–05, pp 1–3.
6. OW Brierly, *'Wanderer' Sketches*, 1833–42, ML A, PX*D 71, p 20.
7. OW Brierly, Journal of a visit to Monaro and Twofold Bay, 1842–43, ML A 537, CY 1067.
8. Brierly, Journal of a visit to Monaro and Twofold Bay, pp 135–40.
9. Brierly, Papers relating to Twofold Bay, 1842–47.
10. Brierly, Papers relating to Twofold Bay, 1842–47.
11. Brierly, 'Wanderer' journal of voyage from Plymouth to NSW 1841–43, p 6.
12. Brierly, Papers relating to Twofold Bay, 1842–47.
13. Brierly, Papers relating to Twofold Bay, 1842–47.
14. Brierly, Papers relating to Twofold Bay, 1842–47.
15. Brierly, Papers relating to Twofold Bay, 1842–47.
16. Clark (ed), *The Journals of George Augustus Robinson*, Vol 4, p 175.
17. Clark (ed), *The Journals of George Augustus Robinson*, Vol 4, p 172.
18. Clark (trans and ed), *Baron Charles von Hügel*, pp 319–22.
19. V Jurskis, 'Decline of eucalypt forests as a consequence of unnatural fire regimes', *Australian Forestry*, 68(4), 2005, pp 257–62.
20. AW Howitt, Unpublished papers quoted in Egloff et al, Biamanga and Gulaga, p 53.
21. D Green, G Singh, H Polach, D Moss, J Banks and EA Geissler, 'A fine-resolution palaeoecology and palaeoclimatology from south-eastern Australia', *Journal of Ecology*, 1988, 76, pp 790–806 and G Hope, G Singh and E Geissler, L Glover and D O'Dea, A detailed Pleistocene-Holocene vegetation record from Bega Swamp, southern New South Wales. In J Magee and C Craven (eds), Quaternary Studies Meeting, Regional analysis of Australian Quaternary Studies: strengths, gaps and future directions, Department of Geology, Australian National University, Canberra, 2000, pp 48–50.
22. B Gammage, *The Biggest Estate on Earth: How Aborigines made Australia*, Allen & Unwin, Sydney, 2011.
23. Burnum Burnum, *Aboriginal Australia*, Angus & Robertson, Sydney, 1988, p 318 and the story is Percy Mumbler's, collected by Roland Robinson, and first published in *The Nearest the White Man Gets: Aboriginal narratives and poems of New*

South Wales, Hale & Iremonger, Sydney, 1989, and more recently in Robinson's *The Whalers*, Angus & Robertson, Sydney, 1997, p 16.

24. R Robinson, *Black-Feller – White-Feller*, Angus & Robertson, Sydney, 1958, pp 143–44, and also arranged as verse in Robinson *The Nearest the White Man Gets*, pp 23–24 and in Robinson's *The Whalers*, pp 24–30.
25. Biamanga's quote comes from Te Whare, *A Bush Cinema: Made in Australia*, Carters Printing Works, Sydney, 1922, pp 46–47 (with picture) and additional material from A Bickford, S Blair, and P Freeman, *Ben Boyd National Park Bicentennial Project*, NPWS, Sydney, 1988 and more generally in Mead, *Killers of Eden*, and Brierly diaries, 14 September 1844.
26. RH Mathews, 'Ethnological notes on the Aboriginal tribes of New South Wales and Victoria', *Journal and Proceedings of the Royal Society of New South Wales*, Vol 38, 1904, pp 252–53.
27. S Wesson, *An Aboriginal Whaling History Project*, NPWS, Sydney, p 26.
28. AW Manning of Crown Lands Office, 31 January 1853, ML A1263, CY 1949.
29. For the blanket return and census details, see quotes from Imlay in EJ Wakefield, *Adventure in New Zealand 1839–1844*, Da Capo Press, Amsterdam, 1971, Vol 2, pp 187–88.
30. Clark (ed), *The Journals of George Augustus Robinson*, Vol 4, 14 August 1844, p 147.
31. Clark (ed), *The Journals of George Augustus Robinson*, Vol 4, p 152.
32. Clark (ed), *The Journals of George Augustus Robinson*, Vol 4, 14 August 1844, pp 150, 145–52.
33. Brierly, Papers relating to Twofold Bay, 1842–47. The Mitchell Library holds various Brierly journals, often one version written immediately as a draft and a more polished second version with more information.
34. Brierly, Papers relating to Twofold Bay, 1842–47.
35. Clark (ed), *The Journals of George Augustus Robinson*, Vol 4, 17 July 1844, p 150, 14 August 1844, pp 147–48.
36. Brierly, Journal of a visit to Monaro and Twofold Bay, 1842–43, ML A 537, CY 1067, pp 0135–40.
37. Brierly, Journal of a visit to Monaro and Twofold Bay, 1842–43, ML A 537, CY 1067, CY 1070
38. Survey of part of a road between Monaroo and Twofold Bay 1845, AONSW, M.73.831.
39. F MacCabe, Field note book, AONSW, 595, pp 91–95.
40. I McBryde, Report on the Greenstone hatchet head from Towamba River, ANU, Canberra, 2007, pp 2–5, and more generally in I McBryde, 'Kulin greenstone quarries: The social contexts of production and distribution for the Mt William site', *World Archaeology*, 16(2), 1984.
41. Wesson, *An Aboriginal Whaling History Project*, p 26.
42. TS Townsend's letter from Camp Coolringdon to Mitchell, 19 October 1842, AONSW 42/65, pp 396–98.
43. AEJ Andrews, 'Surveyor TS Townsend and his work in Australia 1831–54', *Journal of the Royal Australian Historical Society*, 79, Pts 3, 4, 1993, pp 163, 166–68; TS Townsend's correspondence generally in AONSW.

44. Hancock, *Discovering Monaro*, p 41.
45. See generally M McLeod, *Leaving Scotland*, National Museums of Scotland, Edinburgh, 1996; M Plant, *The Domestic Life of Scotland in the 18th Century*, Edinburgh University Press, Edinburgh, 1952.
46. HP Wellings, *The Imlay Brothers (Peter, Alexander and George Imlay)*, DS Ford Printers, Sydney, 1985, p 3; *Australian Encyclopaedia*, Vol 5, p 65.
47. The list of properties is from Wellings, *The Imlay Brothers*, p 6, description of Bigga from *Australian Encyclopaedia*, Vol 5, p 65.
48. J Lingard, *A Narrative of the Journey to and from New South Wales*, J Taylor, Chapel-en-le-Frith, 1846, p 70.
49. Genoa Town Committee, P Allard and G Alves (eds), *Border Tales: Stories from Genoa, Wangarabell, Wroxham, Timbillica, Maramingo, Nungatta, Wingan and Gipsy Point*, Genoa Town Committee, 2000, p 15.
50. CMH Clark, *A History of Australia*, Vol III, Melbourne University Press, Melbourne, 1973, p 178; F Webb, *Collected Poems*, Angus & Robertson, Sydney, 1969, p 20.
51. Brierly, Papers relating to Twofold Bay, 1842–47, ML A 537, CY Reel 1067; J Loney, *The Seahorse Inn*, Marine History Publications, Portarlington, 1986, p 7 and my own inspections.
52. Hancock, *Discovering Monaro*, pp 46, 48.
53. *Sydney Morning Herald*, 2 December 1854, p 11.
54. A Weatherhead, *Leaves from My Life*, Eden Museum, Eden, 1988, p 27.
55. Weatherhead, *Leaves from My Life*, pp 2, 27; J Lambie, Itineraries Moneroo District, X85, 1839–47, 8 October 1839, AONSW, p 4.
56. Weatherhead, *Leaves from My Life*, also MacCabe, Survey field books, AONSW, 586, pp 105, 162 and Lambie's Itineraries Moneroo District, 9 October 1839, p 4, 16 November 1840, p 22.
57. Clark (ed), *The Journals of George Augustus Robinson*, Vol 4, 21 July 1844, p 124.
58. Clark (ed), *The Journals of George Augustus Robinson*, Vol 4, 22 July 1844, pp 125, 143.
59. Weatherhead, *Leaves from My Life*, p 36 and J Winters, *Nungatta South*, NPWS, Sydney, 2001, pp 15–17.
60. Genoa Town Committee, *Border Tales*.
61. Weatherhead, *Leaves from My Life*, pp 48, 49.
62. Weatherhead, *Leaves from My Life*, p 48.
63. M McKenna, *Looking for Blackfellas' Point: An Australian history of place*, UNSW Press, Sydney, 2002, p 42; Keith Brownlie, Bombala, 2005, pers comm.
64. Young, *The Aboriginal People of the Monaro*, pp 393–96.
65. Young, *The Aboriginal People of the Monaro*, pp 393–96; HP Wellings, 'Tailing stock on the Monaro fifty years ago', *Bombala Times*, 1 July 1932.
66. R Robinson, 'Aboriginal tales from Wallaga Lake Mission', *The Bulletin*, 18 September 1957, p 2, and in another form in *Black-Feller – White-Feller*, pp 143–44, and also arranged as verse in *The Nearest the White Man Gets*, pp 23–44.
67. Winters, *Nungatta South*, p 25.
68. EJ Wakefield reported his excitement and findings in 'Genoa River ramble',

The Educational Magazine, 11(8), September 1954. The Bega correspondence is detailed in McKenna, *Looking for Blackfellas' Point*, p 109.
69. G Mosley and A Costin, World Heritage values and their protection in far south east New South Wales, Report to the Earth Foundation Australia, 1992, pp 34–36.
70. Mosley and Costin, World Heritage values and their protection in far south east New South Wales, pp 34–36.

Afterword

1. N Pearson, 'A people's survival', *The Australian*, 3 October 2009.
2. New South Wales Government, Office of Environment and Heritage, 'Declaration of Aboriginal Places in New South Wales', 22 May 2013, <www.environment.nsw.gov.au/conservation/AboriginalPlacesNSW.htm> (accessed March 2015).

Notes on terminology

Some of the words used in the book – people, places, plants, animals and such – are gathered here. The resulting miscellanea or rat's nest might give context to some usages I came across during my search.

At one time the same word might refer to an area, the people, the place, or the administrative region only to be replaced, before long, by another with a different meaning. Aboriginal words were often adopted, then changed, given simplified spellings. The playfulness of the old spoken languages, their richness of wit and poetical usage, have not gone. Many examples survive, for example the gently rounded, undulating downs of the Monaro's treeless plains were said to resemble (and take their name/meaning from) womanly shapes and breasts.

Aboriginal society had meaningful names for everything in the landscape, and yet some features like plants and rivers could have numerous names. Each served its purpose. In the hope that we will take on some of that complexity in our day-to-day understanding of the country, I have preferred to use the old words.

Antechinus A small carnivorous marsupial, acrobatic, quick and cheeky. A number of species found along Bundian Way. Sometimes mistaken for a large mouse.

Arabul Little ravens, well-fattened from dining on bogongs, were prized game.

Artefacts Anything made or modified by people, usually from fine-grained rocks such as quartz, quartzite, silcrete, rhyolite and chert by percussion flaking or grinding, including debris. Stone axe heads or hatchets and flakes most common examples along route. Chisels, saws, knives, spear points, food preparation utensils, mortars and pestles and grindstones have everyday and ceremonial uses. Some tools help make nets, baskets, and other implements or are used in woodworking or set into handles and used as axes. Walkers are asked to leave them where they are.

Balawan, Boolone, Bolloon, Ballun, Mount Imlay A mountain of significance.

Beermuna, Beemere Old district and lagoon, at site of modern day Boydtown.

Bega, Bicker, Bigga A river, district, town and administrative centre.

Bemm, Ben, Bane A river and district in East Gippsland.

Bidawal, Birdhawal, Birtowall, Bidwell, Bidwill, Bidwelli, Biduelli, Beddiwell, Maap A tribe or people of East Gippsland.

Bilgalera, Fisheries Beach A small bay on Turamullerer, beach, inlet and flats with fresh water, host to cultural gatherings.

Boondi, Bundi, Bondi The popular word for a wooden club or nulla nulla.

Budginbro, Budgunburra, Pidjinboro Oswald Brierly's friend also known as Toby, Toby the King or Toby Blue.
Bulda, Brodribb River, Bidwelli River A river of Gippsland.
Bunan A special ceremony and site often marked by one or more circles on the ground.
Bundian, Boondiang, Bondi, Bondia, Bundy, Pundang, Pone de ang, Pone-di-ang, Pandeang, Rockton A district round the south-eastern Monaro and headwaters of the Genoa River, sometimes with -mittong, referring to the Aboriginal people who lived there.
Burragate, Puragete, Parrokeet A small township, Towamba River.
Cann, Karn A district and river south of Mallacoota.
Cathcart, Talaqueong, Talequong, Hibbert's Inn Flats on tablelands near Dragon Swamp, stop-over near eastern limits of the Monaro.
Coolamon A bark or wooden bowl for carrying all manner of things.
Cooma, Coomer, Kuma The central administrative and business hub of the Monaro.
Corrowong, Corrowang, Carawang, Currawong, Kurrabong, Currawang Plains lying between the Snowy and Tingaringy. Hosted a large Aboriginal population and a prosperous station.
Delegate, Dilliget, Delaget, Dziliket Site of Delegate station and the township beside the Delegate River.
Dollikio, Talequong See *Cathcart*.
Dyillagamberra, Djilligambera, Jillicambra, the water-bringer, the spring-maker, the rain-maker Aboriginal Dreamtime character often associated with the area between high country and the Tuross River.
Feldmark Community of dwarf prostrate plants growing on stony wind-exposed, regularly snow-covered sites of the higher country.

Gelantipy, Calantaba Plateau near Wulgulmerang and the Snowy in northern Victoria.

Genoa, Tinnoor, Jinnoor, Tinnoorer, Tin moor Name of river and district at head of Mallacoota Inlet west of Cape Howe, also its people (Tinnoorermittong, Tin moor mit tong).

Gulgin, Calkin, Bare Hill Hill, district and flats at far south-east of the Monaro.

Kiah, Kiar Inlet, district of southern Twofold Bay, East Boyd.

Maharatta, Maratta, Mahratta, Mo.rat.ter A station near Bombala on the south-eastern Monaro.

Mallacoota, Mal lo koter, Mal.lo.ko.tan Inlet district and people on coast south of Cape Howe.

Maneroo See *Monaro*.

Midden Contains principally shellfish remains, as well as bones, charcoal, tools and such. Very common around Twofold Bay, less common inland.

Mittong, Mit tong People, tribe, clan, mob, family group of a place.

Monaro, Monaroo, Maneroo, Manaro, Maniera, Minara, Monera, Maneiro, Meneiro, Meneru, Miniera, Monera, Manera, Treeless Plains In early days signified the place, a changing administrative region and its people; the often treeless plains of the tablelands south of Queanbeyan or Michelago.

Montane Usually relating to plant communities of the mountains and plateaux at an elevation of about 600–1500 metres.

Mount Imlay See *Balawan*.

Moyangul, The Pinch, Nine Mile Pinch Where the Moyangul River meets Nurudj Djurung.

Mur-rowra, Mo.arer Shown as the Esquire of Bundyang by Oswald Brierly. Perhaps also the man known as Moo.ro.rare.rer or Tommy.

Ngarigo, Ngarigu, Monaroo, Maneroo, Ngarego, Ngarago, Garego, Ngarrugu, Ngarroogoo, Nguramal A language, people and place. Would include the Bombala tribe, Menero tribe, Cooma tribe and so forth.

Nungatta, Nangutta, Nan.gut.er A large grassy bowl in the mountain range between the Monaro, Towamba and Wangarabel about 50 kilometres inland of Green Cape.

Nurudj Djurung Lower Snowy River.

Pambulla, Panbuller Place including Pambula Lake and Inlet.

Pinch See *Moyangul*.

Pone de ang, Pone-di-ang, Pandeang A place south-east of Monaro and head Genoa River catchment, the people sometimes referred to as Pone.di.ang.mittong. See *Bundian*.

Pyender Aboriginal people of the forests who lived by climbing trees, usually after possums, from 'pyen' the word for tomahawk.

Ribbony gum, ribbon gum, manna gum *Eucalyptus viminalis*. I call the more rounded form of the tablelands 'ribbony gum' and the tall forest form with its straight white trunk and long strips of bark 'ribbon gum'.

Sacred sites Aboriginal sites that can include mountains, burial grounds, places for ceremonies, increase centres, Dreaming sites and so forth.

Scar or scarred trees Result from the deliberate removal of bark or wood by Aboriginal people. Used for construction of shelters, watercraft (such as canoes) and containers (such as coolamons) or for carving, artefact manufacture, and to aid climbing. Bark was commonly taken in forested parts. Most scarred trees are now well over 100 years old and are disappearing rapidly as they decay with age and die, or burn in fires.

Suggan Buggan, Toonginbooka, Suganbooka, Sugganbooka River and district near the New South Wales–Victoria border.

Talequong See Cathcart.

Teatree Mostly burgan (*Kunzea ericoides*), an invasive species. But also many other *Leptospermum* species along the walk.

Thaua, Thauaira, Dhawa, Daura, Thawa Language and people of Twofold Bay, from about Mallacoota to Merimbula and inland to the eastern Monaro, of the Yuin-Djuin people.

Timbillica, Toombillicer A hill and district beside Wallagaraugh River.

Tingaringy, Dingoringy, Tzingeringy, Dingayringo, Tingi Ringi, Jingo Ringo An important mountain, also spelled many other ways.

Toanho The extensive rock platform and seafood resource adjacent to Bilgalera.

Towamba, Tuamba, Sturt Township on the Towamba River also sometimes described as being on the Kiah or Kiarr River (which usually now refers to the mouth of the river at Kiah Inlet beside Davidson Whaling Station).

Treeless Plains Grasslands of basalt soils where eucalypts and other trees have not as yet naturally grown. They occupy a smaller area than the geographical Monaro region which has numerous other generally treeless plains that vary in extent.

Trerbulender Dead whales recognised by the old Thaua people.

Turamullerer, Turembulerer, Tullumullerer, Thauamullara Southern part of the Twofold Bay between Eden's Lookout Point and Red Point. The other, northernmost part of the double bay is Calle Calle.

Wallagaraugh, Wollokorar, Wollergrar, Wollagerrar The river that runs from near Nungatta into Mallacoota Inlet.

Wangarabell, Wongererbul, Wangrabell, Wongererbil A district about 20 kilometres north-west of Genoa on the Genoa River.

Wiacon, Waokoon, Wecoon, Cattle Bay A place and people west of Snug Cove and Eden Port.

Wulgulmerang A plateau near Gelantipy and the Snowy in the north of Victoria.

Yam daisy, nyamin, garngeg, murrnong, myrrnong, mewan, minngar, native dandelion A variable species formerly *Microseris lanceolata* with an edible tuber and *M. scapigera* (alpine murnong) with its more fibrous but still edible root. Genus undergoing revision and known as *Microseris* spp. Numerous Aboriginal names probably distinguished between different forms.

Bibliography

Andrews, AEJ, *Earliest Monaro and Burragorang*, Tabletop Press, Canberra, 1998

Andrews, AEJ and Wakefield, N (eds), *Dr John Lhotsky: The turbulent Australian writer naturalist and explorer*, Australia Felix Literary Club, Melbourne, 1977

Banks, JCG, A history of forest fire in the Australian Alps. In Good, RB (ed), Proceedings of first Fenner Conference, Australian Academy of Science, 1989, pp 265–80

—— Fire and stand histories. In Jacoby, GC (ed), *Ecological Aspects of Tree Rings*, Columbia University Press, New York, 1987, pp 163–74

Bayley, WA, *The Story of the Settlement and Development of Bega*, Brooks, Sydney, 1942

Bennett, G, *Wanderings in New South Wales*, Vol 1, Richard Bentley, London, 1834

Bickford, A, Blair, S and Freeman, P, *Ben Boyd National Park Bicentennial Project*, National Parks and Wildlife Service (NPWS), Sydney, 1988

Blackburn, A, Blay, J and Dorrough A, AWAY on the Bundian Way. In Williams, N, Marshall, A and Morgan, J (eds), *Land of Sweeping Plains: Managing and restoring the native grasslands of south-eastern Australia*, CSIRO Publishing, Sydney, 2014

Blay, J, *Trek through the Back Country*, Methuen, Sydney, 1986

—— Tapes with Guboo Ted Thomas, Bermagui Oral History Project, National Library of Australia (NLA), 1973–75

—— *Bega Valley Region Old Path Ways and Trails Mapping Project*, Bega Valley Regional Aboriginal Heritage Study, NPWS, Sydney, and Bega Valley Shire Council (BVSC), Bega, 2005

Blay, J and Cruse, BJ, *Eden Region Old Path Ways and Trails Mapping Project*, Bega Valley Regional Aboriginal Heritage Study, NPWS, Sydney and BVSC, Bega 2004

Bonyhady, T and Griffiths, T (eds), *Words for Country: Landscape and language in Australia*, UNSW Press, Sydney, 2002

Brierly, OWB, Papers relating to Twofold Bay, 1842–47, Mitchell Library, Sydney

Burnum Burnum, *Aboriginal Australia*, Angus & Robertson, Sydney, 1988

Byrne, D and Smith, L, Cultural Resource Overview: Aboriginal sites in the south-east region, Report to the NPWS (NSW) and the Australian Heritage Commission, 1988

Chisolm, AH (ed), *Australian Encyclopaedia*, Grolier Society of Australia, Sydney, 1965

Chittick, L and Fox, T, *Travelling with Percy: A south coast journey*, Aboriginal Studies Press, Canberra, 1997

Clark, D (trans and ed), *Baron Charles von Hügel: New Holland Journal November 1833–October 1834*, Miegunyah Press, Melbourne, 1994

Clark, ID (ed), *The Journals of George Augustus Robinson, Chief Protector, Port Phillip Aboriginal Protectorate*, Vol 4, 1 January 1844–24 October 1845, Heritage Matters, Clarendon, 2000

Clark, W, Journal, Reprinted from the *Asiatic Calcutta*, 27 December 1797, 10 January 1798, *Historical Records of New South Wales 1797–98, 1893–1901*

Clarke, WB, Papers and notebooks, 1827–1951, Mitchell Library, Sydney

— Gold localities in the basins of the Snowy River and upper Murrumbidgee, 1851–52, Mitchell Library, Sydney

— *Researches in the Southern Goldfields of New South Wales*, Reading and Wellbank, Sydney, 1860

Clarke, WB and Moyal, A (ed), *The Web of Science: The scientific correspondence of the Rev WB Clarke, Australia's pioneer geologist*, Australian Scholarly Publishing, Kew, 2003

Clery, K, *The Forgotten Corner Interviews*, Eden Killer Whale Museum, Eden, 2000

Clode, D, *Killers in Eden*, CD documentary, ABCTV, 2005, <www.abccommercial.com/librarysales/program/killers-eden> (accessed March 2015)

—— *Killers in Eden*, Allen & Unwin, Sydney, 2002

Costermans, L, *Native Trees and Shrubs of South-Eastern Australia*, Rigby, Adelaide, 1981

Costin, AB, *A Study of the Ecosystems of the Monaro Region of New South Wales*, CSIRO Publishing, Melbourne, 1954

Costin, AB, Gray, M, Totterdell, C and Wimbush, DJ, *Kosciuszko Alpine Flora*, 2nd ed, CSIRO Publishing, Melbourne, 2000

Costin, AB and Wimbush, DJ, 'Trends in vegetation at Kosciuszko', *Australian Journal Botany*, 27(6), 1979, pp 245–54

Cruse, B, Kirby, R, Stewart, L and Thomas, S, *Bittangabee Tribe: An Aboriginal story from coastal New South Wales*, Aboriginal Studies Press, Canberra, 1994

Cruse, B, Stewart, L and Norman, S, *Mutton Fish: The surviving culture of Aboriginal people and abalone on the south coast of New South Wales*, Aboriginal Studies Press, Canberra, 2005

Currie, MJ, Journey southward of Lake George. In Field, B (ed), *Geographical*

Bibliography

Memoirs of New South Wales, John Murray, London, 1825
Davidson, D, *The Davidsons of Kiah*, Self-published, 1990
Davies, P, *Davidson Whaling Station Historic Site Conservation Management and Cultural Tourism Plan*, Paul Davies Pty Ltd for NPWS, Sydney, 2003
Dawson, GH, Recollections of, 1834–90, with additions from his son, HJ of Rockton, Bombala, A1805, Mitchell Library MS, Sydney
Diamond, M, *Ben Boyd of Boydtown*, Melbourne University Press, Melbourne, 1995
Devine, M, A Dissertation on the History of Wonboyn Lake, including the Nadgee and Narrabarba to 1960, Unpublished, 2005
Dunderdale, G, *The Book of the Bush*, Ward, Lock & Co Limited, London, c 1870, <http://gutenberg.net.au/ebooks/e00014.html> (accessed March 2015)
Egloff, B, *Mumbulla Mountain: An anthropological and archaeological investigation*, NPWS, Sydney, 1979
— Report on an investigation of places of cultural significance to Aboriginal people in the southern portion of the Eden woodchip agreement area, NPWS, Sydney, 1987
Egloff, B, Peterson, N and Wesson, S, Biamanga and Gulaga: Aboriginal Cultural Association with Biamanga and Gulaga National Parks, Research Report, Office of the Registrar, *Aboriginal Land Rights Act 1983* (NSW), 2005
Elias, S (ed), *Tales of the Far South Coast*, Vols 1–3, Bega Valley Shire Bicentennial Committee, Bega, 1986
Flood, J, *The Moth Hunters: Aboriginal prehistory of the Australian Alps*, Australian Institute of Aboriginal Studies, Canberra, 1980
Gammage, B, *Australia under Aboriginal Management*, School of Humanities and Social Sciences, University College, University of New South Wales, Australian Defence Force Academy, Canberra, 2003
— '"Far More Happier than we Europeans": Aborigines and farmers', London Papers in Australian Studies, No 12, Bridge, C and Book, I (eds), Menzies Centre for Australian Studies, London, 2005, 27
— *The Biggest Estate on Earth: How Aborigines Made Australia*, Allen & Unwin, Sydney, 2011
Geehi Bushwalking Club, *Snowy Mountains Walks*, 8th ed, Geehi Bushwalking Club, Cooma, 2001
Genoa Town Committee, Allard, P and Alves, G (eds), *Border Tales: Stories from Genoa, Wangarabell, Wroxham, Timbillica, Maramingo, Nungatta, Wingan and Gipsy Point*, Genoa Town Committee, Genoa, 2000
Grainger, E, *The Remarkable Reverend Clarke*, Oxford University Press, Melbourne, 1982
Grinbergs, A, A study of land routes of human movement in East

Gippsland, Report for Australian Heritage Commission, Melbourne, 1993
— The Myth Hunters: Investigations towards a revised prehistory of the south eastern highlands of Australia, Unpublished thesis, Australian National University, Canberra, 1992
Hancock, WK, *Discovering Monaro: A study of man's impact on his environment*, Cambridge University Press, Cambridge, 1972
Helms, R, Anthropological notes, *Proceedings of the Linnean Society of New South Wales*, 10, 2nd series, 26 June 1895
Howitt, AW (1904), *Native Tribes of South-East Australia*, Aboriginal Studies Press, Canberra, 1996
— AW Howitt Papers, Letters to his family 14 January 1966–28 December 1967, MS 9356 Box 1046/2a(3), State Library of Victoria, Melbourne
— 'The eucalypts of Victoria', *Transactions of the Royal Society of Victoria*, 2, 1890
Howitt, W, 'Black Thursday – The great bush fire of Victoria', *Cassell's Illustrated Family Paper*, 1(6), 4 February 1854; 1(8), 18 February 1854; 1(9), 25 February 1854.
— *Land, Labor and Gold; or, Two years in Victoria*, Ticknor and Fields, Boston, 1855
Jurskis, V, 'Decline of eucalypt forests as a consequence of unnatural fire regimes', *Australian Forestry*, 68(4), 2005, pp 257–62
Kabaila, P, *High Country Footprints: Aboriginal pathways and movement in the high country of southeastern Australia – recognising the ancient paths beside modern highways*, Pirion Publishing, Canberra, 2005
Keith, D, *Ocean Shores to Desert Dunes: The native vegetation of New South Wales and the Australian Capital Territory*, NPWS, Sydney, 2004
Kerr, J and Falkus, H, *From Sydney Cove to Duntroon: A family album of early life in Australia*, Hutchinson, Sydney, 1982
Kruta, V and Australia Felix Literary Club, *Dr John Lhotsky: The turbulent Australian writer, naturalist and explorer*, Australia Felix Literary Club, Melbourne, 1977
Kynaston, E, *A Man on Edge: A life of Baron Sir Ferdinand von Mueller*, Allen Lane, London, 1981
Lambie, J, Itineraries Moneroo District, X85, 1839–47, Archives Office of New South Wales (AONSW)
Lampert, RJ and Hughes, PJ, 'Archaeology and physical anthropology', *Oceania*, 9(3), 1974, p 228
Lunney, D (ed), *Conservation of Australia's Forest Fauna*, 2nd ed, Royal Zoological Society of New South Wales, Sydney, 2004
Lunney, D and Leary, T, 'The impact on native mammals of land-use changes and exotic species in the Bega district, New South Wales, since

Bibliography

settlement', *Australian Journal of Ecology*, 13, 1988, pp 67–92

Mathews, RH, 'Language of the Birdhawal tribe, in Gippsland, Victoria', *Proceedings of the American Philosophical Society*, 46(187), October–December 1907, p 346

McBryde, I, Report on the Greenstone hatchet head from Towamba River, Australian National University, Canberra, 2007

MacCabe, F, Survey of part of road between Monaroo and Twofold Bay, AONSW, M.72.831 3753, 1845

McFarland, A, *Illawarra and Monaro*, W Maddock, Sydney, 1872

McKenna, M, *Looking for Blackfellas' Point: An Australian history of place*, UNSW Press, Sydney, 2002

McKenzie, JAS, *The Twofold Bay Story*, Eden Killer Whale Museum and Historical Society, Eden, 1991

Mathews, RH, 'Ethnological notes on the Aboriginal tribes of New South Wales and Victoria', *Journal and Proceedings of the Royal Society of New South Wales*, Vol 38, 1904

Mead, T, *Killers of Eden*, Angus & Robertson, Sydney, 1961

Mosley, G and Costin, A, World Heritage values and their protection in far south east New South Wales, Report to the Earth Foundation Australia, 1992

Mulvaney, DJ, *Encounters in Place: Outsiders and Aboriginal Australians 1606–1985*, University of Queensland Press, St Lucia, 1989

—— 'The anthropologist as tribal elder', *Mankind*, 7, 1970, pp 205–17

Nash, M, *Cargo for the Colony; The wreck of the merchant ship, Sydney Cove (1797)*, Braxus Press, Sydney, 1996

Payten, RF, The festival of the bogong moth: Letter to AS le Soeuf, 15 June 1949, MS (Aa44/3), Mitchell Library, Sydney

Platts, L, *Bygone Days of Cathcart*, Self-published, 1989

Plumwood, V, 'The fight for the forests revisited', *Dialogue*, 23(1), 2004, Academy of the Social Sciences in Australia, <www.assa.edu.au/publications/dialogue/2004_Vol23_No1.pdf> (accessed March 2015)

Preserving historic trails, Conference Proceedings, Friends of Acadia National Park, Olmsted Centre for Landscape Preservation, National Park Service (US), 2000

Prineas, P and Gold, H, *Wild Places: Wilderness in eastern New South Wales*, Colong Foundation, Sydney, 1983

Pulsford, IF, Banks JCG and Hodges, L, Land use history of the white cypress pine forests in the Snowy Valley, Kosciusko National Park, Centre for Resource and Environmental Studies, 1993. In Dargavel, J and Feary, S (eds), *Australia's Ever Changing Forests II*, Proceedings of the Second National Conference on Australian Forest History, Ch 7.

Read, J, Parish Map Preservation Project: The use of digital photography,

CDs and computers to copy, view (and preserve) old maps
Robinson, R, *The Nearest the White Man Gets: Aboriginal narratives and poems of New South Wales*, Hale & Iremonger, Sydney, 1989
— *The Whalers*, Angus & Robertson, Sydney, 1997
Routley, R and Routley, V, *The Fight for the Forests*, 3rd ed, Research School of Social Sciences, Australian National University, Canberra, 1975
Ryrie, S, Moniera & Gippsland Map, 1840, (including tracings after Ryrie), AONSW, M1170 3884 and 3885, M.1.1170, M.2.1170 and M.3.1170, 1840
— Stewart Ryrie; Journal of a tour in the southern mountains, Mitchell Library, Sydney, 1840
— Maps submitted with journal, AONSW, 1840
Seddon, G, *Searching for the Snowy: An environmental history*, Allen & Unwin, Melbourne, 1994
Seebeck, JH, Long-nosed potoroo. In Menkhorst, P (ed), *The Mammals of Victoria*
— *Distribution ecology and conservation*, Oxford University Press, Melbourne, 1995,
pp 131–33
Slatyer, RO (ed), Scientific assessment of the international significance of the eucalypts, Report to World Heritage Branch, Environment Australia, 2000
Smith, BE, *History of Bega Floods*, Bega District Historical Society, Bega, 1978
——— *The Bega Bushfires of 1952*, Florance, S (ed), Bega Pioneers Museum, Bega, 2002
Stanner, WEH, *White Man Got no Dreaming: Essays 1938–1973*, Australian National University Press, Canberra, 1979
Strahan, R (ed), *The Australian Museum Complete Book of Australian Mammals*, Australian Museum/Reed Books, Sydney, 2002
Te Whare, *A Bush Cinema: Made in Australia*, Carter's Printing Works, Sydney, 1921
Townsend, T, Monaro Squatting District 1851, AONSW, M.1.1170 3886
Triggs, B, *Tracks, Scats and Other Traces: A field guide to Australian mammals*, Oxford University Press, Melbourne, 1996
Wakefield, NA, 'Bushfire frequency and vegetational change in south east Australian forests', *Victorian Naturalist*, 87(6), 1970, pp 152–58
Walker, MH, *Come Wind, Come Weather; A biography of Alfred Howitt*, Melbourne University Press, Carlton, 1971
Warren, JW and Wakefield, NA, 'Trackways of tetrapod vertebrates from the Upper Devonian of Victoria, Australia', *Nature*, 238, 1972, pp 469–70
Watson, A, Carver, S, Krenova, Z, McBride, B (2015), Science and

Bibliography

stewardship to protect and sustain wilderness values, Tenth World Wilderness Congress symposium, 4–10 October 2013, Salamanca, Spain

Watson, D, *Caledonia Australis: Scottish highlanders on the Frontier of Australia*, Collins, Sydney, 1984

Weatherhead, A, *Leaves of My Life*, Eden Museum, Eden, 1988

Wellings, HP, *Eden & Twofold Bay*, Magnet Print, Eden, 1965

—— *The Imlay Brothers (Peter, Alexander and George Imlay)*, DS Ford Printers, Sydney, 1985

—— *Sundry Journalistic Writings*, Magnet Print, Eden, see also Papers of Henry Percival Wellings, 1810–1965, NLA MS 3669

Wesson, S, 'An historical atlas of the Aborigines of eastern Victoria and far south eastern New South Wales', *Monash Publications in Geography and Environmental Science*, No 53, Monash University, Clayton, 2000

— An overview of the sources for a language and clan atlas of eastern Victoria and southern New South Wales, Australian Institute of Aboriginal and Torres Strait Islander Studies (AIATSIS), Canberra, 1993

— Alps Oral History Project, Australian Alps Liaison Committee, 1994

—— An Aboriginal Whaling History Project, NPWS, Sydney, 2001

—— The Aborigines of east Victoria and far south east New South Wales: 1830 to 1910 an historical geography, Unpublished PhD thesis, Monash University, Melbourne, 2002

Winters, J, *Nungatta South*, NPWS, Sydney, 2001

Worboys, G, *Trails of Byadbo Mapped on Topo Map*, NPWS, Sydney, 1976

Young, M, *The Aboriginal People of the Monaro*, 2nd ed, Department of Environment and Conservation New South Wales, Sydney, 2005

Young, M, with Mundy, E and Mundy, D, *The Aboriginal People of the Monaro*, NPWS, Sydney, 2000

Index

PS refers to the picture section.

A Boy's Adventures in the Wilds of Australia
   81
Abbott Range 17
Aboriginal
   artefacts 40–41, 67, 92, 118,
      157–158, 190, 234–235, 254, 274,
      278, 280–281, PS
   Australia 12, 289
   blankets 112, 132, 136, 140–142,
      197, 204
   burning 30–31, 80–81, 84, 92,
      147–148, 160, 213–214
   campsites 113, 144, 156, 159, 283,
      294
   ceremonies 11, 23, 55, 85, 111, 179,
      203
   clans 2, 23, 31, 49, 52, 131, 142, 158,
      174, 207, 212, 225, 265, 288
   Country 43, 56, 123, 130, 133, 161,
      171, 178, 181, 237, 290–291
   culture 50, 85, 139, 177–178, 212,
      289–291
   deaths 30, 48, 120, 177, 203
   diet 265
   Elders 5, 11, 52, 55, 56, 85, 155, 160,
      212, 234, 290
   firestick farming 4, 148, 214
   food resources 118, 124–126,
      203, 218–219 *see also* Aboriginal
      whaling; bogongs
   land management 126, 161, 231
   languages 50–51, 114
   massacres 121, 149, 265–269
   mission stations or reserves 50,
      118–119, 132–133, 135–138,
      142–144
   ownership 131
   pathways 2–3, 11–12, 16, 27–28, 36,
      40, 134, 167, 173, 257, 265, 270
   peoples 84–85
   Place 43–47, 50, 56, 67, 160, 164,
      245, 277, 279, 290
   protectorates 132
   rights 49, 52, 108, 123
   settlement 115, 135
   stone arrangements 25
   tribes 48–51, 86, 111, 122, 142,
      166–167, 173–181, 266–268, 274
   violence 266–268
   wells 72
   whaling 143, 201–202, 216–225,
      236, 255 *see also* Aboriginal food
      resources; whaling
Aboriginal Evangelical Church 145
'Aborigine', definition 137
Aborigines Protection Board 236
Aborigines Protection Society 132
Adgery, Charlie 236
Ainslie, James 116
Al.mil.gong 37
Ambyne 73
Ambyne Creek 74
Ambyne Gap 73
Australian Alps Walking Track 28, 33
Australian Museum 24

Back Country 9
Badgerys Swamp 159
Balawan PS
Bairnsdale 159
Banjo Paterson 67–68
Banks, John 92
Bark Camp Creek 60
Barry Way 47, 59
Bass Strait 78
Bega 52, 54, 55, 262
Bega Swamp 159
Bega Times 52–53
Bemm River 267

Bendoc 2, 27, 111, 128, 149, 175
Bendoc Hill 38
Bendoc River 147
Bennett, George 24
Berridale 46
Berrima Ridge 36, 38, 39, 40
Biamanga National Park 56
Bidawal Country 133, 181
Biddi 46, 60, 63, 64, 108
Bidwell 111
Bilgalera 113, 226–227, 277–285, 293
Bililingera 121
'Billy Bamboo' 268
Black Friday bushfires 78–79
Black Range 63, 93
Black Range, Byadbo 90
Black Scrubs 61
Black-Allan line 36
black-birding 255
Blue Lake 103
Blueskin 46
Board for the Protection of the Aborigines 86, 132
Boggy Plain 27, 29, 32, *PS*
bogongs 11, 21–29, 61, 158, 162, 221, 225, 273, *PS*
Bold Granite/Black Range 153
Boldrewood, Rolf 65
Bombala 74, 75, 107, 275
Bombala Historical Society 65
Bombala River 129
Bondi 169
Bondi Springs 156
Bondi State Forest 152, 172
Boondiang station 169
Botanic Garden Palace fire 237
Boyd, Ben 196–204, 229, 239, 251–256
Boydtown 189, 228, 255–256
Bradshaw, Harry 65
Braidwood 23
Brierly, Oswald 3, 167, 180, 192–206, 208, 213, 217, 221, 226–231, 255, 257, 284
Brooks, Richard 46, 150
Brownlie, Keith 276
brumbies 19, 21, 27, 32, 33, 34, 39, 40, 60, 65, 66, 74, 93, 99
Bruthen Creek 45

Budginbro 198–201, 230, 257, 284
Bundian Pass 3, 6, 10, 162, 166–170, 174, 188–189, 215, 231, 245, 256, 271, 275–276, 279–280, 287, 291
Bundian Way Aboriginal Art Gallery 293
Bungel, Billy 152
Burnima 106
Burrimboco Pass 168
bushfires 16, 30–31, 74, 78–83, 92–93, 175
Byadbo 42, 47, 50, 59, 65, 67, 69–76, 89, 98, 101, 106, *PS*
Byadbo Creek 93
Byadbo Gap 62–63, 94
Byadbo Rain 87
Byadbo Wilderness 59, 62, 102
Byatts Camp 17

Campbell, Donald 135
Campbell, Frederick 117–118
Campbell, Jack 55
Campbell, Robert 74, 115–118, 129
Campbell, Sophia 118
Campbell & Co 261
Campbell and Clark 115
Canberra 33, 74, 116
Cann River 142, 169, 173, 267
Cape Everard 84
Cape Howe 5, 36, 84, 114, 239, 261
Cape York 289
Carawang 105
Carr, Premier Bob 269
Carter, Charlie 35, 38
Cascade Creek 32–33
Cascade Hut 33–34, *PS*
Charlotte Pass 20
Cheesman Bros 136
Chinese gold diggers 109, 146–148, 264, 266
Chytrid fungus 20
Circular Quay, Sydney Cove 115
Clark, Manning 251
Clark, William 115
Clarke, Very Reverend WB 3, 29–30, 35, 36, 45, 46, 127, 147, 158, 163–170, 175–176, 291
Cobberas 37, 39, 45, 50, 63, 84
Cook, Captain James 56–57

322

Index

Coolangubra 38, 105–106, 124, 153, 158, 163, 166, 186, 212, 271–273, 275
Coolringdon 45
Cooma 36, 47, 59, 107, 112, 244
Coopracambra-Kaye National Park 181
Cootamundra Domestic Training Home 137
Cootapatamba Hut 18, 21
Corner Inlet, Port Albert, Wilsons Promontory 45
corroboree frog 20
Corrowong 62, 105–106, 108–109, 111, 122, 128, 134
Corrowong Creek 72, 107, 131
Corrowong Falls 107
Corrowong station 112
Cosgrove, John 121
Costin, Alec 273
Cottrell, Clive 64, 106
county maps 170
Cowbail 167
Cowombat Flat 36, 37
Craigie 128, 142, 146–148, 151
Cruse, BJ 3, 5–6, 10, 12, 42, 180, 188, 191, 215, 227, 277–278, 281, 287–288, PS
Cruse, Uncle Ossie 5, 11–12, 54, 144–145, 180, 290, PS
Currie, Captain Mark 115–116

Dalgety 59, 107
Dargal 22
Darrewarra camp 100
Darwin, Charles 109
Davidson, George 187–190, 216, 219–220
Davidson, Rene 209
Davidson Whaling Station 186–188
Dawson, George Henry 23–24
Dead Horse Gap 27–28, 29, 32, PS
Debus, Bob 56–57
Deddick 74
Delegate, Dilliget 50, 74, 100, 122, 127, 133, 134–145, 293
Delegate Aboriginal Reserve 133, 142
Delegate Hill 27, 38, 62, 65, 104–113, 273, PS

Delegate River 118, 129, 142, 146
Delegate station 118, 130
Delicknora 107
dingoes 88, 104, 156, 230, 254, 266
Discovering Monaro 120–121
Divide 32
Dreaming routes 18
drought 92, 108, 117, 125, 130, 136, 150, 175, 264
Drummer, East Gippsland 49
Dulundundu 2
Duntroon 116–117
Dyillagamberra 102–103

East Gippsland 36
Edbo 101 *see also* Byadbo
Edbo Flats 62, 74, 75, 93
Eden 3–4, 10, 155, 188, 195
Eden Local Aboriginal Land Council 3, 5, 145, 227, 234, 294
Eden woodchip mill 54
Egloff, Brian 53, 55
Errinundra Plateau 146–147
Euroma station 125

Farrell, Harold 275
Fead, George 59
Ffolkes 75, 94, 101
Fison, Lorimer 109
Fitzgerald, RD 155
Flood, Josephine 22
food plants *see* Aboriginal food resources
Forbes, Dr 14
Forest Hill 36, 78
Fosbery, EW 136
Freebody's Hut 40
Freestone Creek 45
funnel-web 16, 17

Gammage, Bill 214
Geehi Flats 13, 15–17, 88
Gegedzerick (Gejizrick Flat) 46
Genoa 173, 245, 259–260, 270
Genoa River 181, 247, 257
geology 3–4, 35, 61, 70, 77, 93, 105, 127–128, 160, 165
Gibber, Jemmy 105

Ginau, John 111
Gipps, Governor Sir George 132
Gippsland 45, 47, 78, 84, 105, 135, 142
Gobiam (alias Billy Hayes) 142
gold diggers 109, 128
goldfields 46, 81, 84, 118, 127–129, 149, 232
Gordon, ARL 52–53, 54
Gow, Alexander 105–106
Great Depression 38
Great Dividing Range, Great Divide 25, 29, 60, 239
Greenlands 2
Griffiths, Chris 90
Grosses Plain 28
Guboo, Ted Thomas 158
Gulaga (Mount Dromedary) 56–57
Gulgin Flats 153
Gunnang, Pearly 130
Gunnang's orchard 130

Hagenauer, Reverend AH 85–86
Hammond family 103
Hancock, WK 120–121
Hannels Spur 12, 14–16
hares 66, 150
Harpur, Charles 125
Haydens 66, 75
Hayes family 103, 142
Haygarth, Henry 123–124
Helms, Richard 23
Highlander shepherds 109
Howitt, AW 3, 23, 26–27, 28, 29, 48, 51, 55, 83, 109–112, 142, 175–178, 212, 214, 234 see also Howitt country
Howitt, Godfrey 79–80
Howitt, William 79–83
Howitt country 77–88

Imlay, George 195, 220–221, 240, 262
Imlay, Peter 245–248
Imlay Creek 283
Impossible Flat (The Lookout) 63
Ingebyra 58
Ingeegoodbee River 34, 38–39, 45, 46, 50
Irondoon Range 145–146, 149

Jacobs Ladder 59
Jagungal 22
Jagungal Wilderness 28
James, Frank 111
Jardine, William 24
Jerry's Flats 72, 74, 101
Jimenbuen 63
Jimmys Stairs 60
Jindabyne 23–24, 35, 44, 46, 59, 142, 235
Jingo Mountain 240
Joe Davis Creek 64, 91
Johnson, George James Howitt Patterson (Joker) 65–68
Jones, Rhys 148

Kamilaroi and Kurnai 109
Kangaroo Grounds 101
Kiah 191, 228
Kiah Inlet 284, *PS*
Kiah River 258
Kiandra 128, 264
Killarney Swamp 159
Killers of Eden 187
Kinchela Home 138
King Charley 109, 111
Kosciuszko 16, 20, 22, 28, 29, 37, 44, 46, 66, 108, 213, *PS*
Kosciuszko National Park 10, 47, 88, 90, 98, 100, 103
Kurrajong 63, 284

Lake Albina 22
Lake Bathurst 116
Lake Cootapatamba *PS*
Lake George 115
Lake Tyers 50, 132, 142
Lambie, John 105, 122, 242–243, 247, 258
Land, Labor and Gold, or, Two Years in Victoria 81
Lassie 142
Leatherbarrel Creek 19, 25
Leaves from My Life 258
Lhotsky, Dr John 28–29
Limestone Plains 115
Lingard, Joseph 125, 249–250
Liscombe 172, 249

Index

Little, Jimmy 57
Little Plains River 111, 128, 146, 149
Little River 94, 100
logging 52–55, 147, 230
Lower Snowy (Nurudj Djurung) 42, 67
Lunney, Dan 278

MacCabe, Francis 166, 171, 232–233, 238
Mackay, DH and Mac 65–66
MacKay family 106
MacKillop, George 105
Macleay River 138
Macquarie, Governor Lachlan 138
Maharatta 2, 163, 167
Maher, Bobby PS
Mallacoota 270
Manero 111
Maneroo 26, 45, 48, 99, 102, 106, 114–119, 120–132, 181, 244
Maneroo Squatting District 242
Manning, AW 220
maps *see* county maps; parish maps; survey maps
Marambego 105
Marlo 134
Mason, Rod 103, 213
Mathews, RH 102, 178–181, 218
McBryde, Isabel 234
McCoy's Hut 64
McFarland, Alfred 129
McFarlane, James and Duncan 105–106
McGuigan, Patrick 62
McGuigans Gap 100, 104
McGuigans Stockyard Flat 102
McKay, Lucy 65–66
McKays 75
McKenna, Mark 120–121, 265
McLeod family 143
McMillan, Angus 105
Mead, Tom 187
Melanesian shepherds 255
Merambego 74–75, 90, 98–103, 105, 134, PS
Merambego Ridge 94
Merambego station site 62
Merragunegin 265
Merrimingo 260

Mickey 111
Mila 128
Mitchell, Sir Thomas 44–45, 240
Mitchell Library 194
Moffatt family 142
Moira's Flat 15–16
Moloney, Jack 53
Molonglo River 116
Monaro tablelands 2–4
Monaroo 116
Monderragen 129
Monument Trail 101
Moruya 239, 286
Mosley, Geoff 273
moths *see* bogongs
Mount Cooper 117
Mount Delegate 135, 145
Mount Disappointment 83
Mount Dromedary (Gulaga) 209
Mount Erica 78
Mount Genoa 209
Mount Imlay (Balawan) 153, 190, 209–211, 275, 283
Mount Kosciuszko (Targangal) 5, 15, 24
Mount Pilot Tin Syndicate 38
Mount Townsend 18, 22
Mount Trooper 64
Mountain Top 156
Mowamba River 28–29
Moyangul 22, 36, 44, 49, 58, 68, 90
Moyangul River 46
Mumbler, Percy 55, 158, 216–217
Mumbulla Mountain 52–56, 209
Munday (Mundy) 142
Mundy, Bill 65
Murcutt, Glenn 294
Murray Jack 109–111
Murray River 5, 21, 26, 28, 29, 36, 37, 38
Mutong 28
Myanba Creek 168

Nadgee 151, 153, 235
Nadgee River 114
Nalbaugh 27, 265, 273, 275, 280, PS
Nangutta, Nungatta 38, 142, 164, 169, 172, 245, 258, 261–271, 274, 282

Nangutta Creek 257
Nangutta Mountain 256
National Parks and Wildlife Service 32, 56, 186–187, 234
Native Tribes of South-East Australia 85, 109, 111, 177
Nerrigundah 125
New South Wales Heritage List 293
Newcong (Nuking) 142
Newton family 149–153
Ngarigo, Ngarego 110
Nine Mile Pinch 40, 41, 45, 46, 108
North Durras 78
North Ramshead 22
NSW Aborigines Protection Board 134–139
Nungatta 38, 142, 245, 274, 282
Nunnock Swamp 2, 159
Nurudj Djurung 44, 49, 58, 68, 90

O'Hare, James 106, 107–108, 112, 150
O'Hare Catholic Church 112–113
O'Hares Creek 93
Old Munday 109–112, 142
Omeo 23, 30, 35–37, 40, 45, 47, 49, 51, 84, 105, 128, 142, 159
Omeo Black 37
Omeo Flat 39, 40, 50
Orbost 63, 134
O'Rourke, Bernard 2
O'Rourke, John 112
Ovens goldfields 81, 84, 128

Pambula 235
Pambula River 114
parish maps 2–3, 156
  Beurina 36
  Biddi 60
  Bondi 169, 172
Paupong 63
Pearson, Noel 289
Penrith, Merv 54–55, 56
Pericoe 257, 270
Pericoe Creek 281–282
Pheasants Peak 153
Pinch, Moyangul 50, 58–59, 69, 87
Pinch Gap 91
Pinch junction 58–59

Pinch River 41–42, 44, 46, 47
Plain Statements and Practical Hints Respecting the Discovery and Working of Gold in Australia 30
Platts, Gordon 152, 168
Platts, Neil 156
Playgrounds 45, 47, 84
Pulsford, Ian 92

rabbits 64, 66–67, 69, 92–93, 136, 143, 150, 160
Rainmaker 103
Ramahyuck 50
Ramshead, South 26
Ramsheads 19, 25, 27, 29, 87
Reed, Barrie 100–101
Reed, George 64
Reed's cattleyards 64
Researches in the Southern Gold Fields of New South Wales 35
Researches in the Southern Goldfields of New South Wales 30
Right Hand Creek 63
Robbery under Arms 65
Robinson, GA 3, 36–37, 51, 66, 108, 121–122, 132, 167, 173–175, 221–224, 227, 259–261
Robinson, Roland 217, 268–269
Rockton 172
Rourke, Neddy 111
Ryan, Pat 64, 66, 74, 99–102
Ryrie, Stewart 24, 122, 145–149, 169, 171, 211

Sale, Victoria 65
Sandy Creek 66, 69, 75, 90–91, 107, 113
Sandy Creek Hut 69, 101
Scottish immigrants 242–270
Seddon, George 213
Selection Acts 74
settlers 2, 4, 23, 36, 46, 48, 62, 108–110, 116, 121–132, 147, 167, 190, 201, 236, 241–245, 263, 266–268, 279–281
Severs, Elsie 190–191
Sheep Station 90–91
Sheep Station Creek 63–64

Index

Sheepstation Swamp 275, 277–281
Shoalhaven River 45
Slaughterhouse Creek 60–61, 75
Slaughterhouse Hut 61, 66
Slippery Hole Creek 91
Smithson, Michael 141–142
Snowy 70, 74, 78, 91, 107, 131
Snowy Mountain Scheme *see* Snowy Mountains Hydro-electric Authority
Snowy Mountains 29, 103
Snowy Mountains Hydro-electric Authority 13, 34, 43–44
Snowy Plain 23
Snowy River 5, 41, 46, 47, 50, 58–59, 62–63, 66, 105, 111, 134, 199
Snug Cove 197
Solomon family 103, 143
South East Forests National Park 181, 268, 278, 282
Spring Creek 101
squatters 2, 62, 74, 123, 126, 128–130, 171, 244, 246, 263, 270
Stapylton, GC 238
Stevensen, Captain Henry John 248–251, 261
Stewart, Norman 74, 77, 98, 106
Stockyard Flats 62, 75, 90, 93, 101, 105, 168
Strutt, William 81
Suggan Buggan 40
Suggan Buggan mallee gum 78
Sugganbooka (Suggan Buggan) 45
survey maps 20, 35–40, 45, 90, 165–166, 169–171, 176, 179, 232, 237–238, 243–244, 280
surveying 237–241
Surveyors Flat 40
Swampy Plains 19

Tangaroo 64
Targangal (Kosciuszko), 18, 22, 113
'The Kangaroo Hunt' 125
The Lookout (Impossible Flat) 63
'The Man from Snowy River' 59, 65, 67–68
The Moth Hunters: Aboriginal prehistory of the Australian Alps 22
The Pilot 27, 35, 37, 47

The Pilot Wilderness 37, 40
Thomas, Guboo Ted 52–53, 55, 57
Thompson 142
Thredbo 5, 21, 28
Thredbo River 28, 29, PS
Timbillica 258–262
Tin Mine Creek 34, 38
Tin Mine Falls 37, 38
Tingaringy 27, 38, 70–71, 73, 77–88, 107, 129, 131, 167, 273, PS
Tingaringy gum 78
Tom Groggin station 21, 26
Tombong 84
Tongaroo (Jacobs River) 58
Tongihi (Tangiai) 266–268
Tongio-mungie 37
Tooginbooka 45
Towamba 226–236, 245, 257, 283
Towamba River 4, 167–168, 208, 213, 240
Towamba Valley 238
Townsend, TS 20, 29, 36, 39, 40, 45, 46, 47, 59, 90, 171, 238–240
Travelling Stock Reserves 107, 113, 151, 156
Treeless Plains 3–4, 38, 106–107
Tubbut 84, 107
Tungai, Maggie 142
Turamullerer (southern Twofold Bay) 193, 205, PS
Tuross River 102
Twofold Bay 3–5, 22–23, 30, 37, 118, 122, 167, 186–191, 195–196, 207, 218–220, 236, 239, 245, 258–259, 284–285, 294, PS

Victorian Alps 21
von Hügel, Baron Charles 45, 208, 209, 220, 247
von Mueller, Baron Sir Ferdinand 14, 207

Waalimma 265
Walker, Gordon 75
Wallaga Lake 50, 52–53, 54, 55, 56–57, 133, 138, 159, 268
Wallagaraugh 258–260
Wallagaraugh, Wallagara 245, 258–260, 265

Wallendibby 64, 104–106, 110–111
Waratah Creek 167, 271–272
Weatherhead, Alexander 256–266, 279, 282
Webb, Francis 251
Wellings, HP (Harry) 266
Whale Beach 219, *PS*
whaling 245–248 *see also* Aboriginal whaling
White Rock River 280
Whittakers 84
Whittakers, William 126–127
Wilderness Area 36, 47
wildflowers 77–78, *PS*
Wilkinsons Creek 17, 87
Willis 46, 63, 74–75, 87
Willis-Biddi Creek 91
Wimbush, Dane 20
Wog Wog 38, 168, 186, 245, 259, 265, 274, 276, 280
Wog Wog Pass 188
Wollondibby 75
Wollondibby Creek 105
Wollondibby Station 105
Wombat Gully 29
Worboys, Graeme 90
Wran, Neville 55
Wright, Judith 79
Wulgulmerang 40, 46, 107, 112

yam plants 100, 126, 154–162, *PS* *see also* Aboriginal food plants
Yambulla 265
Yambulla State Forest 282
Yarramgun 158, 272–273
Yibai Malian (Murray Jack) 142
Youngal 22

www.ingramcontent.com/pod-product-compliance
Lightning Source LLC
Chambersburg PA
CBHW040745020526
44114CB00049B/2931